*Voting About God
in Early Church Councils*

RAMSAY MacMULLEN

Voting About God
in Early Church Councils

Yale University Press
New Haven &
London

Published with assistance from the Kingsley Trust Association Publication Fund
established by the Scroll and Key Society of Yale College.

Set in Sabon type by Keystone Typesetting, Inc.
Printed in the United States of America by Sheridan Books, Ann Arbor, Michigan.

Library of Congress Cataloging-in-Publication Data
MacMullen, Ramsay, 1928–
    Voting about God in early church councils / by Ramsay MacMullen.
        p. cm.
    Includes bibliographical references and index.
    ISBN-13: 978-0-300-11596-3 (cloth : alk. paper)
    ISBN-10: 0-300-11596-2
    1. Councils and synods. 2. Church history — Primitive and early church, ca.
30–600. 3. God — History of doctrines — Early church, ca. 30–600. I. Title.
    BV710.M28 2006
    262'.514 — dc22   2005034666

A catalogue record for this book is available from the British Library.

The paper in this book meets the guidelines for permanence and durability of the
Committee on Production Guidelines for Book Longevity of the Council on
Library Resources.

10 9 8 7 6 5 4 3 2 1

Contents

Figures

Preface

How did Christians agree on their definition of the Supreme Being, Triune? It was the work of the bishops assembled at Nicaea in AD 325, made formal and given weight by majority vote and supported after much struggle by later assemblies, notably at Chalcedon (451) — likewise by majority vote. Such was the determining process. Thus agreement was arrived at, and became dogma widely accepted down to our own day.[1]

The process has been often described: studied to death, one may almost say. But the level I choose to focus on is not quite the usual one. I have nothing to add about the intricacies of doctrinal debate, high up, nor the shaping of the most important participants' views in their own minds and writings, nor their gaining and applying of influence in the lead-up to council meetings and at the most crucial sessions. Such matters I leave to others, who are many.

I leave to others also the view that the shaping personalities were in some sense superhuman: Saint Ambrose, Saint Dioscorus, Saint Constantine, or Saint Cyril. Revered by members of this or that party to theological dispute and by reverence raised to a plane above history itself, along with the events in

---

1. Time has brought change, witness the words of the present pope, "truth is not determined by a majority vote," quoted in P. J. Boyer, "A hard faith," *New Yorker Magazine*, May 16, 2005, p. 59.

which they were involved — surely their elevation must provoke a historian's protest, though the protestant deprives himself of all sorts of familiar lines of explanation, all sorts of certainties and dramatic touches.

Rather, I focus on those persons who made up the great mass of any council, by no means superhuman. Many were not in the least prominent. They remain for us nothing but names, as, in the past, some were no doubt hardly more than names even among their fellows. All participants together, however, were necessary to the outcome. Without a majority of them duly subscribed and tallied, no view could claim defining authority.

In the making of any event such as emerged from Nicaea or Chalcedon, figures great and small, high and low, had all to contribute. Of course. There can be no leaders without followers, no followers without leaders. It is for readers of history then to decide who counted the most, or perhaps whom they find most interesting. But writers like readers may have a choice, too. My own preference has always been some level not too different from my own. To look up at the past never suited me, any more than looking down on it.

Which means, not biography. A thin narrative line, following not the community that makes an event but rather some single actor's progress, doesn't suit my sort of curiosity. It is the whole contributing mass that I like to understand — how people, lots of people, really behaved. I might plead Fashion. As Orlando Figes put it, a few years ago, "History has long ceased to be the record of the achievements of extraordinary men: we are all social historians now."[2]

Accordingly, I have done what I could to understand what might be in the mind of less-than-eminent persons participating in church council decisions. Granted, information about them is available only in tiny disconnected bits; and these have to be aligned with and interpreted in the light of other tiny bits. The result can only be pointillist; but a pointillist portrait of a composite figure engaged in composite events may be as fairly representative of the truth as attempts at the biography of some one historical figure like Cicero or Augustine. What is required is enough dots, connected. Let this excuse or explain my multiplication of instances of this or that sort of behavior. I aim only to satisfy the sceptic.

In contrast, statements about large groups or characteristics of some historical period, supported airily by no more than an anecdote or two, aren't worth much.

Looking into the mind of those council participants who are my subject, I find four shaping elements: a democratic, a cognitive, a "supernaturalist", and

2. *A People's Tragedy. A History of the Russian Revolution*, New York 1997, 455f. (speaking, no doubt, of historians of periods closer to the present than mine).

a violent. Explanation of each of these four terms makes up my earlier chapters; and in each of the four there is something of major historical significance to be discovered, as I try to make clear. Thereafter, I turn to scenes from various particular councils to show the four elements at work.

The logic governing the general flow of the book is Summarized in its last few pages.

Voting About God
in Early Church Councils

Introduction

Before getting very far into a subject so familiar as the formation of Christian creeds, it may help to think of it for a moment in a detached way. If the distance between it and ourselves can be brought out — if we can try to see the scene and its actors afresh and in all their strangeness — we may bring a more curious eye to our observation, we may really *look*, taking nothing for granted.

Suppose for a moment that a visitor from Mars asked about the setting for this essay — and no one more detached can be imagined — might he not need to be told the most obvious things? First, to situate the matter in time, we would want to declare a convenient starting point, a certain year. The 325th according to our most usual convention would suit very well. As to space: our focus would fix on lands encircling a great sea, and their resident population of fifty or sixty million human beings, most of whom lived on or near the eastern shores.

Now, among these residents (we would explain) prevailed a universal belief in the existence of an equal or even greater population of other beings — all invisible, superhuman, greater or smaller, malign or (mostly) benign, able to shape life in every detail and so requiring to be obeyed and conciliated.

To one of these and to one only a special title "God" was fiercely reserved by a minority calling themselves "Christians". All other superhuman beings (except their own God's angels) they declared to be enemies, and evil, or lacking any reality at all. They drew sharp boundaries around themselves, at first around only their individual scattered tiny groups but increasingly, also, around all of their groups thought of as one whole. Definition of this whole which we call "Christianity" they sought in turn through definition of their "God". He was the reason for their being. This much, they determined by consensus.

But just how was the Christian consensus arrived at? The answer, well known, is: by majority vote of group leaders in occasional assemblies.

The Martian visitor, a space traveler and a scientific type in the habit of thinking quantitatively, would no doubt have more questions to propose of a quantitative sort. As to these assemblies, now, just how many were they? With how many persons attending? At what intervals? And where in the social grid did the participants come from?

From the two and a quarter centuries post–325, surviving evidence allows the location of 255 councils on the map and in time (on the locations, see Figs. 1–2). Two or three might better be called conferences; and, besides, the great majority of the rest were not focused on theology; rather, on internal government: as, what were the rights of deacons against presbyters? or what office should determine the rites of baptism? Yet their procedures and participation were no different than in those assemblages focused on credal questions. To understand one sort is to understand all.

The list that follows, beyond date and site of assemblages, sometimes adds in parentheses the number of bishops attending. Where this is known, participating clerics of a lower rank are not counted and the frequent uncertainties in the count are not spelt out; for sometimes a number given in one historical source doesn't agree with another, and there's no choosing between them; or often, the names of later signatories to the resolutions of a council may have been wrongly counted as if they had been present. More will need to be said elsewhere about such confusions and the reasons for them; more, too, about the designation of five councils as "ecumenical". They are shown in bold face with Roman numerals in parentheses; and they are underlined along with other councils which were called or authorized by emperors (below, Chap. 6).

Three Centuries of Synods = Councils[1]

253 Carth. (18)	305 Cirta	312 Carthage
255 Carth (30)	306 Alexandria	312 Rome
256 Carth. (87)	307/311 Carthage	314 Arles (26/33/44)
264 Antioch	?310 Elvira	314 Ancyra (18)
368 Antioch	311 Cirta	320/1 Bithynia

Three Centuries of Synods = Councils[1] (*Continued*)

314/20 Neocaesarea (Pontus) (20)
320 Alexandria
321 Caesarea (Pal.)
?324 Alexandria
325 Antioch (56/59)
(I) 325 Nicaea (?200)
328 Alexandria
330 Antioch
332 Antioch
334 Alexandria
334 Caesarea (Pal.)
335 Tyre
335 Jerusalem
335 Tyana
335/6 Cple
336 Carthage
   (Donatist) (270)
338 Cple
338 "Mareotic" (Eg.)
338/9 Alexandria
339 Antioch
341 Antioch (97)
341 Rome (50+)
341 Alexandria
343 Rome (50)
343 Philippopolis
343 Serdica (165; 170/176)
345 Carthage
345 Antioch
345 Milan
346 Jerusalem
346 Alexandria
346 Cologne (14)
347 Carthage
347 Sirmium
347 Milan
348 Carthage
349 Sirmium
351 Sirmium
353 Rome
353 Arles
?355 Gangra
355 Milan (300+)

356/7 Baeterrae
357 Antioch
357 Sirmium
358 Sirmium
357 "Gallic"
358 Antioch
358 Ancyra
359 Ariminum (400+)
358 Nike (Thrace)(300+)
359 Seleuceia (150/60)
360 Cple (72)
360 Paris
361 Paris
362 Alexandria
363 Carthage
363 Antioch
364 Caria
364/5 Lampsacus
365 Sicily (Soc. 4.12)
366 Nicomedia
366 Antioch (27)
366 Smyrna
366 Singidunum
367 Tyana
369 Rome
370s Armenia
374 Pazoukome
374 Rome
374 Valentia (Fr.) (20)
375 Ancyra
376 Iconium
376 Rome
378 Antioch (Caria)
378 Rome
378/9 Antioch (146/153)
380 Caesaraugusta (12)
380 Milan
?381 Side
381 Aquileia (24/34)
(II) 381 Cple
   (140/150+36)
382 Rome
383 Cple

384 Burdigala
?385 Capua
385? (S)angarum
   (Bithynia)
385 Caesarea
386 Rome (80)
386 Trier
389/90 Side (25)
390 Carthage
391? (S)angarum
   (Bithynia)
392? Caesarea (Pal.)
392 Capua
393 Hippo
393 Cabarsussa (Afr.)
394 Rome
394/6 Nemausus
394 Cple
394 Bagai (Afr.)
394 Cple (37)
394 Carthage
394 Hadrumetum
396 Nemausus (21)
397 Carthage
398 Torino
398/9 Diospolis (Pal.)
399 Carthage
400 Cple
401 Carthage
402 Ephesus (70)
402 Milev
403 Carthage
403 Cple (40)
404 Chalcedon "The
   Oak"
404 Cple (60)
404 Carthage
?404 Thessalonica
405 Carthage
406 Carthage
407 Carthage
408 Carthage
409 Carthage

Three Centuries of Synods = Councils[1] (*Continued*)

410 Carthage	449 Arles	504 Rome
411 Carthage (571)	449 Rome	?504 Byzacena prov.
412 Zerta	449 Tyre	506 Agde (35)
412 Carthage	449 Berytus	511 Orleans
415 Jerusalem	450 Cple	512 Antioch
415 Diospolis	451 Arles	512 Sidon (80)
(=Lydda) (14)	**(IV) 451 Chalcedon**	515 Illyria prov.
416 Milev	(350/360? 413; 500+)	515 Antioch
416 Carthage	452 Laodicea	515/6 Tyre
418 Suffetula	452 Alexandria	516 Epirus prov.
416/8 Thysdrus	453 Angers	516 Tarraco
417 Rome	455 Arles	517 Eponum
417 Carthage	458 Narbo	517 Lyons
418 Rome	459 Rome	518 Jerusalem
418 Carthage (217)	459 Cple (80)	518 Tyre
419 Carthage	461 Tours	518 Cple (44)
419 Ravenna	463 Cple	519 Apamea
421 Carthage	464 Gallic	519/20 Cple
422/3 Carthage	465 Gallic	520 Tournai
425 Carthage	465 Rome	523 Carthage
426 Cple	471 Antioch	523/4 Iunca (Afr.)
427 Hippo	470s Vienne	524 Arles
429 Tricasis (Troyes)	470s Arles	527 Carpentoractum
430 Rome	470s Lyons	527 Toleto
(III) 431 Ephesus I (150–160; 200+)	475 Ephesus (?600)	529 Arausio
431 Ephesus II (130–35; 150)	?478 Cyrrhus	524/530 Valentia (Fr.)
433 Anazarba	478 Cple	532 Rome
433 Antioch	478 Rome	532 Cple
434/9 Reios (Provence)	481 Antioch	533 Orleans
437/8 Antioch	482 Antioch	536 Jerusalem
441 Arausio (Orange)	482 Alexandria	536 Cple (65)
442 Vasio-Vaison	?484 Carthage (466)	538 Antioch
443 Arles	484 Rome (27)	538 Orleans
444 Rome	485 Rome (43)	539 Gaza
445 Besançon	495 Rome (45)	541 Orleans
445 Antioch	495 Cple	547/8 Cple (70)
446 Astorga (Sp.)	496 Rome (55)	549 Orleans
447 Toleto	497 (498?) Cple	550 Mopsuestia (14)
448 Cple (31)	499 Rome (71)	**(V) 553 Cple** (152–
448/9 Berytus	501 Rome	161)
449 Cple	502 Rome (76/80)	
449 Ephesus (150)	503 Rome	

Fig. 1. The western empire's council sites

The tabulation offered here doesn't aim at any perfect combing through of the surviving sources; no more than is needed to satisfy a Martian curiosity — but also, to help in understanding a bishop's ordinary life experience. That is my target.

For the resulting list, the evidence is evidently incomplete. It can be roughly corrected, however, through quantifying the existing sees = bishops. Their total in the western provinces rises across time. We can count, then, in Gaul a mere 16 in AD 314, but 70 by the end of the century and well above a hundred in the mid-fifth century; in north Africa from modern Tunisia westwards, above 450, reflecting a regional tradition of placing bishops in charge of even quite small centers. In contrast, Italy: here, there were up to roughly 110 sees in the mid-fifth century, although population centers of one to five thousand residents numbered perhaps 400, while the larger towns and cities would add another 30 to that total.[2] Thus Africa was over-episcopalized, we might say, while Italy was the opposite. It is worth noting, too, how urbanized the peninsula really was.

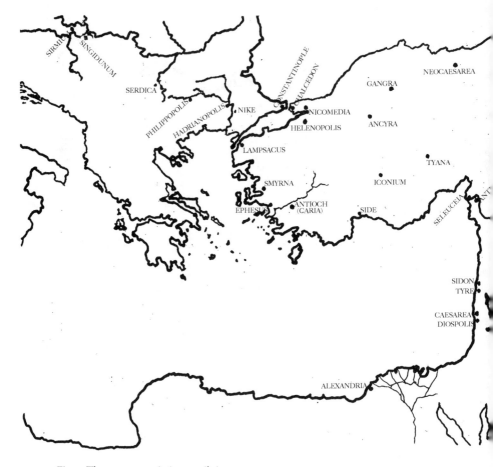

Fig. 2. The eastern empire's council sites

It is, however, the Greek-speaking provinces which count for most, by far, in the conciliar story. Sources provide good figures for the total of bishoprics in Egypt. They numbered just under a hundred.[3] For other parts of the East there is unfortunately no comparable evidence. The fact might seem to rule out any over-all estimate; but at least an approximation is possible. The reasoning in its support can be left to a long note, but the yield is a grand eastern-empire total of seven or eight hundred, as my best guess.[4]

Some duplication of bishops must be mentioned: a full century of it in north Africa, where there were as many Caecilianists as Donatists sharing towns more or less angrily; a decade and more of duplication in the east when Arian bishops outnumbered the Nicene, and often competed with them in the same city; and many other scenes and periods of rivalry on a lesser scale, which increased the episcopal ranks. But to my knowledge competitors didn't turn up at councils in antagonistic pairs, except only at Carthage in 411.

All the bishops of a province were supposed to meet together twice a year, spring and fall. This was commanded by the Nicene council (can. 5), repeated at Antioch (AD 363, can. 20) and at Chalcedon (can. 9) and elsewhere, and observed in Cappadocia in the mid-fourth century as in Gaul in the mid-fifth (but there, only once per year). We happen to know this from Basil's and Hilary's letters.[5] We hear of complaints that compliance was burdensome; but also, that such councils might be called back for successive sessions, as in Bithynia in AD 325–26. So, some compliance or provinces fell below the average, some above.

Multiplying by 120 provinces, where the actual number of them was a little lower in AD 325 but higher in 553,[6] the councils over this time-span cannot have totalled less than 15,000. As one whole phenomenon, they must be of general interest to historians of the later empire. For one thing, they must have encouraged a common way of life through the bringing together of people in situations both social and governmental. But my own concern is only with the degree of involvement of individual bishops, experienced in most sees as something at least frequent; more often, as annual or semiannual. Council-attendance was certainly a completely familiar fact of life.

So much in answer to those questions that a visitor from space might ask: How many assemblies? How frequent? As to the numbers of participants, the council-list given above provides a generous sample of what is known at both provincial and so-called ecumenical assemblies. Attendance by clergy of all ranks ran from 12 up to 1,000 and more. We can't say how nearly complete the response to a summons may have been, except that it was generally very full. Clearly a large majority of bishops of a given province or region were often assembled, as it is manifest also that only a handful can have escaped all experience of participation over the term of their service to their sees.

To confess the gaps in our evidence, in reply to a Martian inquirer, is to arouse further curiosity about the record as a whole; for if so much information has been lost — if we can name only a little more than 250 councils out of 15,000 — how on the other hand did any information at all survive from so long ago?

Knowledge was originally very full and widely dispersed, as will appear in a later page; for conciliar proceedings (*acta*) were all taken down verbatim in short-hand, transcribed, often translated at the time from Greek to Latin or vice versa, and duplicated for preservation in both ecclesiastical and some-times civil archives. The whole process was carefully seen to.

But here again, much more of the record has been lost than preserved. Reasonably complete *acta* from only a dozen or so meetings can be read today. Most of them can be found in the first nine (of 54!) gigantic volumes, collected with other relevant bits and pieces and with no sparing of vellum and elegant typography, by Gian Domenico Mansi. His was a work of the eighteenth century. In the earlier twentieth, Eduard Schwartz drew on this and on other manuscripts and editions for a much better version of *acta* and attendant documents. The spoken parts even without the attendant documents run to well over a half million words. Schwartz, however, offered only the so-called ecumenical councils I–V. Subsequently, and still more narrowly, these councils' canons or decrees were published in careful editions of both the Greek and Latin text or of the Latin alone.[7]

In explanation of the steady narrowing of our window on the subject, over the centuries and even into modern times: it should be remembered that councils of any sort met over controversial business; and it is the rule across time that the record of controversies will survive or not at the pleasure of the winners. It should be no surprise, therefore, that some of what we know of Aquileia (AD 381), deplored today as unedifying, survived only as marginalia to one single manuscript, brought to light in the 1980s; or that a meeting that gave a voice to both sides of a certain theological argument lay hid only in a Syriac manuscript, published also in the 1980s; that *acta* of a third meeting dominated by persons later judged losers, at Ephesus II, survived only in the same language, off in a corner of the empire; similarly preserved, some of the letters of a loser; and not preserved beyond a few fragments, the letters of another such figure; while a church historian representing the ostracized today speaks to us only through excerpts made from his lost work, excerpts in which he is, for each passage, introduced to the casual reader as "the impious."[8]

Obviously there was a screening process separating us today from the abundance of antiquity. How it worked in detail, others may say who know more about manuscript transmission. My small sampling is enough to show, however, that the chief treasure to be preserved from conciliar *acta* was thought to be the final, agreed-on legislation, not the lead-up argumentation. Outcome counted, not process. Indeed, it was best not to revisit the process, for reasons only a Martian would need to have explained. So, for example, Nicaea's proceedings were duly taken down at the time and duly published; but they were allowed to perish, all but the creed and canons.[9] These of course were much copied.

Selection has continued to operate in its own way. In Mansi's day you could still widen your readership for Greek documents if you provided a parallel translation into Latin. That was done in his volumes. But translation stopped there, for a majority of the surviving *acta*. They remain little visited in the ancient tongues. Fortunately, a substantial minority is available in French, with some editing and abbreviation; some in English; a little, in German; and a still smaller quantity, once in Syriac, now in French or German.

As to the last question raised from outer space, Who *were* the participants? or, in more scientific terms, where on the social grid would the council participants fit? — a safe answer would place them generally in the upper ten per cent but not quite at the top, as measured by their families' estate-value, their occupation before joining the clergy, their command of wealth as bishops and their place then in the public eye. Information is of course very incomplete. The upper and lower extremes of the group are, however, worth indicating to define it.

A description by one of the most privileged tells us about the bishops he found floating loose in the eastern capital in the 380s:

> Some, sprung from the change-tables and the icons you find there; some from the plow, blackened by the sun; some from the never-ending toil of the mattock and hoe; others, off the galleys or the army list, still smelling of bilge-water or with the scourge-marks on their backs . . . ; still others who have not yet cleaned off the soot of their fiery trade [as smiths], fit only for a beating or the work-mill . . . now on their upward path, dung-beetles headed for the skies . . . babbling stupid phrases while not up to counting their own fingers or toes.[10]

Other sources indicate a small percentage who couldn't even sign their names; some from the most obscure hamlets or callings.[11]

But these were few. And few, also, at the other extreme, bishops who could count imperial senators among their acquaintance. Ambrose is the example that will be most often offered.

There were others not too far beneath him. Episcopal rank, after all, in towns of any size brought not only renown and respect but some degree of luxury, too: a staff of slaves and secretaries in an ample, perhaps gigantic residence (containing at Ephesus one public room able to receive more than a hundred persons); pay at least for a metropolitan bishop above a provincial governor's; at least in Rome, pay equal to that of the lower clergy of all the see put together, equal to the whole of the monies set aside for the poor; access to big fees, up to twenty pounds of gold for participating in an ordination; access to big fees also as an invited preacher; and at least in the largest of sees, Alexandria, a treasury able at need to provide a strategic gift of more than a ton of gold along with a huge value of various exotica.[12]

In consequence, and quite in keeping with the practices of their world, bishops sometimes acted out their wealth with extravagant behavior and pomp in their public appearances. As one of them said of their place in the world, "Prefects and city magistrates do not enjoy such honor as the magistrate of the church; for if he enters the palace, who ranks the highest, or among the matrons, or among the houses of the great? No one is honored before him."[13] The posturing and wealth suitable to a really great see, making celebrities of its successive occupants, of course were on a scale all of their own. In small sees, however, relative to their small size, the rank of bishops was still that of a principal citizen, still in the top tenth.

An apparently significant number of bishops had had what we might call post-graduate training in rhetoric with the idea of a career as a professor of rhetoric or as a lawyer. Among these were included some who had actually begun such a career before ordination, such as Augustine, bishop of Hippo. Others, or the same, had studied philosophy.[14] Advanced schooling was valuable. To be able to argue forcefully was a great help in getting up in the church; so was that way of speaking and writing that set apart the privileged from the common lot, so as to command instant respect from those lower in society, and recognition as an equal from the privileged.

Yet it is one of the rewards of reading the *acta*, that a great deal of common speech is on display, because of the stenographic quality of the text. Nowhere else in the written record of antiquity is there a match for this. All sorts of grammatical constructions, word choices, meanings of words, and departures from a careful, educated style turn up in both the Greek and Latin. The explanation is a reminder of how human beings speak, whatever their schooling, when they have not specially prepared their thoughts. Unselfconscious expression proceeds in short chunks and limited word-choice, even today among academics where it can be scientifically studied; similarly among the ancient bishops.[15]

A passage from a sort of ancient Polonius (yet, like Polonius, with something sensible to say) illustrates the quality of the record. We have the aged Emeritus in the early fifth century entering a discussion in what he intends to be the best manner of speaking — and he is no stranger to proper style — on the question of the on-going *acta* themselves and their stenographic quality; and before he is done, he has most terribly confused himself:[16]

> Emeritus, bishop, said: "There are indeed human minds which operate so fast that they can easily grasp, by seeing or hearing, everything presented to their attention, but this is in the powers, it may be, of the educated or learned, considering the nature of the thing. I must admit, however, that I am not well suited to this thing; for who can catch with his senses or

understand what is a mere fragment of speech or quick spoken word, barely as it passes, Noble Sire? [addressing the president of the session] — while the words and meaning and essence of the business are to be scrutinized, throughout their course and the flow of discussion? That's why, when a fair copy [of the proceedings] is being read and quick remarks are, so to speak, released into the air, our perception can't grasp or hold them. Where and to whom is the power given? If they are so fortunate in their powers of mind, they shouldn't boast in pride of their memory. Anyway, mine isn't good enough unless I review it, many times and by a slow reading, so I can get to the real truth of what is said through a re-reading and what the other party proposed in objection. You can see how the record of the proceedings is made, so that they are laid out for the recall of testimony in writing, and memory which can't be adequate by itself, through loss by forgetting, may know what went on. And it's no different with the careful arrangements for the knowledge of written evidence and public testimony, by a wise provision, unless I have trouble grasping what is read aloud, perhaps because of omissions or perhaps because so much time has gone by — or because of the flow of the proceedings themselves, which can hardly be followed, both from the reading and their very compression in itself — one can comprehend what was expressed in the hearing. So you see, Noble Sire, our requests are fair and the trial mustn't be conducted in a hurried way, but the proceedings must be presented to our attention when they are made public, all of them carefully scrutinized, for the trial to be comprehended. . . ."

Possidius bishop of the catholic church [with a mocking little smile, no doubt] said, "The bible says, 'In too much talk there's always sin.' [Prov. 10.19] And since we have this scripture before our eyes, we would rather not appear long-winded — with God's help. . . ."

The bishop Emeritus said, "Since we've had scripture, it is also written, 'In wisdom that is hidden or treasure that is buried, what is the use?' " (quoting Sir. 20.32; 41.17).

The questions proposed by the visitor from space, it may be hoped, served to open up the subject of my study in a nice quantified scientific way; but the conversation of Emeritus and Possidius seems somehow better suited to make those church councils intelligible.

2

The democratic element

Political power in the Roman world, *kratos* defined as a claim on compliance by or upon those in public office, was no simple thing. Most obviously it was exerted from the top down by the few. These were imperial bureau chiefs, governors and garrison commanders, ex officio, or great persons without office, through their influence, wealth, and friends. But from the bottom up the many wielded power, too — the *demos*. To this extent the empire was democratic.

At first sight the idea appears paradoxical. The emperor's was an absolute monarchy. No one said otherwise. He commanded his generals and governors, they commanded others in turn, without challenge. In a parallel structure, the rich and pedigreed lorded it over civil society. They hob-nobbed with generals and governors, arranged things, and got their way. Everywhere one saw the sure, known signs of office or of social rank displayed in dress, behavior, accent. Everywhere one's sense of one's place was acted out in gestures grand or humble, in deferring to or insisting on titles or one's mere name, a name with connections.

In this world so unmercifully vertical, how could democracy find a place? Yet it was possible. In the very face of the ruler of all, and in the most public places, democracy found a place. Successes, well remembered for their drama, entered the record of the empire's earlier centuries again and again: the *demos* massed outside the palace or in some place of entertainment, the race track or the like in some great city, behaving just like a political assembly and getting what they wanted.[1] Lung power was people power, however informal it all appears.

Later, here is Constantius in Rome in AD 355 intervening in a church dispute to recall one of the contestants for the see from exile; let everyone accept him along with the incumbent, the pair to live together in peace. "The decree being read aloud in the *circus maximus*, the crowd shouted, 'The King's decision is the right one!' But the spectators were split in two according to the colors designating them" and in support of one or the other candidate; and they ended on the side of the exile, demanding him as their bishop. "In derision at the King's decree they exclaimed in unison, 'God is one! Christ is one! The bishop is one!' They spoke the truth in these very words; and after such shouts by the Christ-loving populace, expressive of such piety and justice, the reverend Liberius did return while Felix retired to a different city."[2]

A second scene, in the eastern capital, in reaction to the charges brought by the praetorian prefect against a popular favorite, Isokasios, in the hippodrome: "the Byzantine *demos* standing and watching listened to Isokasios and [at first dutifully] hailed King Leo with many acclamations, and then freed him."[3] Leo we know as the emperor Leo I (457–74).

A third in the same setting, to show the emperor conciliating the masses in the hippodrome, but honoring the Greens over the Blues (those colors identifying the two blocs of race-track fans): "Members of the Green bloc chanted in Constantinople to the King, 'To each his own!' He replied with an announcement through his chief herald, saying, 'It was to honor you that I moved you to the left [the place of honor] of the box from which I watch the races;' and they acclaimed him."[4]

A fourth: the emperor in the suburbs of the capital is obliged to pay homage to a pillar saint Daniel at the insistence of the crowds of the pious, "the *demos*, who cried out saying, ' . . . Why are the orthodox bishops in exile? Theoktistos the *Magister* to the Stadium [to be lynched]! . . . Burn the enemies of orthodoxy! . . .' and while the *demos* loosed a thousand other shouts of this sort, the King and the bishops stretched themselves prone upon the ground at the feet of the holy man."[5]

And by far the most famous, the exchange in AD 532 in the hippodrome. Present were the usual blocs, with the Blues by now enjoying imperial favor; seated in the imperial box, the emperor's herald and a secretary to take notes in shorthand. The trouble began with the Greens, voiced by their choral master Antlas and answered by the herald, both speaking in accentual phrases like "rappers" today. From the Greens, a dutiful commencement: "Long life to you, Justinian, may you conquer! We have been wronged, O Uniquely Good! We can't bear it, God knows! We're afraid to name a name lest he flourish all the more while we suffer for it!'

Herald: 'But who *is* he? I do not know him.'

Antlas: 'It is Calopodios the Palace Guard Secretary, who does us wrong!' And the Green party and Blue traded many insults and abused the King a lot . . . ,'' with protestations of orthodoxy on each side, mutual accusations of impiety, name-calling and threats: "accursed blasphemers" (boldly from the herald), "It is better to be a pagan than a Blue, God knows!" (from the Greens, against the other bloc, a safer target).[6] There follow bitter exchanges with insults from the herald. He defies the crowd. The next day but one, in the emperor's presence, further shouts are not dignified with any response at all. As an indication of the rules that should have been observed but were not, at this point the crowd grows seriously ugly. By nightfall the great "Nike" riots engulf the city in flames.

And from all of these incidents, a view into the conventions of power. From the *demos* due deference was required as a sort of introduction to whatever they had to say. In Greek settings, they would perhaps add a word or phrase in Latin to show respect for the language of the conquerors of long ago, the masters now (so we have, regularly, the transliterated title "Auguste" for the ruler; or to Justinian, *tu vincas*, "May you conquer!" transliterated in the record as *tou bingkas*).[7] And they would make an attempt at unison, so as to be both loud and intelligible.

Those who shouted would try to follow the phrase first called out by one of their number, their leader. By the third century the practice had been taken up even by the Roman senate in its more subservient transports; less surprisingly, it had long been common and in later centuries it continued at theatrical productions applauded by hired claques. At Alexandria when doctrinal differences split the city, unison was taught to give proper force to the intransigence of one party, whose leaders "prepared the others to cry out, 'Not one of them [the opponents] shall set his foot here, neither shall the transgressor be received!' "[8] At least some such directing voice is needed to explain the incidents recalled, above and to follow. Given the testimony to claques in Pompeii as well as Rome, in Ephesus as well as Constantinople, a general familiarity with them empire-wide can be assumed.[9]

After the civilities, next the demands. These easily took on a sharper, noisier quality as they were reiterated.

Kratos which could prevail even against the emperor in his capital, western or eastern, could certainly prevail against one of his servants, mighty though they all were. As his agents they could claim his absolute authority as their own. They generally did so without challenge. In Antioch, however, the assembled citizens chanted their demands rhythmically and got their way; in Alexandria the governor yielded to them in disregard of the law; in western cities as well as eastern, unspecified by the jurist Ulpian, a governor might yield to shouts when he knew he should not properly do so.[10] It is a short step to the best known moment in Jerusalem (Mk 15.8ff.; Mt 27.15ff.) where "the crowd began their demands as they usually did," for a prisoner to be released, and the governor wanted to give them one man but agreed to release another, just to keep them quiet. It was a moment with its rules: the crowd spoke and he listened.

Finally, in the very substantial city of Egypt, Oxyrhynchus, a later-third-century meeting of the council took place in the presence of the citizenry, to make certain decisions and appointments. At one point in the proceedings "the meeting shouted out, 'Noble minister! You have administered well! Witness has been made to a man who is true, upright, a patriot!' Menelaus, the minister: 'This account has been laid before you and it shall also be publicly displayed and entered in the records.'" Follows, his report. It is interrupted often by the meeting's repeated acclamations; then more business, with protests and disagreements and wavering by the speaker. "The assembly cried, 'Yes! Yes!'" to move the debate in one direction, as more arguments were offered in another — only to be overridden by still more massed exclamations, "That's the way! That's the way!" *houtos! houtos!*[11] In effect a majority had voted and so determined the outcome.

In the *acta* of the same council a century later the procedures emerge a little more clearly, though the conflict didn't involve any high person. It was in fact only a horse-breeder who had been given, against his will and certainly against his interests, the job of producing army supplies on call from the city. No, said he, not me, I'm the wrong sort of nominee, it's illegal. But en masse and without dissent "the councillors shouted, 'What is on the nomination is valid, what has been properly ordered mustn't be altered.' Ptoleminus, former City-Accountant, said, 'What has been ordered by our lord the Most Illustrious [governor, Flavius Eutolmius] Tatianus with the approval of the whole council must stand fast. . . .' Gerontius, former City-Collector, said . . ." (essentially the same thing). Eight more councillors, each with his title recorded even if it is no higher than that of Policeman, explain their concurrence in a sentence or two, and the presiding officer then wraps it all up with the statement, "What you collectively and individually urged is in the safe keeping of the *acta*. . . ." So the meeting concludes — unless, after these closing words, as we see in other Egyptian *acta*, the persons present all stayed on for a moment to sign the record of their sentiments individually.[12]

The reason for calling attention to all this material is of course to prepare for a later discussion of church councils. Their participants, it will be seen, behaved as they were all used to doing in secular decision-making groups or assemblies. Their rules and procedures developed along the lines of secular equivalents. But discussion of this can wait, perhaps, while one point in particular is stressed: the fact that acclamations did really function as votes.

What we would today call "votes" seem to have been the most frequent business of civic assemblies, *vota* or *psephismata* offering welcome, praise, or grateful honors to high personages. As for instance in a little town to the north, in the late second century. Here "in a full meeting, the people and assembled councillors hailed him aloud in the agora with joyful cries," the "him" being a new governor, their recent benefactor.[13] Or again, the citizenry who massed in Antioch's theater, there to "liken the greatness and flow of his [the honorand's] civic generosity, in its abundance, to the waters of the Nile, and they call him a very Nile of gifts, and some . . . bring in the Ocean, and say that is what he is."[14] Or in the not inconsiderable city of Oxyrhynchus in Egypt: on the occasion of the governor's visit, the *acta* of an open meeting to record the shouts, "Oceans to the council president! Oceans to the glory of the city! Oceans to Dioscorus our First Citizen! With you, all good things and increase! To the fosterers of good things! Isis loves you and brings a high Nile! . . . Let the decrees, the *psephismata*, be voted for the president! Let the decrees be voted on this great day! He is worthy of many *psephismata*!" (and so forth). The honorand responds graciously; yet his admirers' feelings overcome them again. "The *demos* shouted out, 'He deserves many *psephismata*' " and they go on to hail the provincial governor similarly, and the emperor, the Romans, and again their own First Citizen, for a total of some three dozen benedictions. When they fall silent, the syndic promises, "we will pass on what you say to the council" — which was the city's highest authority.[15]

It has been suggested that the text was taken down for use in an honorific inscription, of a sort that has been found very widely. Some were posted up in public places in red-painted versions. Time has not quite erased those in Aphrodisias and sites in the provinces of Caria and Pamphylia, and in Delphi in Greece. Others were stamped on the Greek cities' small change. Still others, the most commonly surviving, were inscribed on stone, not only in the east.[16] The emperors' honors naturally got the most attention and appear often in the historical accounts, Tacitus' or others'.

No account of acclamations is more extraordinary than that which introduces the law-collection published in AD 438, not, it is true, because the emperor himself was on hand but because the senate house of Rome was the scene. The senators were there assembled and the occasion was an act of what amounted to legislation on the grandest scale. Here to offer the Theodosian Code for publication, the Most Noble and Most Illustrious Praetorian Prefect, three times Ex-Prefect of the City, Consul Ordinary, delivered a speech interrupted at an early moment: "the assembly shouted, 'Thou art newly eloquent! Truly eloquent!;'" and with this encouragement he was able to proceed to an explanation of just what the emperor had done, greeted by the "assembly shouting, 'It is right! So be it! So be it!'" Followed, then, the emperor's own words that were the introduction to the book, read aloud. This at the time of its publication in the eastern capital a decade earlier had been hailed by the assembly there with shouted sentiments of loyalty and admiration, 43 in all, some of them only a couple of words in length, some two or three times longer, all of them repeated eight to 28 times to a total of 748, requiring close to two hours from the audience and now repeated before the senators in Rome. All were then written into the minutes of this senate meeting, as was the practice with such august *acta*.[17]

The number of repetitions has been doubted, but the doubts removed by looking at accounts of other, only slightly less awe-full moments signalized by a 60–times repeated acclamation (this, for an emperor, naturally) or 23, 16, 26 . . . to a total of 159 times for successive salutes and hopes expressed in support of a mere priest. He was being appointed co-adjutor to his bishop in AD 426.

There were similar moments awaiting The Great, new-come to a city: Alexandria, it might be, or Antioch; or Edessa in 449, visited by the Great and Glorious Chaereas, Count of the First Rank and Governor of Osrhoene.[18] At his appearance, the men and women of the city "all shouted, 'One is God! Victory to the Romans! Our God, have mercy on us! Our rulers, may they ever be victorious!'" and so forth, individually cheering for the consul in Constantinople, various governors, the imperial court, the bishop of Antioch, all Christ-loving people, the orthodox, the imperial Commander-in-Chief, and "One is the God who guards you!"—a total of 82 acclamations, *phonai*, of which the last 28 focus on their own bishop and on their very passionate views about church governance. Two days later, the city's "workmen and ordinary residents of the capital city [of the province], Edessa, who requested leave to enter [Count Chaereas' hearing-chamber], shouted 'May our Lord have mercy on us!'" and went on from there to deafen the Count with 148 shouted sentiments, a mix of dutiful praise but also of supplication for his justice. These will require mention later on.

But these sentiments were also mentioned immediately on the Count's return to Constantinople. It was necessary and expected that he do so; for he served not only as the emperor's voice but as his ears, too, and the Edessenes, understanding the fact, had thus been exercising their democratic rights in an approved fashion, with all their might. Constantine had decreed long prior, "We grant to all persons the privilege of praising by public acclamations the most just and vigilant judges . . . [while] the unjust and the evildoers must be accused by cries and complaints . . . ; We shall carefully investigate whether such utterances are truthful . . . the praetorian prefects and the counts who have been stationed throughout the provinces shall refer to Our wisdom the utterances of Our provincials."[19] In the same way, we have seen the acclamations in a public meeting in Egypt written down for a reading aloud before the city council. They would count, there. That was the point of them: a bit of *demos*-power, not just lung-power. The same understanding governed church-council action routinely, as will be seen.

Since everyone knew the rules, sometimes their application is provided for in so many words. The Syrian governor in AD 518 concludes a council over which he has been presiding by a promise that "what the Most God-Loving Clergy of the Holy Church of God in Apamea have determined, a true account of everything done shall be reported" to both the Throne and its high officialdom; to which, he says, please "add on also to these Proceedings the acclamations forthcoming from the assembly of the Undefiled Clergy of the aforesaid Most Holy Church"; whereupon, the undefiled clergy oblige with seventy-odd shouts, including specifically, "These Proceedings, *acta*, for the King!"[20]

Turning to *kratos* on display, not in city plazas, amphitheaters, race-tracks, theaters, and the like, nor in the production of decrees, nor in complaints and charges pressed upon some high official — in none of these common forms but rather in trials: here too was some measure of democracy. It is of interest to the student of the church since the most important of councils so often took the form of a judicial hearing, whether as the sole item of business or occupying only one session among several.

Indeed the Roman senate was a model. The fact is generally agreed on; it is already clear from the mid-third century when we get our first look inside an ecclesiastical council or synod. Not that bishops had observed what Tacitus was familiar with in Rome; rather, they had observed local imitations to be seen about them in their own municipal senates.[21] Where the setting was western and Latin, as it was for our earliest glimpses in detail, the civic term to convene, *cogere*, was picked up by those in charge; other terminology, too; likewise the mode of delivering one's vote standing, the use of supporting documents and the echoing of a discussion-leader's words. They were to sum up each proposal in very neutral terminology, while the meeting shouted *placet*, "Yes!"

These scenes were all Roman; Roman, the number of witnesses where they were needed in answer to charges; Roman, the *sententiae*, the "opinions" or individual votes which participants delivered upon invitation, after the *placet*; decision by a majority and by massed shouts which had replaced the older senatorial usage of physical division into two parts, to be counted (the *discessio*); finally, the writing up of the proceedings, *acta*, to be made known thereafter in a public notice or letter.

Strange, that no *acta* should survive from the tens of thousands of Roman senate meetings that we know took place.[22] There are, however, many revealing anecdotes or glimpses in literary sources: in Cicero, the younger Pliny, Dio Cassius. These suffice to show why, if not exactly when, the older Roman *discessio* should have yielded to massed shouts, similar to the rumbling "Hear! Hear!" of Parliament. To stand up for the wrong cause was simply too dangerous under bad emperors — emperors in a long list, a list close to all-inclusive, as Tacitus would have said. Better to sense which way the wind blew; better to make out just who wanted what action taken on a given day. One could stand silent if one chose, or even shout twice, after an ill-judged support of a first, defeated opinion. No one need know the error. So it must have been in Rome; so it evidently was in local town-council meetings, although what governed conduct there was not so much fear of dire punishment as the calculation of the costs in "clout". Public loss in a debate meant loss of face.[23]

The risk was unwelcome, perhaps more serious than that; so the general aim was unanimity. All those "demands by the people" referred to above, with no hint of a minority, constitute the epigraphic result. The papyrological result is no different: in Egyptian town council meetings we find no sign of a division being taken, but instead, discussion until everyone has fallen into line or, alternatively, postponement of a decision until, we may suppose, the back-room arrangements have been better nailed down.[24] It may be supposed, too, that the back-rooms could help in advance of a meeting. This speculation may be turned on church debates.[25] They certainly aimed at unanimity.

Nevertheless and inevitably, minorities made their appearance from time to time. They could prove stubborn, they might need steam-roller treatment, as an old hand at councils describes it — where "those who seek the truth with due care [regarding some dispute] should note that statements are often made by people in synods from partisan sympathy or opposition or sheer ignorance; yet no one pays attention to what is said by some minority but only by common agreement, as determined by all. If anyone chose to take seriously such contrary statements, as those people would have it, every synod would be found to contradict itself."[26]

Alternatively, minorities might be forced into the majority. Cyprian presiding at Carthage in the 250s speaks frankly of unanimity arrived at "not only by our united feelings but by threats."[27] Of course, it was important to him to have his way; and the subordinate bishops were docile. Again, two long generations later and only a dozen years after the persecutions had ended, a group of recalcitrant bishops at Nicaea confronted the emperor, himself attended by his great judges and military commanders in his own palace and speaking in Latin, the language of command. He anticipated no trouble. A minority present, however, were unwise enough at first to offer their own credal text for consideration which "all the bishops tore to pieces on the spot," making "a huge uproar." After the ensuing debate, the emperor's High Panjandrum, by name (in Greek) "Beloved", then personally carried round the creed the emperor had approved for everyone to sign if they wished to be spared the penalty of exile; which, needless to say, most did — to be condemned later as hypocrites. There were 17 (or 22?) of these latter. With a little reflection, they were reduced to four; and, as they had no doubt foreseen, those four were carted off to some part of the Roman Gulag, some obscure corner of semi-desert away west or far south, there to repent.[28]

In this and, for later discussion, in a good number of other instances of split councils, two common assumptions are evident: first, that the participants acting as a *demos* would exercise *kratos* (and some would win and some would lose); second, that universal endorsement of what the majority wanted was considered of such importance, it must be extorted if need be by plain force. The two assumptions were often in conflict.

They can be seen also in episcopal elections, through which council members had all risen to their role and by which they had all experienced democracy in action. The experience was part of their mental baggage; and their model was, once again, secular.

Members of the Roman *demos* had once filed past tally-keepers to declare their preference in popular elections; but eventually they adopted a secret ballot. Greeks instead had always raised and counted hands, the act of *cheirotonia*.[29] No doubt, being Greeks, they weren't silent about it. *Cheirotonia*, or alternatively the rough measuring of shouts equivalent to "The Ayes have it," were both methods adopted by the church. They were adopted in preference to Roman balloting quite naturally; for the Christian community had its birth and early growth in the Greek east. In councils, then, a show of hands was occasionally asked for by the presiding person; but a show of preference by shouting seems to have been the rule, and certainly prevailed in episcopal elections.

In these latter, three groups can be seen in action: the local aristocracy, the clergy, and the populace. The first of these groups, over the course of the late empire and more markedly in the west, increased their influence (and the same increase can be noticed in other areas of life in the period); but their power was never absolute.[30] In what way their voting was kept separate or folded into the general process isn't clear. Of the second group, the clergy, some were bishops summoned from around the province, some local, none of whom should try to impose their choice. Instead, they should sense which candidate(s) would prove acceptable, then to be hailed by the crowd and so offered to them for confirmation. Such was the prescribed procedure. Yet bishops sometimes simply appointed a successor; they named a brother or nephew; so they enjoyed more *kratos* than anyone else, at the expense of the populace.[31]

This last, the third group, when it agreed with the other two, was the most easily acknowledged. In theory, at least, "an active lay participation was considered necessary and normal, albeit troublesome."[32] Indeed, the electoral role of the people was described increasingly in terms borrowed from secular equivalents. That is, choosing a bishop was always and ultimately a democratic process. It could involve supporting parties, leaders of these, deals to swing votes, bargains rather distrustfully confirmed in written contracts.[33] However, our sources which speak from among the leaders of the church are in general agreement that the process worked best when the *demos* was least active and engaged — best, if the people enthusiastically but submissively requested a bishop, if they perhaps suggested possibilities, and the higher-ups made the choice.

It was a delicate matter. It went one way at one time and place, differently at some other, depending as much on personalities and influence as on merits or rights. True, the *demos* outnumbered their betters, a hundred to one; if *kratos* meant sheer physical force, as sometimes it did, of course they won; and many instances of this sort will be described in due course; but normally that was not the case. Some measure of religious awe inclined the power of deciding toward the clergy, before whose house, the Lord's house, or actually within it, the lead-up to the election and the decision itself took place; a sense of up and down, of rank and deference, slowly asserted itself even beyond the degree prevalent in the middle centuries of the empire. And still, unanimity couldn't be expected always to prevail.

Two glimpses, now, so as not to be so blurry about the whole matter: in Constantinople at the ordination of a bishop in AD 390, "many of the throng present, instead of [the expected and conventional acclamation], 'Worthy!' *axios*, shouted 'Unworthy!'"; and, once installed, when he tried to ordain another new bishop, "he was unable to get anything agreed to by the people, whose belief lay with the similarity of [Christ's] substance, *ousia*, according to the teachings of [their former bishop] Eleusinius." So the new incumbent and his supporters had first to produce public statements and anathemas so as to satisfy the people about his doctrinal position, and only then did "they permit the election, but would allow no other person to be raised to the episcopal rank unless by their votes, *psephoi*, and provided the elected person would promptly and openly preach the similarity of substance."[34]

Which all serves to show how theological debate wove itself into episcopal elections. The point is important to my subject. In elections indeed all parties might consider rather their personal attachment to some well-known candidate with a record of long service to the community, a tried and true archdeacon long ripe for promotion; or perhaps they preferred some different sort, able to promise a rich flow of favoring influence and gifts, his own or his grand friends'; but doctrinal questions often intruded and determined the outcome.

As the moment came for decision, we must imagine someone presiding who is chief in the church of the area or province, inviting comments from colleagues summoned to the ordination. They speak. In what order? It is minutely determined. The church loved ranks as much as secular society and most minutely served out its duties and privileges among lectors, exorcists, presbyters, deacons and archdeacons. Some must never speak or always stand in the presence of others.[35] To seniority in office among the bishops, such close attention was paid that certificates of appointment had to be exactly dated with duplicate records in scattered archives, "so no fights could arise."[36] *Democracy?*

The paradox acknowledged in the opening paragraphs of this chapter makes the picture confusing. On the one hand were the claims on compliance made by both secular and ecclesiastical authority; and these were not contested in so many words, whatever the fact in action. On the other hand was the claim of the greater number to prevail over the lesser *in* an assembly, and *of* an assembly, over its presiding officials whether secular or ecclesiastical. This too was not challenged directly — rather, confirmed by the most common experiences in every city, often in a given year and well publicized, too, when there was any joint business to be done. In the welcoming of important visitors as in the recognition of important acts of public beneficence, even people well below the ruling class were likely to have played a part at some point in their life, cheering as they were supposed to do; and people of a class likely to be recruited to the clergy had at least a good second-hand knowledge of how things went in city council sessions, and the way decisions were there signalized.

Those who attended church councils brought with them, then, as their mental baggage, all of these experiences governing their expectations of what would and should happen there, and of what their own behavior ought to be.

It remains only to add as a final comment, that the most obvious problem in democracy was never consciously addressed: that is, the inability of the majority always to understand the business before them, so as to judge wisely among arguments and alternatives. Scattered in my third chapter and elsewhere, below, are a few out of the many statements of ecclesiastical leaders rebuking or deploring the limited grasp of those beneath them, the "simple-mindedness" (or some such term or phrase) which rendered discussion of anything complicated too much for *hoi polloi*. The Church Fathers, however, never went on to say, Let us therefore openly and expressly rule from above. No more did the Founding Fathers, in an American analogy. Almost at the opening of the Constitutional Convention (May 31, 1787) they too rebuked, they deplored "the follies of democracy . . . the people, [who] want information and are constantly liable to be misled . . . They are daily misled . . ." (so, Edmund Randolph, Roger Sherman, Elbridge Gerry, great leaders at the moment and for decades to come). But in the morrow, such misgivings were not voiced again. It would have been politically impossible to impose or even seriously to suggest the rule of the "best".

3

The cognitive element

Why should Christians when they met together debate and inquire about the nature of their God? Were they acting under God's instructions? Did God care what they thought?

Perhaps only a visitor from Mars would puzzle over such questions. They find no answer in the sources because evidently they were never asked.

In early times the church's leaders did indeed speak up for unity of command and doctrine. Paul did so more than once, and Ignatius, too. Later, emperors and bishops on their behalf repeated the plea on behalf of the empire's safety.[1] Yet peace was continually disturbed by views not accepted among the prevailing majority; and from the beginning the majority judged it right and proper to abominate such novelties and their proponents, without having to explain why.

A "heresy", *hairesis*, in those times was something quite neutral, nothing more than a "choice"; but it came to mean a choice that divided a religious community; and the writers who established this meaning show "a remarkable preoccupation with correct doctrine — even if their notions of correct doctrine vary."[2] By the mid-second century in the Christian community, sharp boundaries had been set up around what a speaker would call orthodox and permissible. The war was on, almost unnoticed by the persons all around who were not Christian and never could see why the definition of one's worship had to be warred about at all.

An observer of such a philosophical mind, later a bishop, a generation before the council of Nicaea set down his thoughts on the subject:[3]

> The philosophy of the Christians is simple. It devotes most of its efforts to ethical instruction, and regarding the more rigorous discussions of God it uses metaphorical language. In ethics also they avoid the more difficult questions . . . They devote themselves principally to moral exhortation . . . piling up their rather crude injunctions hit or miss. Ordinary folk who hear this as one can see for one's self make great progress in virtue. But this philosophy has been much fragmented by its subsequent adherents; many schools of thought have emerged just as in academic philosophizing, with the result that some of these men developed beyond others in their skills and, so to speak, in their more vigorous inquiries. Indeed, some have risen to leadership of schools of thought, *haireseis*, and thus ethical instruction has declined as it has become less clear — since none of those who wanted to head up schools of thought were able to attain the necessary rigor and since the common people became more disposed to factious strife. So, as each was eager to surpass his predecessors through the novelty of his teachings, they converted this simple philosophy into an inextricable tangle.

The writer, a certain Alexander, lived at the very center of serious intellectuality in the empire, Alexandria, where one would most naturally look for those tendencies in the church that he describes.

In a quite general description, however, and not just of Egypt, there is an echo of Alexander's account offered by a well-known church historian. Looking back some generations to the 320s, he reports "everywhere confusion reigned; and not only were church leaders to be seen entangled in disputes but the masses were divided, some inclining to one side, some to the other. Things reached such a wretched state that in public, in the very theaters, Christianity was a target of ridicule." Concerns of this sort continued to bother the church throughout the centuries of my study.[4]

Next in the series of comments, a rhetor in the 360s addresses a Christian monarch and commends him for tolerance by praising Christian wrangling: "Consider how by this variety [in beliefs] the very Maker of All is gratified. He wishes the Christians of one sect ['Syrians'] to shape theirs in one way, the non-Christians ['Greeks'] in another, the Christians [of another sect, 'Egyptians'] in still a third; and the Syrians themselves, not all in the same way but cut up into little parts. No one thinks just like his neighbor, but one man this way, another, that."[5] Such was a polytheist's view; while another, in an opinion often quoted, notes much the same thing: "the straightforward, simple Christian worship he [the emperor Constantius in the 360s] turned upside down with the silly dread of old women, and provoked many splits through anxious quibbles instead of sober peace-making."[6]

Last, another church historian of the mid-fifth century saying in retrospect:[7]

> As to the East, though it had been divided after the Antioch synod [of AD 341] and differed openly on the Nicene view, I think that in truth most people agreed about it and concurred in the Son's being from the Father's substance, *ousia*, but for argument's sake some disputed the term *homoousios*, consubstantial. For some opposed the word from the start, as I surmise, considering it shameful to be defeated — as most people are prone to do — while others from a custom of continually discussing the subject were drawn into these opinions about God, and then their minds couldn't be changed. Still others, aware that their quarreling was misguided, inclined toward one side or another because of considerations of influence or family or whatever it may be that makes men adopt something unsuitable or to suppress their preferences where they ought really to stand up. And there were many, too, who thought it ridiculous to chew away at such quibbles and continued serenely in the view of the Nicene fathers.

The church's thrashing out of theology is at the center of all these quotations, as it is at the center of my study. They are to my knowledge our only contemporary or near-contemporary sources to shed light on the earlier phases of the process (though not on the violence of it). Thus they are important. Modern accounts may pass them by too quickly, to get to the personalities and publications that emerged during the thrashing out — publications by those very leaders who are missing from my own pages. It is, however, clear from the passages offered in the series above that not only the reasoning elite but an increasing part of the Christian masses concerned themselves with doctrine. They had somehow been drawn in; their interest, their passions, had been engaged in new thoughts and sophisticated argumentation. How did this happen?

The term *homoousios* in the last quotation of the series may serve as a convenient starting point. This, an adjective, was formed in the usual Greek way to mean "same-substance-y". It comes to notice first in the later 260s in the course of proceedings against the bishop of Antioch, Paul from Samosata. Four years later (AD 272), after his enemies had secured his excommunication and on their appeal to the emperor to clear him out of church property, he was sent packing. The whole affair gave notoriety to his principal offense. He had been guilty of defining Christ in relation to God by terms that other Syrian bishops thought were demeaning; he had asked if Christ was a distinct being from all time, or rather the substance of God implanted in a human form; and he had done all this loudly and offensively. His position like his deposition qualified him to be the arch-heretic for ever after, the very type of the species; consequently his writings were before many generations suppressed and can today be reconstructed only in bits and pieces and with many uncertainties.[8] For my purposes, however, it is enough that he did use the term *homoousios*, and in the connection indicated, and in service to future debate that required the word again; so it was in some circulation for Constantine to hear it and thrust it into the Nicene deliberations, exactly at whose suggestion, no one can say.[9]

It was the emperor's intent to end all arguing about the "god-ness" of Christ. This had been called in question in the course of the preceding decade by one Arius, in a manner recalling the bishop Paul of ill fame. Arius, senior presbyter in Alexandria, had used his authority, his great energies, and his eloquence to publicize and persuade others of his views; and in the process he had divided the chief of church communities. It was this division that provoked the calling of a council at Nicaea.

The solution there proposed was wrapped in the term *homousios*. It worked for a time; that is, the church accepted the neologism to describe the relation between Christ's nature and the nature of God the father; which was the emperor's object. The novelty itself was wisely kept out of a creed agreed on at Sirmium some years later (AD 359) and little heard of for a time after that; yet it was to have a life indeed, still later. At Chalcedon, for example, as at Sirmium a sharp challenge to it was raised: the word could not be found at all in the bible.[10]

What lay behind its invention was the need to make clear the ideas being talked about, in Antioch in the 260s as in Alexandria in the teens of the fourth century. Yes — but lending urgency to this need, in AD 325, was the fear felt by Constantine and widely preached in the church, that things would go well for him and his reign only if God were pleased; and wrangling among bishops of the realm was certain to bring down divine wrath. He expressed his anxiety and the reasoning behind it more than once. So did his successors on the throne. In particular, he shared his views on the divisions in Egypt, which he found incomprehensible, therefore all the more to be dealt with impatiently. In a public letter, he described what had gone on in the capital there, where the bishop had invited his clergy to declare,

> what each thought regarding a certain bible passage, or I should say, regarding an idle speculation therein . . . But from the start, it was not proper to inquire about such matters nor, once asked, was it proper to

respond. In an investigation of such a sort, where there is no legal necessity but only the chatter of unproductive idleness to occasion it, if it were
for the sake of some healthy exercise, still, we should keep it all locked
away inside our own minds and not bring it forth recklessly in public
assemblies, or entrust it imprudently to a general audience. For how few
they are that have the abilities for such great matters, so very profound,
either to see them distinctly or to expound them as they require! Or if
anyone should suppose he could do this successfully, how many among
the populace could he persuade? Who could command the needed preci-
sion in an inquiry of this sort without danger of missing something? In
such matters we should thus say as little as possible, where our natural
inadequacies prove incapable to explain, or the dullness of mind among
the people whom we teach may fall short.[11]

And Constantine goes on in other publicized statements to rebuke those who
ventured to talk about theology at all unless they did so "in words divine that
are kept hidden" as in cultic initiations. He dismisses the points raised by or
against Arius as "extremely trivial and quite unworthy of so much controversy", "small and quite minute points".[12]

The conclusion is surely right, then, that "we must dismiss the myth of a
Constantine obsessed by theology, finding his delight in the quarrels of specialists. He didn't even understand, for instance, how the trinitarian problem could
unleash such violent passions. For himself, these were tedious matters about
which no one understood anything and which it would be better not to raise. He
is forever repeating his appeals for unity: *concors, fraternitas* . . ."[13] — for on
unity depended his personal safety, not to mention the commonweal.

Such an emperor might be put down as a very stupid man, unable to enter
the mind of anyone different from himself. His particular origins, however,
and his life's experience must be remembered; and more, the cultural gulf that
divided the empire into west and east. It was not a matter of language. In fact
Constantine could express himself adequately if not elegantly in Greek; and
such a degree of competence was nothing unusual in at least the larger western
cities. He had spent much of his early life in eastern courts, too, which were no
doubt bilingual. More consequential was the west-east difference in the valuing of a legal education above a philosophical — in the valuing of political over
intellectual power. It shows in the western training of bishops as it does in
Constantine's asking (above), Is there any *law* that requires us to debate these
ridiculous Arian or anti-Arian points of doctrine?[14] Generally speaking, western churches did display much less interest than the eastern in credal definition
and logic-chopping (as it would have been called, contemptuously).[15] There is
thus something to be said in excuse for the emperor's incomprehension.

There are witnesses from the east on his side, too. The historians Ammianus and Sozomen, pagan and Christian, were quoted above on the "quibbles" or hair-splitting they saw at the heart of the church's problems. A third witness, Jerome, joins these two to deplore how "the simpler-minded are easily deceived" by Arian argumentation. "Both bishops and laity are deceived equally," he says; and there is much to show that he was right to include some at least of the clergy among the confused or ignorant.[16] "But bishops must not go wrong. And in fact," he goes on, turning to the trouble-makers, "they are introduced into the episcopal rank from the very bosom of Aristotle and Plato; for how often will you find one of them not educated to the hilt? . . . Arian heresy consorts better with secular wisdom. It borrows its flow of argument from the fonts of Aristotle."[17]

Complicated thought, strange vocabulary, drawn-out proofs, the multiplication of provisos and conditions, everything that Jerome objected to in doctrinal controversies is again clear in an attack by his contemporary, the bishop Epiphanius, on the Arians of the day:[18]

> For if, they say, he [Christ] is from God and God has begotten [a Son] from himself, which is to say from his own *hypostasis* according to nature or out of his substance, *ousia*, then he has been expanded or divided in two or broadened out in the process, or suffered compression or some other bodily experience; and they are thoroughly ridiculous in attributing to God by analogy with themselves and in trying to make God like to themselves. But there is nothing of this sort in God, for God is Breath, *pneuma*, and from himself he has begotten the only-begotten in a manner beyond words, beyond comprehension, and undefiled.

For my purposes it matters not which side of the argument here is right or wrong. Rather what counts is the quality of it, the level of sophistication — this, the cognitive element which one could expect to find in the minds of any ordinary bishop. Since it was so much and often on display, it seems fair to repeat, that the public had been somehow educated in a new style of theological analysis.

How well educated is of course another matter. The church historian Socrates (*HE* 1.23), with access to archives now lost, learnt "from various letters which the bishops wrote to each other after the [Nicene] Council that the term *homoousios* had reduced some of them to confusion." They hadn't really understood what they had signed on to nor, Socrates continues, did they now understand each other! It was an indication of the different cognitive levels to be found in the episcopal ranks and the differing capacities to handle theological debate. Controversy only continued.

To give an idea of the challenge it presented, consider a sampling of questions raised by Arius and his succession. These have appeared, seriously argued by someone of influence at some point in time, in my reading of the primary sources. One must imagine oneself an ordinary bishop, listening to these matters being parsed, disputed, fought over; one must imagine, and then ask one's self, Would I not be truly perplexed? — perhaps quite at a loss to know what to make of them?

> Did Christ exist before his incarnation?
> Is Christ begotten the equal of God unbegotten?
> Did Christ collaborate with the Father in the Creation?
> Is God the Father before the Son's existence?
> Was the coming into being of the Son the same process as the Creation?
> Is Christ's divinity or humanity merely notional, an external seeming?
> Was Christ man in flesh alone?
> Is Christ's human nature only in the flesh?
> Is Christ's likeness to the Father the same after incarnation?
> Is Christ anointed as man or as God?
> Is Christ begotten as other men, or made?
> Is Christ begotten of the Father or of the Pneuma-Spirit?
> If Christ is begotten of the Father, then by the Father's will?
> Is God one or two unbegotten beings?
> Is Christ a copy of the Father or an image?
> Is Christ a perfect copy of the Father?
> Is Christ the Logos?
> Was Christ created or born?
> *Is* Christ, as God, God of his substance, or only *made* of his substance?
> Is God's substance increased or divided in begetting?
> Is Christ of one will with the Father, or separate?
> Is Christ of one substance with the Father?
> Was Christ begotten once or twice?
> Was Christ a man indwelt by God?
> Is Christ one nature from two? or one nature in two, united?
> Is Christ's human nature separate from the nature of the Logos?
> Is the Pneuma-Spirit the equal of Father and Son?
> Is the Pneuma-Spirit of the same nature?
> Did the Pneuma-Spirit take the place of a soul in Christ?
> Is Christ's soul/mind (*psyche*/*nous*) human and impure?
> Is Christ one in properties, names, and operations, when incarnated?
> Did/can Christ's mind suffer? or only his body?
> Did the Father suffer on the cross?

Is there any separation in Christ between his self and his flesh?
In Christ are two natures resident in touch with each other, or fused?
Is "subject"/*hypostasis* the same as "subsistence" or "person"?
Is there one *hypostasis* or are there three?
Is "nature"/*ousia*, the same as "subsistence" or "person"?
Is one or the other of these terms the same as "substance"/*substantia*?
Is one or the other of these the same as "personality"/*persona*/*prosopon*?
Are the *hypostaseis* mere names?
Does "like" mean "identical"?
Is God a monad containing the dyad, or the triad?
Is Christ who suffered the same Christ who performed miracles?
Is Christ's nature, by birth, from Mary or by creation, from the Father?
Is Mary the mother of God, or of Christ, or of Jesus?
Is Mary's nature divine in any aspect?
Did Christ's existence begin in the womb or at birth?
Was Mary of the same substance as human beings?
Must all theological understanding be supported by terms in scripture?

A less ambitious, simpler approach to doctrine which all of the western and some of the eastern witnesses would have preferred was in fact quite familiar. For admission to their community, the churches everywhere employed a process of teaching and a ritual in which no very close examination of the divine *ousia* was insisted on. Consequently there were a lot of local differences in baptismal creeds and day-to-day theology for everyman — differences, however, of a sort generally tolerated as harmless or insignificant.[19] They continued for a very long time unchanged.

Their very simplicity insured their success, no doubt; this, and their basis in the best-known parts of scripture. Scripture, however, was no guarantee of peace. Even "heretics" drew on it.[20] For in the bible's words of unchallenged authority lay apparent contradictions. They were familiar, through such doctrinal questions as were listed above: how could two or three beings be one being at the same time? or how could the same being work miracles and feel pain? Even bishops were not all well equipped to respond. The minority who couldn't read indeed knew the essential texts, scriptural or other, well enough to stand up with the more literate like Emeritus. We saw him in my second chapter trading quotations with his supercilious opponent. Others too appear at moments bringing to bear the right parts of controversial tracts from memory, verbatim.[21] The majority had enjoyed a better than average education, true; and a handful were privileged beyond this, through long schooling. They knew Greek, of course, so they could handle words like *ousia*; or they thought they could, sometimes in mistake.[22] It was recognized as the language of exact reasoning, often not translated but transliterated into Latin.[23] They would know something of formal logic and about the arranging of thought in a flow. But these very skills of the elite fitted them as much to discover new uncertainties and to publicize them among their less gifted colleagues and congregations, as to resolve the old. That was where the problem lay.

Hence those questions. They should perhaps never have been asked at all. Being once asked, however, how could they be ignored? They multiplied, then. How they multiplied! and as they did so they imposed sharper choices of belief to be made at a deeper level of understanding and with more complex consequences in logic. Response, a little repressed by Nicaea, became again vocal and engaging. It is not too much to say "a great revolution now takes place."[24]

To show the consequences, a single, representative publication may be of help. It is a letter of AD 452 from the emperor Marcian in the months after Chalcedon addressing theological problems which had become problems of good order as well, in Palestine and its patriarchal capital (Jerusalem or Aelia by its Roman name). The most unruly of the people there were the scores of thousands of monks, whose leaders his letter addresses. He recalls the recent murder of "a deacon of venerable memory, whose body had been dragged around and subjected to further blows," followed a little later by a bishop's death at the hands of his rival's followers. Sectarianism run wild! that was the picture. But Marcian goes on,[25]

> Our Serenity has not called for anything similar [to this violence] to be directed against the monks, but only to bring peace to Jerusalem so far as it may be secured by general tranquillity among its citizens. Your outrageous behavior, in violation of the rules laid down for monks, has brought on a regular war levied against the common good order; has collected crowds of gangsters and other such habitual criminals; has stirred up arms for slaughter and devastation and every ill amongst those resident in the countryside. Thus it is that Our Power has been roused by such malefactors. . . . You have undertaken to teach rather than yourselves to be taught, oblivious to the divine counsels manifest in what is said [Mt 10.24], "a pupil does not rank above his teacher". . . . Hearing about "two natures", you spread the report that your souls have been assailed with new-fangled terminology strange to your ears. You should know, however, that it is not proper for yourselves to meddle into the examination of such matters, incapable as you are of understanding the subtleties involved. Ourselves on the other hand have received the teachings of the Fathers and so We know that Nature is Truth, . . . just as the

holy apostle Paul taught [Gal. 4.8], knowing Nature is Truth: . . . "pagans worship beings that are not gods by their nature (*physis*)". . . . Thus it shows clearly that Nature is the Truth even if (as you say) there is no inclusion of this regarding natures in the declaration of faith set forth by the 318 Fathers [of Nicaea]—for no one at that time was moved to inquire into this nor, at the present time, is any innovation against that faith intended. Rather, the determination authorized is that of the holy Fathers, so illustrious for their sound doctrine. You, however, who say there must be no theologizing are caught in that very act yourselves, demanding to know, "How could a virgin give birth and still be a virgin?" "How could she in a natural way give birth to a being above nature?" and so forth. . . . And herein, too, lies your sin, that you falsely assert that the doctrine of two Sons and two Christs has been determined [at Chalcedon]. But this is not so. We curse this doctrine as we deny it also and those who write or speak or dare to say such a thing . . . We have no wish to bring anyone into the path of truth by threats or force, whereas you for your part, to the contrary—beyond those actions of yours in the past with your swords and other injuries, through your outrageous conduct and cruelty to noble matrons and dedicated women —have not hesitated to force them into compliance with your perverse teachings, and by your clamor and by signed petitions have directed your obsecration at the holy council [of Chalcedon] itself and at the most holy patriarch of the apostolic throne in great Rome, Leo.

Such were Marcian's fulminations. Stick to Nicaea! Let it be only discerned in Chalcedon's creed as well. No one was trying to tamper with the Nicene text; no one was reaching beyond scripture, either. Trust in the council and stop thinking, for Heaven's sake! He repeated himself to the churches of Egypt, adding for that audience a reference to the deceits practiced by their former patriarch Dioscorus and other supporters of false doctrine which were packaged "in a way to fool the unsophisticated with their lies."[26]

And to repeat a piece of the quoted letter, "it is not proper for yourselves to meddle into the examination of such matters, incapable as you are of understanding the subtleties involved." Marcian sounds just like Constantine, surely; just like other persons in high positions in the church who will be instanced below: Gregory of Nyssa, for one. But the emperor as the man in charge perhaps better understood the very serious consequences of doctrinal debate evident in the wake of Ephesus I (AD 431): a part of Christendom might be broken off, for good and all; and again and in fact, another huge part was broken off in the wake of Chalcedon, and the east made into three churches, three populations.[27] No wonder he exclaimed against the stubborn ignorance, or simple piety as it might just as well be called, which confronted him among his subjects. People of quite ordinary intellect, ordinary bishops and archimandrites and monks and deacons and all those other folk who followed their lead, seemed able to control church history — and had, as any emperor must see it, no right to do so.

The problem was not of their making. The "subtleties involved" were the creature of sophisticated theology as it developed over the centuries of my study. Yet it is no part of my purpose to pursue this point into church history in its broad outlines. It is enough only to draw attention to the gulf, and the importance of that gulf, separating the elite (as they may called) from ordinary Christians. It was a question of the cognitive element; and it was a question, too, of a critical mass of involvement.[28]

Controversialists had first been drawn into the debates post-Nicaea through bishops circulating their sermons to be read aloud from other pulpits. They did so by the authority of their metropolitan status; equally, because of their individual merit as teachers. They communicated with their friends or colleagues all the time by what has been called "an epistolary spider's web uniting the churches," the ancient equivalent of the post: as an example, the output of one individual estimated at several letters sent out each week over a period of decades. And when in trouble over their teachings, they wrote more or less public letters, disseminating these as widely as they could to "all the clergy" of this or that other see. From time to time the emperors also wrote letters widely disseminated, naturally, and read aloud to whole congregations.[29]

One emperor toward the mid-fourth century assisted more actively in stimulating debate. He summoned a bishop whose beliefs he favored to meet before him with several others on the opposite side, shorthand writers at hand, so they might thrash out the merits of their differing theologies; and the results were then copied out to be consulted in major cities of the east. The winner, the bishop of Sirmium, had been earlier itinerant in his own cause, which became well known and a match for Paul's from Samosata.[30] Missionizing by bishops is casually reported as a common thing (below, Chap. 6). They were especially drawn to the imperial courts and seats of power but didn't ignore the odd corners of the world, either. Local authorities had to worry about contentious clerics on the loose, "lest I go about among the churches, win over the people, and contrive a split," so says one such under suspicion.[31]

A "running pamphlet war" which broke out in the sequel to Nicaea, between two of the prominent bishops there attending, was only the first of many such in the east, in which the leaders of one interpretation or another engaged with furious vigor: leaders such as Theodore of Mopsuestia, "said to have written more than ten thousand books." "He was," his enemies went on, "a regular plague of a man, *aliquis pestis homo*, or rather a wild beast with the shape of a man in the devil's fashion, known by the lying name 'God's-Gift', *theodoros*, who gained the form and name of bishop, lurking in a sordid little corner of the earth . . . , truly and chiefly a descendant of Paul from Samosata."[32] It may be seen from the style of this description how a rejoinder might be provoked, how rivalries might grow more heated, how other persons would be drawn in from the sidelines and the original issues become entangled in explosions of antagonistic passion.

And in any survey of intra-church communications, councils merit a particular place through their final reports, their synodal letters. Dozens survive. One or more by authorized writers would be sent round to key persons or groups in one or more provinces to explain what had been accomplished. At least, this was the case where the business addressed had been controversial. Sometimes the most notable news to be published was the text of a new creed. Many such creeds emerged: ten in the first generation alone post-Nicaea, many others in succeeding generations of struggle. The speed of their dissemination became in itself a problem, when they had to be revised or withdrawn and proved impossible to police because they had been too promptly entered in too many churches' archives.[33]

Knowledge of them could not in any case be erased from men's minds. It is known that many synodal letters when received were read aloud to a congregation. It is likely that most were. So were letters sent to subordinate sees from a metropolitan, dealing with doctrine? The bishop of Alexandria, superior to Arius, had set the standard in his angry encyclicals, with copies, some seventy of them, dispatched not only to the sees under his care but to a number in Palestine as well, still more in Cilicia, and so on around the east.[34] The writers of such publicized statements had risen to eminence most often thanks to their eloquence, their power to move and persuade their readers as well as to inform. Moving was half the point. Their views were presented from pulpits, discussed, and copied for wider circulation.

Circulation almost too wide, one may say, involving too many, in matters almost too important to bear talking about! A success easy to applaud too much; at the same time, easy to underestimate. Our sense of how absolutely wonderful we ourselves are in our modern world may lead us to discount the capacity of the ancient: for example, the capacity to disseminate ideas so as to engage popular interest. We should take account of the *weight* of their content; of the *quality* of thought; of significance, which is the historian's proper yardstick. Significance in ancient times lay in the urban population, that fourth or less of the empire's citizenry who lived in anything that could be called a town. Of all these, a majority could in turn be easily reached by a bishop, at any point after Nicaea, directly or indirectly through rapid word of mouth. The substance of the more controversial councils then held an interest, a threat, an urgency at least as they were advertised, which must seize on people's attention; for the advertisers, the bishops, were themselves seized and urgently informed, almost to a man. Their reading of their weekly or monthly "mail" (call it) persuaded them of its importance; they pondered it, whether it reached them in tracts or letters; and the way in which they responded to it, the seriousness of their thinking, reflected that importance. They themselves had very likely attended some such council as had generated the news, or they had listened personally to some such controversialist as had given it form. Their understanding of such major realities as these beyond their own back-door — of realities that counted — was not like the modern sort confined to meretricious photo ops, celebrities, or babies stuck in wells. Hence my supposing more *consequential* communication in this period of the empire than generally in our own world today.

In the process of publication, however, bishops might excite a public generally unfit to control its own reading or hearing of a given dispute. Witness the unfortunate spread of mistaken beliefs on which a certain bishop comments. He held out hope the converts might repent; "and it is enough for persons heading in this direction to declare their anathemas on the Messalian heresy; but anyone working with them very closely and trying to go beyond this with, perhaps, passages read to them from books, confuses someone lacking a clear intelligence. Most people don't have any educated knowledge and can't think out how thoroughly to condemn what needs to be condemned." His was not too harsh a judgement of the public, perhaps. Certainly he himself, Cyril, was in an exceptional position to judge and generalize: himself bishop of a great city and in touch with or personally present at events in several centers of ecclesiastical controversy.[35]

His observation finds an echo in the next century. Evagrius explains how a terminological debate could be misunderstood; for actually "the one of the two expressions [involved in Christology] does fit completely with the other; but among the masses the difference has been considered a great one."[36] It was thus, he adds, that the Devil could make trouble with a single letter (in *ek* or *en*, Greek "from" or "in");

> — for a person who says Christ is *in* two natures, declares him explicitly to be *from* two, and granting Christ to be both *in* divinity and humanity, thus declaring, says he is composed *from* both divinity and humanity. But the person who says he is *from* two, thereby entirely concedes Christ

is *in* two natures, since he is declaring him to be from divinity and humanity and thereby agrees he consists in divinity and humanity; for there is no transformation of the human flesh, to divinity; nor again does any passage of the one to the other take place, so as to produce that unity which words cannot express.

To read these words of Evagrius is to forgive the confusion of "the masses". Among the propositions that circulated were many truly difficult to take in. As Cyril himself says to the emperor regarding a related question, "The manner of [Christ's] incarnation is a deep thing, truly beyond words and beyond the grasp of our intelligence."[37] In support or excuse, often Isaiah will be quoted, "Who shall describe how he (Christ) was begotten?"[38]

An indiscriminate sharing of theology with the population at large could result in the situation that Edward Gibbon describes in words borrowed from a visitor to the eastern capital.[39] Here,

> The city is full of mechanics and slaves, who are all of them profound theologians, and preach in the shops and in the streets. If you desire a man to change a piece of silver, he informs you wherein the Son differs from the Father; if you ask the price of a loaf, you are told by way of reply that the Son is inferior to the Father; and if you inquire whether the bath is ready, the answer is that the Son was made out of nothing.

The passage, often taken to reflect a moment of tender amusement at the depths of innocent piety, is in fact rather more caustic. The bishop Gregory of Nyssa registers his shock that such base people in base settings should presume to discuss matters more properly left to their betters. His reaction was not uncommon among the clergy and not unreasonable, either, given their interest in maintaining their control over opinion. But it escaped their hand, sometimes. Such was Gregory's discovery; such was the discovery of a visitor to another eastern capital, Petrograd, in February of 1917: "You cannot buy a hat or a packet of cigarettes or ride in a cab without being enticed into a political discussion. The servants and the house porters demand advice as to which party to vote for."[40]

Hoi polloi had become involved. Their own leaders were the cause of it, the matters agitated were of such huge importance. But, to repeat with Cyril and others: not all questions that might seem urgently interesting ought to be submitted to untrained minds. People might not be really up to it mentally. They were "simple," a polite way of saying "simpletons"; and in their attempt to understand and participate they might endanger their right beliefs, their salvation. Accordingly the emperors forbade public debate of theology.[41] In vain. No decree no matter how harsh could bring controversies to an end. They would persist so long as they were unresolved.

For, beyond all the means of advertising their ideas reviewed earlier — letters and tracts and sermons — bishops might speak to a wider than usual audience through two devices that indeed reached to a very simple-minded audience. The target included or consisted mostly of ordinary citizens, whom the bishops' class called poor, and who were not often addressed in sermons.[42]

Of the two devices, one was song, winning prominence for the first time in the east just before Nicaea. The emperor there, the embattled and ambiguous Licinius, saw an angel in a dream instructing him (as only the emperor himself could have reported, later) that he should memorize the words now given him for a hymn to be sung by his troops. He woke up, he had the words copied down, they were sent around in his army, and were then used to raise morale:[43]

> Highest god, we beg you, holy god, we ask you, to you we entrust all justice, to you we entrust our salvation, to you we entrust our realm, through you we live, through you we conquer, you are our fortune. Greatest holy god, hear our prayers, our arms we stretch out to you, hear us holy one, highest god.

It is easy to pick up the reminiscences of acclamation-style here, and anticipations of liturgical exclamations, too: "Hear us, Christ!" and the like, best known in the chanting of lauds today. But enough was said of all this in the previous chapter.

Enough, except to notice one feature: the punchy, sloganeering short phrases employed. The very same may be assumed in songs by Arius, "songs," a church historian tells us, "written for sailors, millers, travellers and all such folk" (whom the historian holds in contempt) "arranged to tunes as he thought each was best suited; and by this style he drew over the more ignorant folk to his impieties."[44] The scene was Alexandria at about the same time as the angel's appearance to Licinius; and what was so successful for Arius offered rewards to others attested later in Antioch, Hippo in Africa, Constantinople, Edessa, Nisibis and Milan — that is (we may safely say) everywhere, in service to religious instruction; adapted to the teachings of every conceivable faith, too, whether Nicene or other.

The composers sometimes glory in reaching down to the most humble and ignorant of their city's people; so, Ambrose and Augustine. Such compositions aimed at changing minds but also at confirming and inspiriting the converted; or they were used, perhaps invented on the spot, in contests over doctrinal wording, "praise the Father *in* the Son," and so forth. Monks in massed ranks advanced to their sound in street-demonstrations, as if they were launching missiles of war. It is a pity that the systems (yes, plural) of musical scoring in antiquity are preserved in such meager fragments, so that we have almost no idea of what music really sounded like. We are only told that tunes for the hymns just described were often taken over from popular ones, that is, popular in theaters; and we know they often supported two choirs in answer to each other. Acclamations too were often uttered antiphonally.

Obviously such songs couldn't accommodate much content; what they taught could only be a very partial understanding of the matters in contention. It might be supposed that bishops offered sermons to accompany them in a similarly simplified voice. One was instanced by Augustine, who also composed songs. There were various attempts of that sort; but the conventions or necessities of preaching favored a higher tone, because directed at a much higher audience.[45]

The second device by which bishops could expect to reach a wide audience, necessarily one ill-informed and not good at following any sort of complicated statement, was by personal names: Arius' teachings were Arianism, and so forth. A good text to show how it worked is the law of AD 435, where the emperor in fulminating spirits declares,[46]

> Nestorius, the author of a monstrous superstition shall be condemned and his followers shall be branded with the mark of an appropriate name so that they may not misuse the title of Christians. But just as the Arians, by a law of Constantine of sainted memory are called Porphyrians from Porphyrius, on account of the similarity of their impiety, so adherents of the nefarious sect of Nestorians shall everywhere be called Simonians [after Simon Magus of the bible].

The same collection of laws which preserves this text also preserves a dozen names and more of credal parties designated by the name of their founder, Pricillianists, Pelagians, Novatians, Valentinians, Marcellians, Macedonians, and so forth, "reducing beliefs," as Brent Shaw says, "to 'aberrations' of one individual".[47] The intent is, as he says, "marginalizing"; but it is also didactic. It encapsulates a cluster of ideas in a single word, as today the specialist speaks of binitarianism, dyophysitism, dissimilarian and so forth (hardly an improvement!); thus providing a neat convenient handle by which occasionally to recall with veneration, or more often to offer for attack, or to throw away in disgust, whatever the named individual had defended. A typical piece of condensed name-calling can be instanced from the mid-fifth century. The target happens to be the bishop from Alexandria "most of whose teachings agree with Arius, Apollinarius and Eunomius."[48] No need to say what these various blasphemers had taught; everyone knew it or had once known; anyone could at least tell you that whatever they had taught was to be accursed, *anathema*.

By a matching practice, to compress approved views into bare names, bishops made use of "the holy diptychs" during the recitation of mass. They were official lists, periodically emended, of persons whom each church revered, and included its own past bishops as well as the most generally known and acceptable teachers. Since their names were read aloud, every congregant would be familiar with them. Questions came up at repeated councils of the fifth and sixth centuries regarding inclusion of this or that person, amounting to a declaration of his orthodoxy. This would of course be noticed in local liturgy, but notice did not amount to explanation.[49]

Confessions of perplexity from bishops were sampled, earlier; more will appear in a later chapter. No one can speak with certainty about the cognitive level of the higher clergy over-all; yet it seems safe to say that a lot of them had trouble understanding a lot of the doctrinal debate in which they were obliged ex officio to participate. This did not prevent their voice, their vote, from registering in conciliar decisions; but it added to the importance of loyalties which were rather political and personal than doctrinal.

As to *hoi polloi*, the cognitive level among them was obviously much lower; they might not always follow the arguments whirling around them; but this didn't deter them either from holding a strong opinion and acting in accordance with it. Ancient historians understood better than modern that people in fact do things of the very slightest or greatest importance, historically, out of their feelings, not out of calculation. Action is the outcome of the affect or emotional colors in which an idea is wrapped, not of the cognitive content of it.[50]

4

The "supernaturalist" element

At Nicaea in AD 325 some 200 bishops assembled. The total is not certain: perhaps a little below that figure, probably a little above it. Not all who attended signed, as was not unusual at the end of councils nor surprising at this one, given its special difficulties. The exact number doesn't matter.[1] It was soon inflated, to 270, to 300, and so to 318 within a generation. In the Greek system of numeration by letters of the alphabet, it was noticed that a tau, iota, and eta standing for 318 began with a cross 'T', went on to "Jesus" (IE . . .), and also recalled the number of Abraham's servants at Genesis 14.14. In this, Hilary and others saw the significance. So at 318 the total was stabilized and became a sort of shorthand for the council and its published creed. It is often referred to in that fashion in subsequent councils: Chalcedon, for one. Similarly "The 150" (rho-nu in Greek numbers) attending the second ecumenical council served as a designation.

To ourselves, the active interest shown in the Nicene attendance figure, or at least the wish to inflate it, would seem a natural part of those habits of voting and other forms of popular expression that bishops were familiar with in the world around them, in town councils and so forth. Wherever there is debate, there must be force in a majority. Not only physical force is in the balance, by which one side could ultimately be tested against the other; there is the more civilized respect for a preponderance of minds. Democracy teaches the equation, many = good; therefore, more = better. Yet a truer understanding of the Christian community suggests instead, or also, the equation, many = God. In voting a power beyond the human might assert itself.

Certainly bishops in conflict with each other insisted, if it were the case, that there were more of them than of their antagonists. This was a constant refrain; so a bishop long before Nicaea defended the rightness of his views because they had been agreed to "among churches with the very largest congregations"; so, later, the synodal letter of Tyana gloried in the number of their friends at Lampsacus in 364/5 being greater than of their enemies at Ariminum in 359; again, at Aquileia one party pointed out (quite untruthfully) that they represented almost all the bishops from almost all the provinces of the west; while at Carthage in AD 411 the competing parties vying for numerical superiority even counted off by pairs in public.[2] *More* trumped *less*: there was in the end "validation from numbers," as a council president reminded a minority who were slow to give in.[3] Consequently the deposing of a bishop remained in effect if re-instatement had been voted only by a smaller synod; appeal from a conciliar decision could only be to a council with a larger number attending.[4] Majority mattered; everyone must agree to an opinion "of so very many bishops in attendance." But to these words the speaker added, "in attendance with the Holy Spirit, too."[5]

His reminder sheds light on accepted reasoning among the bishops as they tried to settle their differences. They were convinced of a divine force present and at work to assure a preponderance in the first place; it was divinity that prevailed, or at least not a total by mere mathematics; hence, the choice of Pentecost for the convocation of the council at Chalcedon.[6] The Spirit, the Breath, the Pneuma would be there.

This conviction expressed itself in shouts at a moment of high drama, when a great bishop was torn down by his opponents in defiance of the emperor's representatives there present — present and declaring that the decision must be accounted for with God himself. But they replied, "God has deposed Dioscorus!"[7]

Their belief fits well with that celebrated moment when Ambrose was chosen bishop in a big assembly in the Milan piazza on the instant, no one even thinking about it till a universal shout arose for the choice; or with the choice of a bishop in Rome in AD 238, when a dove, the *Ur*-pigeon of the city's flocks today, settled on the head of a certain Fabianus, whereupon "the whole people as if at the impulse of one breath, one divine *pneuma*, with all enthusiasm and a single mind, shouted out, 'He is worthy', *axion*."[8]

The *pneuma* in the form of a copy of the bible was brought in at councils, from a date not to be firmly fixed, perhaps. The practice seems to be implied in Carthage in the mid-third century; it is shown in Fig. 3 (but the depiction

Fig. 3. The Council of Constantinople AD 381. Courtesy Bibliothèque nationale de France

belongs to the AD 880s); it is regularly attested from Ephesus I on (AD 431);[9] and it would have been natural at any point, given the weight and regular use in debate of quotations from scripture. All the proceedings in councils might therefore be attributed to the presence of the Holy Spirit, at least in the judgement of bishops who approved of the outcome. Such verdicts are liberally spread across synodal letters. They speak of the bible almost as a person, brought forward to the center of their meeting. On it, bishops called to testify might place their hands as they spoke. It and its presence are "fearful".[10]

Contrariwise, if bishops disapproved of a council's work, then it must be the Devil's. Ariminum of AD 359 and Chalcedon were so characterized by critics who opposed their outcome.[11] Beliefs held to be wrong were always blamed on the Devil, by everyone from the emperors on down, and in that remote sense he was the instigator of all councils that had to deal with doctrine. So, Arius' bishop warned in a letter to another see in AD 324: his enemies "are possessed by the Devil", father of lies; and this was echoed at the time by Constantine writing to the churches in Alexandria and elsewhere to explain the effects of Arius' preaching.[12] Scripture could be quoted, teaching that Satan himself spread "weeds" meaning wrong beliefs; and his workings could be seen also in the too-elaborate argumentation of too-learned proponents in debate, where Greek cleverness won out. Across the centuries, such were the causes credited for dissension.

And why not, in all common sense? At the moment of baptism, through the rites of exorcism, every convert, every child in crossing the threshold into Christendom testified to the ubiquity of the Devil and his minions. In Satan, evil of every sort had its origin. It was he, once, who had urged on the persecutions; no one doubted that. Now he attacked equally the pious in their study or the solitary ascetic in the desert (there were a hundred reports of these latter assaults from the mid-forth century on). By satanic instigation the populace of whole cities could be thrown into uproar or riot, even civil war. So much was known and accepted. There were eye-witnesses in Edessa, Constantinople, or Antioch. Among other ills, epidemic disease was of demonic doing. Taken far enough, popular fears could indeed credit the Devil and his armies with a kind of universal rulership — fears that a bishop of the eastern capital took as a worthy target for correction in a series of sermons toward the turn of the fifth century.[13]

What priests and, by special assignment, exorcists in every church could do in church by rites, others could do singly out of their particular powers. They demonstrated it through the driving out of furious demons from the possessed, in scenes of terrifying uproar and drama. Many bishops did so, many ascetics, many plain people of adequate confidence in their own faith, as their admirers had reported from the earliest times of the church. The invaders as they quit the possessed threaten them and vituperate; the possessed shriek and tear their hair.[14] Unforgettable moments! Even more, a bishop or someone else of power knew where demons lurked and could manhandle them, subdue them to his will, drive them to distraction. People who saw these acts attested to the impression they made, overwhelming as it was.[15] As Augustine tells his readers, writing in AD 426, because he had it directly from an eye-witness, a demon when he is confronted speaks "with a horrible yell," "huge howlings" (*City of God* 22.8)

The same qualities of person, that is, bishops of many cities and ascetics especially of Egypt, notoriously did good in the world, beyond exorcism — above all, through healing. There was no concern more urgent than health; none, so far beyond common comprehension; none, closer to the center of most people's active worship.[16] Some benefactors could raise the dead to life.[17] In other areas of life, too, if flooding became less common in some region or if water once again filled the wells, if hailstorms or pests were averted, a bishop or an ascetic was the cause; or bishops turned attacking armies from a city's walls.[18] The world was competed for by opposing forces, forces beyond the human, to which the testimonies were so numerous and authoritative, no one could withhold belief; and the dramatic nature of this whole area of experience, or of report, insured everyone's attention.

A cautious summary of all this material will be familiar to many readers, offered by an observer so widely known and admired: Arnold Hugh Martin Jones.[19]

> It is difficult to make any generalization which is both true and significant about the religious temper of an age, but it may at least be asserted with some confidence that the later Roman empire was intensely religious. Sceptics and rationalists, if they existed, have left no mark on history and literature. All, pagans, Jews and Christians alike, believed, and it would seem believed intensely in *supernatural* powers, benevolent and malign, who intervened actively in human affairs; all were anxious to win their aid and favour, or to placate or to master them, as the case might be. This had probably been true of the great mass of the population; by the fourth, and indeed probably by the third century, the educated minority, who had in the late Republic and early Principate ceased to believe in the gods, had become religious once more.

Jones' analysis, here, brief though it is, drew on immense learning. As the story was once told to me, he liked to work propped up on his bed. The setting was Oxford University. He had an awestruck student to supply him there with a quantity of books to go through every few days in the course of research for the three volumes from which the paragraph above is drawn. In his own dogged way he thus got through something above a hundred thousand two-column folio pages of Greek and Latin relevant to the period of my study and a bit beyond, too — quite enough to support general conclusions. They are cast

Fig. 4. A. H. M. Jones. Courtesy The British Academy

in his usual un-showy, matter-of-fact style. The tradition in which he had been trained, and in which he trained others, gave readers the evidentiary base for whatever was asserted, without eristics or cleverness.

But the italics in the passage are mine, *"supernatural"*, to tie in the quoted passage to the present chapter. The word should make clear the tenor of all the little scenes and details laid out in the pages above. It should perhaps be added that *natural* evidently designates for Jones, as indeed in common speech, the whole realm of experience untouched by superhuman beings — the realm within which science operates, as we would say today. My term *supernaturalist* therefore designates the tendency to reach beyond nature — beyond the material world — in any attempt to explain our experiences.

As, for instance, earthquakes. When one struck the capital in AD 532, "The entire populace in supplication shouted, 'May Christians' good fortune prevail!' 'Crucified one, save us and the city!' 'Justinian Augustus, may you conquer!' 'Away with the Chapter [of doctrines], burn it, the Chapter which the Chalcedon council published!' " — for clearly it was this that had brought down God's punishment on them all. Similarly, a quake that shivered the capital in the wake of the exiling of a revered bishop, to the terrification of the people and the empress herself. This too was God's sign. Again, a terrible hailstorm had the same meaning.[20]

Theological argument that went off the tracks invited God's rebuke. The proof to ponder most fearfully was Arius. All the ancient church historians expatiate on his hideous end, his guts spilling out, with every circumstance of degradation and horror. Generally God's vengeance was seen as striking at the victim's genitals and bowels, with a confusion of feces and urine in the mouth, it might be, and worms pouring out of disgusting sores and orifices. Such was Arius' fate, arch-heretic. The latrine where he died was shown as a sort of tourist point. As to his teachings, Ambrose in a council could demand a curse on them: "Are you hesitating to condemn, when after divine judgement he burst open at the middle?!" A similar fate would surely visit proponents of any impious belief, Nestorius for one; such persons could expect a sudden death, *nutu divino*; punished, too, would be those emperors who lent their support to error — even entire populations. Those that were wickedly Arian or Chalcedonian were seen to suffer for it under barbarian assaults.[21] Events public and incontestable taught a lesson in the supernatural which bishops — the ordinary like the elite, whether in councils or before their congregations — must ever bear in mind: there were consequences to one's choice of belief, in this life as well as afterwards. This was the teaching, as urgent as it was universal, that underlay the fear, the need to placate and earn the favor, of divine powers. This was what Jones discovered in our sources.

There had once been contrary teachings. Non-Christians in the Greco-Roman world, so far as we can enter their thoughts, evidently accepted the possibility of superhuman beings at work in great events, earthquakes or military disasters; but the possibility had had little reality, it was little considered. Minor events causing loss or pain might also be blamed on superhuman agents, invoked by magic. That too was a reality off to the side, so to speak: a rare thing, forbidden, a resort for only wicked and credulous people. In fact, superhuman beings were beneficent. So the philosophers said, and common piety agreed. The common word, "gods-fear", *deisidaimonia*, pointed the finger of ridicule, sometimes of shock, at any denial of this wonderful truth. Gods were only beneficent. Granted, they were not omnipotent. Therefore bad things might simply happen. To blame evil on the gods, however, was deeply impious; and it made no sense.

Into this Greco-Roman thought-world, Christianity introduced an alternative view: one of opposing forces, God's and Satan's, alike able to smite and confound. It established itself in step with Christianity itself, and was as universally spread about as other Christian beliefs, through the preaching of the churches' leaders and the elaboration of stories about the church's heroes.[22] They too were as well able to hurt as to heal.

Another and related change Jones draws attention to: the tendency increasingly to see about one the intervention of superhuman beings, both the good and the bad stirring in to the life of this world of ours. The old gods and their benevolence were steadily displaced, most obviously through the miraculous acts of persons known for their ascetic ways, their heroic devotion to God, or through their relics, able most often to heal, also to repair a loss, to predict the future, and so forth.[23] More and more of life and its incidents could and should be explained in this fashion; less and less was left to nature unassisted. To attribute something unusual to mere chance showed a lack of any religion at all.[24]

In illustration, a moment in northern Greece, reported by the non-Christian historian Zosimus. A traveller on foot had been evidently attacked, beaten badly, knocked senseless. There he lay by the edge of the road·without speech or apparent ability to move a limb. The emperor happened by attended by all his retinue. "They supposed the man must be a portent and pointed him out to the emperor who was at hand and who repeated the question to the man:" Just who was he and what had happened to him?

> But he remained unable to speak, seeming to be neither alive (since his whole body was inert) nor entirely defunct, since his eyes seemed alert. Suddenly the portent disappeared, and, while those who were standing about were at a loss what to do, those who happened to be very good at explaining such things said it foretold the future condition of the state: that it would continue to exist, battered and bruised like a man in death-throes, until it was at last destroyed.[25]

The company had come upon something odd, certainly; but it, the speech-less injured traveller, was at least tangible. They could inspect him. Then most likely he recovered his wits and fled. But such an explanation as this didn't seem most likely to the particularly knowledgeable folk in the emperor's en-tourage. Instead, they reached beyond the natural to the supernatural and found a message left for them, we may suppose, by God — by God, not Satan, since its intent was not to hurt them.

How different, Plutarch's encounter with a comparable oddity. The contrast helps in the understanding of late-empire habits of mind, which are the focus of this chapter.

Plutarch (ca. AD 46–127) was himself something like a bishop, or as close as ancient paganism could get to that quality of person. For a great many years he had served as officiant-in-chief at a place of worship of great importance, Delphi. He qualified as one of "those who happened to be very good at ex-plaining such things" as oddities, not only through his piety but through his great learning as well. An honorary citizen at Athens, the empire's university town, and himself a popular lecturer in Rome, he was a voracious reader all his life and an inquirer into every sort of question sacred or profane. Witness the friends he chose to dine with and the style of their conversation. They often turned to curious questions which he enjoyed recalling. We may picture him one evening, then, with a half-dozen others recumbent in a square 'C' where,

> At a dinner in Elis, Agemachus served us some giant truffles. Everyone present expressed admiration, and one of the guests said with a smile, "They certainly are worthy of the thunder that we've had lately," obviously laughing at those who say that truffles are produced by thunder. Several of the company held that the ground splits open when struck by thunder, the air serving as a spike, and that afterward the truffle-gatherers are guided by the cracks in the earth. This is the source, they continued, of the popular notion that thunder actually produces truffles instead of merely bringing them to light. It is as if someone were to imagine that rain not merely brings out snails where we come to see them, but actually creates them.
>
> Agemachus, however, upheld the popular theory and advised us not to regard the miraculous as unworthy of belief. For indeed many other marvelous effects are, he said, produced by thunder, lightning, and other meteoric phenomena. . . .
>
> Here I remarked . . . that fertile rains often accompany thunder . . . That explains exactly why these phenomena have generally been supposed to be *supernatural.*

— and Plutarch goes on to develop the theory that weather conditions associated with the one phenomenon, in everyday experience, account also for the other, in ways that have no mystery about them.[26] There are indeed forces to account for thunder or wind or a spring welling up; but they have no will, no intent. They are not like us; or, as we would say today, they are not anthropomorphic. Only, notice that the quoted translation slightly misrepresents what he says: the concluding word, "(of the) supernatural", *theiotes*, more properly means *divine-ness*, "having the quality of god about it".

Plutarch confronts something strange along with the explanation offered for it by *hoi polloi*. They wanted to place its origins somewhere and somehow among superhuman beings. He considers their belief, not to dismiss it too quickly. In the end, however, with a great deal of learning and what we would call common sense, too, even of science such as it was in those days, he prefers to stay within the boundaries of "nature" — whenever possible.

The point at which it is *not* possible defines his difference from *hoi polloi*. Certainly he has no doubts about *theiotes*. The gods indeed exist; theirs is a realm to be acknowledged. But, limiting that realm, his wide reading and patience in searching for "natural" explanations induced him to extend them far beyond the reach of the common man's understanding. Had he extended them indefinitely so as to exclude all influence or presence of superhuman powers whatsoever, what would have been left over would be "nature"; but his thought never reached so far.[27]

Paul Veyne describes Plutarch as a convenient mid-point between A. H. M. Jones' "educated minority" on the one hand, "who had in the late Republic and early Principate ceased to believe in the gods" — men such as Cicero, extreme sceptics or atheists — and on the other hand those figures of the third century and later whom Jones offered in contrast: the "intensely religious."[28] The change of mind across the centuries, looking only at the elite but recognizing their importance, has been often detected; the names most useful in illustration are well known.[29] There is ready agreement that more of both superstition and irrationality can be found progressively across time from Cicero to the Byzantine and medieval world. Consensus, however, has stopped short of defining just what is meant, and what is wrong, in beliefs characterized as "superstitious" or "irrational". So long as Christian beliefs in themselves appear to be threatened by any such discussion, or even insulted, the "darkening" of the West is bound to remain little explored. The so-called scholarly literature on it would hardly amount to fifty pages. Contrast between the treatment of our Western "darkening" and our "enlightenment" is certainly very striking.

Bishops of the late empire, who are my target, of course fall within the definition of Jones' "intensely religious"; among them, the likes of Plutarch, still less of Cicero, could never be found. There is not a church historian of the time, there is no biographer or panegyrist of piety, who does not have stories to tell of divine power visibly at work in tangible reality. Many come forward as they write to say they have in their own person sure knowledge of what they describe. Let none of their readers, then, persist in doubts about the miraculous. Superhuman forces for good and ill are to be looked for at any moment, in any experience the least out of the ordinary: a speechless traveller by the roadside, or gigantic truffles. Reports of something truly wonderful are to be readily credited: walking on water, actual visible dragons in your city or along the highway, or the greatest rulers and officials suddenly struck down.

A. H. M. Jones further draws attention to a related fact often noticed: that the difference in religious beliefs between elite and *hoi polloi* diminished and then simply disappeared, one can say, by some point within the period of my study. The balance of surviving evidence by then had tipped toward the western provinces and Latin, but the phenomenon is noticeable everywhere in the empire. In the same period and for related reasons, the reach of reading and curiosity among the elite diminished. All those resources of second-hand experience which Plutarch commanded, from Aristotle as from his own widely informed friends, were very greatly reduced; consequently, analogies were also reduced through which educated people like himself could interpret their experience and resolve their perplexities within the boundaries of nature. The universities were shut down. Books of the pagan past were not copied or they were destroyed; the mere knowledge of them could be dangerous.[30]

The knowledge rather praised and cultivated was increasingly scriptural and theological, of course providing explanatory resources of an entirely different sort. Among ten thousand illustrations of the change in habits of thought one alone may be enough (since the whole subject is after all quite familiar): it is Augustine in his great *City of God* (15.28) drawn into the subject of demons by questions from his congregation. Yes, demons exist everywhere, he says; they account for crop failures as for the sickness of some draft animal. As to who or what they are, the answer may be found in Genesis. They are the offspring of God's sons who took "those fallen women" to wife. Which is possible, Augustine supposes; for after all,

> There is the very widespread report, one that many people say they know of through their own experience or declare to have heard it from others who have experienced it and whose credibility is beyond doubt — a report that the Woodland and Backwoods deities whom the common folk, the *vulgus*, call *incubi* have often conducted themselves wickedly with women whom they have sought out and gained intercourse with; and certain spirits, *daemones*, whom the Gauls call Dusii, are forever on the lookout for this depraved pleasure and succeed in it. Such a number of persons and of such quality vouch for this that it would seem defiant folly, *impudentia*, to dispute it.[31]

"Whose credibility is beyond doubt. . . ." What is unmistakable here is the acknowledgement of popular wisdom, not to be dismissed.

A growing anti-intellectualism makes itself most clearly evident in the creation of a culture hero quite different in mind and background from the traditional elite — a hero ready with the *vulgus* or *hoi polloi* to credit reports of demon lovers. Anthony of Egypt (d. AD 356) is the first and very model. Others like him appear from the second quarter of the fourth century on, in unending series throughout the eastern provinces and, before long, too, in the western as well. Legend introduces one such saint at the council of Nicaea itself to assert the new wisdom, the wisdom of the simple. Others fill the pages of many authors in scenes to show the acumen of the unlettered, triumphant over the pretensions of human learning. The latter is routed by some telling short words of pure piety; theirs is true philosophy.[32]

They also represent that quality of "intense belief", "intense religion", discovered in the later empire by A. H. M. Jones. They were the "grazing saints" and ate only the grasses of the field; they roamed the desert wastes stark naked; passed much of their lives in some great storage jar or walled up in a cell to which access for food and drink lay only through a sort of mail-slot; or they stood for days in an unmoving posture, or endured nights without sleep. Even those who chose moderation (by far the greater number) imposed a Spartan diet on themselves, long prayers, and long periods of solitude.

Response to the example of such practices proved rapid and enthusiastic, especially in Egypt, Palestine, and Syria and especially in rural areas. Here, there was little call for reading and writing. To monastic life as to a peasant's, bookish skills were irrelevant; the lack of them needn't prevent a rise even to the rank of archimandrite, witness Eutyches for one;[33] nor did it deter the most educated observers from describing both solitary and coenobitic ascetics with reverence. Chrysostom and Jerome themselves tried the path trod by Anthony, at least for a space, and earned general respect for their efforts; Athanasius and the historian Theodoret sought out the company of ascetics to learn from them. By other visitors and apprentices, their sayings, quoted below, were elicited, recorded, and passed around.[34] In these several ways they served as a vehicle for the transmission of peasant piety and assumptions about the supernatural, into the mainstream and general conversation of the later empire.

The mainstream of course included the episcopal ranks, both the great like Athanasius or Chrysostom, and the ordinary. The ascetic movement in the late empire thus fits within the bounds of my chosen subject.

To continue: at the heart of the ascetics' way of life was the felt need to placate, a need to which A. H. M. Jones calls attention — in a word, *fear*, the fear of God and his judgement. No other explanation of their settled conduct, rules, and excesses can be easily imagined; nothing among them was more emphatically taught than this; nothing better stimulated a response in action.[35] They must attack the very root of danger, the cause of sin: that is, the needs and appetites of the natural man.

By their lives, they often attracted a following, some of whom they might admit to a sort of apprenticeship; or they found it practical to live in clusters of two or three or more, and so communities took shape in bleak remote places in the eastern provinces, first, and then in the western. In monasteries and nunneries, defeat of the appetites could begin with one's daily bread.[36] The less you ate, the better. Thirst should be mastered, too, and the longing for sleep or shelter or for human company and conversation, or sexual urges and thoughts, all should be mastered under the spur of fear.

Their conversations often dwelt on this essential subject. "Why is your body so dried up?" ask aspirants; "and the old man," Father Macarius, "answers them, '... if a man cleanses his mind through fear of God, that very fear of God consumes his flesh.' " Or again, "Father Moses said, 'If a man has it not in his heart that he is a sinner, God will not hear him.' " Or "Father Matoes said, 'Pray God to grant you heartfelt grief and abasement, and give mind always to your sins . . . bewail and grieve, for the time draws nigh.' " And at greater length, the question is asked, "How may I become a solitary?" The answer made, requiring total denial of a natural life, seemed too hard. Then, "If you can't do as we do, settle down in your cell and bewail your sins."[37] So taught the veterans of an ascetic life.

One of their most celebrated champions makes this teaching explicit. When his companions try to relieve the pain of the agonizing wounds, maggot-infested and noisome, which he has inflicted on himself,

> the holy Symeon cried out to them, saying "Leave me be, sirs, my broth-
> ers! Let me die thus, stinking like a dog! — for according to my deeds I
> shall be judged. Everything that is unjust, all covetousness, are mine. For
> I am an ocean of sins."[38]

Through such and similar self-punishing efforts, more and more extraordi-nary but always with the same object — so as to become super-natural, one may say — Symeon achieved a fame that spread from Syria to Rome, just as the fame of Anthony spread from Egypt to Milan.

Monks were sometimes accused by bishops of being insubordinate or worse: thugs and fanatics. They seemed to come from another world, with their lowering looks and heavy staffs: formidable in their silence, equally in their massed shouting. They could be mustered by their leaders in the streets or at a council by the hundreds, making them even more intimidating in doctrinal conflicts of the fifth century and later. A synodal letter recalled their reaction in the capital to the deposition of a bishop popular among them, in AD 431, "whereupon all the monasteries rose up together in company with their archi-mandrites, to go to the palace, singing their hymns antiphonally."[39]

Among these black-robed figures singled out for mention was one known for his recent miracle-working. His presence indeed deserved notice. Belief had long prevailed in "the gift of miracles as the visible sign of the author's orthodoxy and, consequently, of the person he has come to defend." From Anthony as the model appearing against Arius in Alexandria and miraculous-ly healing the sick and suffering in the streets, now in Constantinople the monks borrowed strength for their own street demonstrations. In the same Antonian tradition, on his way into exile, a certain bishop of Alexandria worked miracles, miracles which proved him a martyr wrongly deposed; and again, "a voice was heard" speaking for yet a third victim in doctrinal conflicts, the bishop of Gaza and founder of a monastery, he too an exile and martyr for his beliefs.[40]

To secure the support of such special piety in time of doctrinal strife, at Constantinople, "the King [emperor Theodosius] and the bishops stretched themselves prone upon the ground at the feet of the holy man," Daniel the Stylite (Chap. 2 at note 5). The same emperor earlier sought support from that model for Daniel, the great Symeon himself whose name was on everyone's lips.[41] The invitation in the turgid tortured style favored by imperial ghost-writers, begins,

> Having found that Your Reverence's life is totally given to God and that you so conduct it that you may draw down the Divine favor upon Us by your firm faith, We are unable now to withhold Our Letter from you, whereby affairs that very much depend on Divine Providence, especially at this season, you may conclude as quickly as possible, thus that peace may be, by your efforts, firmly established and that dissent, introduced by the Devil's arts, may be removed from our midst . . .

Or less ornately: Symeon's sitting for so very many years atop a pillar and subsisting on so very little to eat and drink — allowing himself so little of any bodily comforts of any sort — enabled him to direct a superhuman power at the Devil and his works, which were the "weeds" of heresy. He could, in A. H. M. Jones' words, master those supernatural forces that were malign. By the same token he could invoke the benign. Thus, later, looking into the future after Chalcedon, the emperor Leo also turned to Symeon for his views on doctrine.[42] Why? There is no reason to think that the stylite had actually read anything from the council, or leading up to it, or discussing its issues. That would all have been irrelevant. He commanded attention rather because he had drawn the Pneuma itself into his very mind and thoughts.

Before the fourth century ended, monks were being appointed as rural bishops and occasionally to head regular urban churches in Seleuceia or Mopsuestia. Nestorius was a monk, later bishop of Constantinople (AD 428–431). In Egypt the patriarch ordained some dozens in the AD 340s and 350s and his successors in the fifth century did so as a general custom — bringing from the desert the most famous to head the church of Alexandria, Dioscorus (AD 444–54). By the mid-fifth century a Syrian monk, the archimandrite Barsumas, was admitted to vote at a council. Others enjoyed positions of trust and prominence at court. By AD 532 in the Constantinopolitan council of that year they were sitting together with bishops in large numbers; more generally, from the sixth century on, in the East, bishops were recruited only from monasteries.[43]

And this development in the church constitutes a second reason to include the ascetics of the later empire in my pages: not only did they exert influence on the religious views of ordinary bishops, but they might be ordinary bishops themselves — a few, indeed, extraordinary.

In Jones' thumb-nail sketch of the Late Antique thought-world, and in some expansion of it in the pages above, a causal connection is discernible. Belief in "the active intervention of supernatural powers" led to or produced a great "intensity" of religion.

And why not? — since even we who may not be great theologians or deep thinkers take seriously what may seriously affect our lives, especially what may hurt us. If those powers are really likely to intervene, to bless or more particularly to harm or destroy or punish, to do so instantly or for all eternity, then the common sense of the thing is to pay attention, to insist, to press for action or one's self to take action in some strident or urgent or extreme fashion. It might be asceticism, it might be rioting and demonstrations. These phenomena were of the times.

5

The violent element

Our sources for the two and a quarter centuries following Nicaea allow a very rough count of the victims of credal differences: not less than twenty-five thousand deaths. A great many, but still only a small minority, were clergy; the rest, participants in crowds. The total cannot be less if the sources are to be read in the usual way, discounting round numbers a bit and treating adjectives rather conservatively. Some of the evidence gives us only "many" or mere plurals, "deaths" and "slaughters" without specifics.[1]

All those who died met their end irregularly as targets of fury, not of legal action. Of bishops who died for their faith while in the custody of the secular powers, the examples can be counted on the fingers of one hand. Their killers had no wish to make martyrs ex officio. A few of the victims were, however, remembered and are to this day venerated as saints.

The recoverable reports reach us from all but two of the twenty-four decades included (and these two, in the sixth century when the surviving record thins out). In north Africa for about a century the point at issue centered in the sacrament of ordination and re-baptism, about which Cyprian, once, and then Augustine had so much to say. The troubles of this region may be set aside as having nothing to do with my chosen title, "voting about God", though they had everything to do with "the violent element". In all other regions, however, the issues that were fought over were strictly theological.

They were contested in many scores of recorded incidents and touch a great many centers: a half-dozen Italian cities, a half-dozen in Egypt beyond its capital, a dozen in Syria including Palestine, and so forth. It is naturally the empire's largest cities about which we are least ill-informed (one can't claim more than that, of course). They are Alexandria, Constantinople, Rome, Antioch, and Ephesus. The disproportion of evidence in favor of these five may or may not reflect the realities of religious temperature. We can't say. They were (and not by accident) the home towns of many writers of the time on whom we rely: John Chrysostom, John Malalas, and others. Towns very much smaller also got into the news for murderous clashes, sometimes because they were reported in the course of councils as assault charges against bishops or partisans. All such reporting was very hit-or-miss, suggesting that a survey halfway methodical, if it were possible, would produce much evidence now missing; but the ancient world, as everyone knows, can be observed only through chinks and chances.

The rise of religious violence is nevertheless prominent in the sources. It was obviously interesting and important. Indeed in the cities, which were the very heart of the ancient world, the phenomenon as a whole surpasses any other one can think of for historical significance over the course of the empire's latter centuries. No aspect of economic history, of family or class or labor relations or mortality rates—nothing brought such changes into people's lives. It disrupted them not only by ending so many of them, once and for all, abruptly, but in other ways as well: through arson, wounds and injuries, displacement, losses of property, rioting, disorders, and deep abiding splits in communities.

The whole matter has been quite ignored. Specialists tell us, "we know of only two occasions during the fourth century when tensions led to violence"—tensions of any sort, in Antioch. Only two secular occasions are instanced; yet the city in question was often torn apart by church disputes. Or again, "The commonest sort of factional disturbance in the late Empire . . . is the battle between partisans" at race tracks, and "the history of popular disturbances in the late Empire is in large measure the history of the Blues and Greens" (fan clubs).[2] In the face of the facts about quite another sort of violence, centered in charges of heresy and attested everywhere, the only response has been to wave it aside as the work of what in other contexts we are used to calling, dismissively, "outside agitators," hirelings, thugs, and the like. And such bloody-minded people cannot have been *Christians*, for Heaven's sake![3]

While victims were killed in many strange ways, stabbed by styluses or burnt alive or trampled under foot, of course the most serious losses of life followed upon the use of cold steel. That mostly meant soldiers. They appear to have been stationed in every city of any size whatsoever, directly among its streets or in its suburbs. Thus there was never a problem in finding force, provided one had the authority, of one's self, or influence over authority, to give the orders; and one could assume some friendliness among the garrison rankers toward their own bishop. This is mentioned with relief by the rather anxious friends of such a person at Ephesus I. If the details of the connections are never made plain, still, a local commander would always be welcome at dinner parties among the elite, where the bishop would certainly be included. Power seeks out power. And it will be seen later how much involved the emperors were, too, and with them, their armies. An army role is thus very often attested; but even this has been denied.[4]

Strange! the evidence denied being so abundant and so strident. For then as now, violent death must make news, the flash of steel must be talked about and remembered. Listeners shudder and imagine not only the scene itself, the blood on the altar or in the baptismal font (as is often given special mention), but the motive as well. Such awful things to happen! To account for them, awful passions must be imputed. If these were in the service of some cause, then the cause itself must be considered, in itself bloody. So acts turned into thoughts and possessed the mind of the times.

It will be clear, of course, why these matters are raised: to help in understanding the conduct of councils through understanding the ideas and assumptions, the sense of the usual and permissible — in short, the mental baggage — brought to their work by the participants.

For the participants, instruction in the realities of life, at least within what could be called their profession, began with their very election. It prepared them for the physical dangers and furious explosions that attended the murderous moments so far described. Certainly the choosing of a bishop was a democratic affair; the reality of this and its limits were explored in the second chapter, above; but beyond any counting of majorities there remain the appropriate colors to be added: the blood-reds and jagged blacks in which the electoral scenes are so often presented to us.

"It is hardly surprising," as Henry Chadwick says, "that episcopal elections were *normally* a source of unrest and disorder." His generalizing statement echoes others made by contemporaries, Chrysostom, Augustine, Sozomen, or the assembled bishops at Chalcedon.[5] They were familiar with the *slaughter*, as it was called, incident to a disputed throne such as Rome's — here, fifteen years before Nicaea, with a much worse repetition of violence to follow in the generation after Nicaea, notorious for the total of bodies left on the cathedral floor by the rival parties: one hundred and thirty-seven by the lower of two accounts. There were still more to come around the end of the fourth century.[6]

In other centers the story was much the same, and for much the same

reason, namely, that whoever presided over a see represented a credal preference. Where this might be in dispute, he could expect to be challenged and
perhaps removed. Thus creeds could be at least a contributing factor, sometimes really the only one, in street fights, stabbings in the church, brawls in
public squares, and general rough stuff.

We have Jerome to explain how all bishops would be tempted to resist
removal, "so long as they had a clear conscience. Who indeed would let himself be deposed? — especially since every body of citizens, in love with their
own clergy, wouldn't hesitate an instant at the stoning or murdering of anyone
who was deposing them?"[7] On occasion the hostile effort had to be backed up
by armed forces, since the populace did resist just as Jerome said; and in
consequence, serious bloodshed.

Supposing there were fifteen hundred bishops in the empire at a given moment, in very round numbers (above, Chap. 1), then the enforced turn-over
among them may not seem very great, so far as it is known. It was the celebrities who generally suffered the loss of their see, and as a result of conciliar
action: thus, mere single individuals like Athanasius or Hilary. However, they
might later be vindicated and returned; and then deposed again; and so on — a
number of them, twice, and some for a third or forth or fifth time. Beyond such
disturbed careers, a few died in the course of being taken to their place of exile,
being old and hard-driven on the road.[8]

And at several junctures, substantial numbers of bishops suffered all together. The cause might be a ruler who took religion seriously. It might be
Constantius (AD 337–61) sharing and trying to impose the doctrinal prefer-
ences in which Constantine had died;[9] or under Valens (AD 364–78), "those
times of flights and confiscations, exiles, threats, fines, dangers, imprisonment,
manacles, flogging and whatever not, that was most terrifying to inflict on
those who did not subscribe to the emperor's wishes";[10] under Gaiseric in the
AD 430s and 440s, with the exiling en masse of clergy opposed to that king's
credo;[11] the deposition of fourteen in eastern cities for not subscribing to
Chalcedon, or Justin and his adopted son Justinian in the opening year of their
reign (AD 519–20) sending 54 or more into exile.[12] The agent might be a
vigorous metropolitan, occasionally a vigorous council.[13] In any case, across
the period of my study, we can point to some hundreds of bishops forced off
their thrones. As a percentage of the episcopal population, perhaps this may
count as a total of consequence.

Hearing of actions of the sort through the exchange of letters, bishops or
lower clergy in a given region could hardly misunderstand what sort of threats
they might have to face, themselves, once they were elected. *Might.* It should-
n't be supposed from the record of physical danger that most of them had to

deal with it in their own careers. They didn't. Nevertheless, they could not help thinking about the possibility, which was not easily dismissed. It was not an uncommon thing. Being seated on an episcopal throne, being seen as the servant of the Almighty, the object of honor and genuflection, set over a force of slaves and dependants and commanding the wherewithal to pay them, with something left over, too — all this was no doubt very wonderful. But so was life once for Damocles.

Besides, what of the tongues torn out of the mouths of bishops found to have uttered blasphemous opinions? and bishops worked to death by a sentence to the mines?[14] or scarred for life by the beatings they received, sometimes a judicial flogging, sometimes a blow from a sword that missed its mark — to be seen on a fellow-bishop's body, a sight to bring shivers. At one council, survivors displayed their scars.[15]

Personal witness, oral or at first offered in writing with the injured party present to speak to it, could be highly dramatic. There is the bishop Bassianus of Ephesus describing the moment of his forcible deposition by the partisans of his rival:[16]

> Certain persons among the ranks of the priesthood along with others as well have done terrible things, forbidden by the laws. For, despising any fear of God and the power of the Immaculate Mysteries which are received from the humble hands of myself, from a merciful God . . . , they suddenly seized me and tore me away from the holy church and beat me, dragging me to the public square; for a while they locked me up; they struck me with their swords. . . . Afterwards [when the rival had been ordained] they inflicted death and grievous wounds on many of those attached to me, whose remains were left before the doors of God's holy church.

— whereupon his successor, who is believed and supported by the council, says instead that his accuser "was not ordained in Ephesus, but when the holy church was empty he gathered a riotous mob with swords and some other pugilist types," arena fans, *eranarii*, "and came in and occupied it." Questions are then raised which connect the dispute to a bitter quarrel over the prior deposition of another bishop, whose long arm even from the grave is seen stretched out to avenge his own unmerited defeat.

Whatever may be the truth about the *eranarii*, a bishop did need friends, sometimes. He should make his face known to the local garrison, he should walk about the town, share his views with all. Especially through his church he should build a base of respect and support. By it he could defy even imperial commands and forces; they flinched, they didn't dare face the size and anger of the crowds. Many surprising such retreats could be instanced.[17] If the passions of credal preference reached and stirred his people, he should make his own views clear from the pulpit in the ways described above (Chap. 3), simplifying them for mass consumption and if necessary infusing them with a passion that worked to the right ends.

Among the descriptions of how this could best be done is the following, drawn from the eastern capital at the turn of the fifth century:[18]

> The Arianizers, as we said, held their meetings outside the city. As the festal day of each week came around, meaning the Sabbath and Lord's Day in which assemblies in churches are usually held, they gathered inside the city gates around the public squares and sang responsive songs composed of Arian teachings; and this they would do throughout most of the night. Toward dawn, reciting these they trooped through the city center and out the gates, to gather in their usual places of meeting. Since, however, they went on with their infuriating songs against the Homoousians, repeatedly demanding, 'Where are those who say the Three are One Power? [bishop] John took thought against the drawing off of simple people from the church by such chanting, and opposed to them some of his own people, so that they too should engage in nocturnal hymn-singing and drown out the zeal of the Arianizers, on this score, and at the same time make his own people steadier in their own faith. His intent was a good one; but it led to disorders and dangers. The Homoousian hymns appeared the more striking in the nocturnal singing, since he thought of the idea of his people carrying silver crosses with wax candles on them, supplied by the empress Eudoxia at her expense; and the Arianizers, being so numerous and in the grip of rivalry, tried to strike back and engage in conflicts. From their past domination they were the more fired up and ready for combat, and scorned their opponents. Without delay, then, one night they engaged, and one of the empress' eunuchs, Briso, was struck on the brow by a stone as he participated in the singing. Some in the crowds on both sides were killed.

Every detail in this account could be amply illustrated from other times and settings: the likelihood of stoning, the role for civil authorities, the more or less orchestrated provocation of physical acts. And the psychology is right. Anyone who has been a party to demonstrations, standing on one side of a street with his like-minded at his back, while across the street, antagonists with their chanted phrases challenge the crossing of that street and dare it to be done — everyone knows how these things happen.

Bishops must be easy about addressing an audience, if not with educated eloquence, then at least with natural force. This they needed to move people to action. Their logical arguments and scriptural proofs counted for nothing as against passion, to raise the temperature of men's minds, inflaming them with a sense of urgency. Written attacks might make the attempt but within the bounds of more or less clever abuse and name-calling; and of this, much survives, once relished but unpleasant and tedious today (for illustration, yards of Basil and his brother writing against Eunomius). Oral attacks, much simpler, hit much harder. Any belief and its sect could be called Manichaean or Jewish or whatever was thought to be universally detestable; accuracy in the accusation was not the point; and there was a rich black lexicon available for use, perhaps by the very emperor. His anti-heretical fulminations were of course read aloud in public places before being posted, and so could be given the force of the voice.[19] However, it was in preaching that strength of feeling was most often expressed and aroused. Sermons could do the job; and their success is the less surprising, given the habit of audience-participation in the empire's society. From top to bottom, all ranks were used to expressing their reaction to whatever was being said in its assemblies. The scenes and shouts have been described, above. Listening was in fact often a back-and-forth affair, all the more likely therefore to stir people up.

For example, in Constantinople, Chrysostom in his pulpit rebukes while yet lingering on the loud approval he keeps getting, and likens it to what one could hear in the theaters for actors and musicians.[20] There too performances were interactive. Again, at Alexandria in AD 432 at a time when the city's hero Cyril was elsewhere under attack, a visiting bishop of Emesa from the pulpit offers encapsulated controversy to suit his auditors — as it were, raw meat — and does so in a provocative not to say combative fashion:[21]

> "Mary Who-Bore-God, *theotokos*, gave birth to Emanuel." The crowd shouted, "There's the faith itself! Cyril is orthodox! Cyril is the gift of God! This is what we wanted to hear! Whoever doesn't say this, curses upon him!"

"*Theotokos*" was a war-word, Cyril had been a great champion of one side of that war. And as the speaker resumes, he is again interrupted: "The crowd shouts out, 'Welcome to you! The bishop is orthodox!'" He continues, "'For I declare the One Christ, the One Lord, compounded of two perfect natures, *physeis*, the divine and the human' [and again, from the crowd:] 'The worthy for the worthy! It is Christians who speak! God's gift! Cyril orthodox!'"

In Cyrrhus in the AD 430s quite opposite teachings from the pulpit are welcomed with cries, "This is the Apostles' belief! This is the belief of the orthodox! We believe as Diodorus [bishop of Tarsus] and Theodorus [of Mopsuestia, another of Cyril's targets]! . . . Away with heretics! Away with Eutyches and Maximian!" Written down, the opinions were preserved for use in their bishop's contests, even for recall at a later council.[22]

Or earlier in Antioch in AD 361, a new bishop focusing on doctrine for the first time is assaulted by his own archdeacon, holding opposite views, who tries physically to muzzle him; whereupon the bishop, his mouth stopped, signals his teaching by holding up a hand with three fingers extended, closes it, and then holds it up with one, in token of the Trinity being a unity; at which the party in agreement before him "lets out a huge shout, exulting and jumping up and down."[23] They understood.

And if the reaction had been hostile? A bishop must be ready for that, too. Chrysostom recommends, no doubt to applause, that his listeners should not hesitate to give a good punch in the face to misbelievers. Equally bellicose words are heard from other bishops in eastern and western pulpits. They occasionally join as combatants in the riots they have aroused or which they have certainly directed and sustained. Their clergy have been seen, above, beating and stabbing each other in the cause of Bassianus at Antioch.

At Antioch, too, in behalf of another embattled bishop, his men "made a dictation of praises [for him] and carried it around among the clergy to get signatures. Some of the clergy, fifteen or eighteen, didn't want to sign, saying, 'We're being asked something and we don't know what to say, and we can't lie.' He took them into the church and incited angry shouts against them, that they should be turned out of doors because they hadn't signed, and he excommunicated them in the presence of the whole church and turned them out of doors."[24]

And in the capital, despite the emperor's known and settled enmity, supporters of a bishop recently deposed for heresy had the courage still to preach his gospel.[25]

> Since here we are, anyway, we haven't ceased from our cares for his cause, with all our energies, mindful of the injustice brought on him by the atheists . . . — though there's not much to be hoped for here, given that everyone's decision is for sale and the very judges are arguing that Christ's God-ness and human-ness are but one nature, *physis*. The people as a whole are all right, God be thanked, and flock about us all the time, and we've begun speaking to them, have gathered very large meetings, and for the fourth time preached to them about the faith, thanks to the prayers of Your Piety [fellow bishop in another city]. They listened with such pleasure that they didn't leave till the early afternoon, but stood the day's full heat. The throng being gathered in a vast court with porticoes on its four

sides, we made our remarks from the second floor. But the entire clergy with those lovely monks commenced a violent attack on us to force one single creed, when we were coming back from the Rufinian Palace, after our audience with the Most Pious King; and a lot of people were wounded, both the laity on our side and the so-called monks.

A final church instance of the excitement generated by definitions of faith in groups, this one in Tyre in AD 518, where the bishop reads to his congregation certain polemical letters from colleagues, arousing "votes" as they are called in the report of them:[26]

"Long life to the Augustus! Long life to the Augusta! . . . [and so on through a list of great officials to the Constantinopolitan bishop John]. One is the God who did this! Great is the God that granted this! . . . Whoever doesn't say this is not in the faith! [adding a score of more shouts, among them scattered curses]." And with the bishop mounting to the pulpit, they shouted out, "A good God brought you!" [with six more acclamations, and other bishops joining him in the pulpit, followed by 97 more acclamations, including:] "Accursed be Severus and John [the monk]! . . . Throw them out of the city! Throw out the Egyptians! Throw out the den of robbers! Burn them! Out with Romanus! Out with the Manichaean! Cursed be Severus, Eutyches, and Nestorius! If they had won we'd be dead! The cross has conquered and there is no disorder!" And himself the bishop addressing them, "I beg of Your Charity to bear with me and permit me and the bishops with me, beloved of God, to curse [Severus] the Acephalus . . ." [in which the speaker is joined by another bishop, with more assertions of credal loyalties and complementary:] "curses invoked on all heretics together with all their impious ideas and the people who join them in believing their pestiferous teachings . . ." [now to be cut off by interruptions from the people shouting] "One is the God who made everything! . . . Curses on [John] the monk!"

In this way eventually end these hours of mutual excitement between the pulpit and the nave, bishops and people, as night falls on their assembly.

In all such scenes we see determined, energetic, articulate men in charge. They are willing to take real risks to gain their ends; are good at judging crowd reactions; are sure they are right; and can persuade their audience of their sincerity — otherwise, why should anyone follow them? Some of them evidently possess that mysterious thing called charisma. The record in dealing with masses of people allows a guess at the effects of their powers and personality on their colleagues in councils, who are my proper subject. It is above all useful to consider their success.

They were indeed successful in generating the strongest feelings, capable of breaking all restraints and challenging all authority. The result was those deaths with which the present chapter began. Their total indicates the desperate seriousness of doctrinal disease, call it, which so repeatedly afflicted the empire's towns and cities. Deaths, yes, the most dramatic; but another symptom was the physical destruction that went with it. Arson was generally the cause but by no means the only one.[27] The target might be a residence, a monastery, a church, or whole sections of some town.

Social division, too, was a symptom, in much broader terms — the splitting of communities into two or more angry parts. Since cities in the Greek-language provinces were the worst afflicted, it is proper to use the word so often found in contemporary documents, *stasis*, amounting to "seditious faction".[28] Everyone would be drawn into it, in scenes familiar from previous pages. To recall them, this last: "Troops with their swords occupied the church and ranged about everywhere in the building. Confronting them, a thoroughly aroused populace. . . . The streets outside were crammed, the avenues and squares, every place, and from second- and third-story windows the young and old, men and women, craned down."[29]

A crime problem, as we would say today, but a crime problem afflicting half the empire. The emperors could hardly close their eyes and ears to it; by its victims they were constantly reminded of it and of their own responsibilities, too. However, in their view much more was involved than crime. God's anger showed. Their realm and reign together were under threat of destruction, and heresy was to blame.

To control it, public discussion could be forbidden. Laws to this effect have been cited, above. The burning of theological tracts or the minutes of misguided councils, ceremoniously in public squares, were good measures, and much resorted to from Constantine on through the period of my study. So, "Justinian Augustus, may you triumph! Away with it!" shouted the throngs in the capital, enraged by a certain creed being circulated; "Burn the Chapter issued by the bishops in the Chalcedon council."[30]

Beyond efforts at censorship, however, armed force might be needed against the purveyors of detested beliefs, themselves. Had the moment for it come? Was violence the right way to end violence? Resort to it meant taking sides; the question was difficult. Emperors never lacked for advice in their court, but advisers themselves had to decide what to say; and, as we heard from a deputation to the palace, on their leaving, "Everyone's decision is for sale," for gold, *toi chrysoi*.

In illustration, we have a letter with particularly striking figures in it. It shows that something above 200,000 gold coins, at a time when a man could live for several months on one such, had been paid into the inner circle of the emperor to retrieve the throne for a deposed bishop, no less than Cyril of Alexandria. The payments were not a closely held secret, and indeed were of a size no more to be hidden than an elephant, amounting, let us say, to $500,000 in a not-rich country today, or $15 million in a developed economy.[31] They showed Cyril in both a good light (he was a power to be reckoned with) and a bad (payments to authority being a universal but dubious thing). His agent referred to them as "blessings" and "eulogies", two of the many euphemisms current in the period.

Purchase of favor on such a scale was of course far above the reach of the everyday bishops who are the focus of my own study. It was a thing they wouldn't ordinarily hear about in any detail. What did they make of it? At the least they must see the importance of the emperor in doctrinal debate — importance given numerical expression by men who really knew the world, great metropolitans and patriarchs. The emperor's weight was quantified, his power could be totalled up, as if we ourselves heard that the cabinet officers of our president had pocketed specific gigantic sums before some specially interesting decision was arrived at. And to make conclusions more obvious, there at councils, enthroned up front, were the emperor's men flanked by great metropolitans — the latter with gold to offer by the ton.

6

Preliminaries

The councils of particular interest to this study were all more or less under the emperors' thumb. The fact was due to the nature of doctrinal disputes. They involved bishops who claimed some following. It was one thing to decide who was right by majority vote, and for the purposes of some one church or one diocese; quite another thing, to speak out more widely and to enforce the decision. To what, then, other than a superpower could there be appeal? In the third century one of the five most storied churches, Antioch, looked for help to one emperor (Aurelian), as other churches did to another (Constantine) immediately after the edict of toleration (AD 313). Constantine called bishops together in large enough numbers to carry weight, with his own weight superadded. The model served for Nicaea and thereafter whenever nothing else would do. Within the period of my study, the occasions for it — twenty-five identifiable among ten times that number of known ecclesiastical assemblies (Chap. 1) — were rare; but they were most important.[1]

The Christian communities in the two halves of the empire, Latin and Greek, were quite different. The western was ruled by an unchallenged primate enthroned in a secular capital long left to itself, and in a church relatively undisturbed and unengaged in empire-wide doctrinal debates. Represented by its spokesmen, Rome was not to be ignored; but western representation was rare or insignificant in councils advertised as empire-wide, and eastern delegates to western councils need not expect a friendly reception.[2] Initiative as well as determinants of style for theological debate lay clearly in the east.

As for secular power: since it was generally shared among two or three emperors, sometimes one of them in the west — a Constans, a Gratian — might intrude on general ecclesiastical debate. But that too was rare.

The nearest approach to a western capital was Milan. There, in AD 390, something took place quite unimaginable in Constantinople. It was that famous full surrender to Ambrose by Theodosius I, seeking re-entry to communion. In contrast, consider the statement by the head of the church in the new capital, Menas, a half-century later: "None of the matters considered within the most holy Church should be settled contrary to the emperor's views and command."[3] True, Menas' church was only one of four competing for preeminence in the eastern regions. Moreover, it was inevitably watched and dominated by the imperial court; therefore dependent. Or one might rather say, it was the best situated to make friends among the great. That was how the reality was understood by the best of observers: the historian Socrates, explaining that the bishop of a certain city "was especially powerful at this time because that was where the emperor was resident."[4] The connection didn't have to be explained. Dependence of the sort that Menas endured, then, was no bad bargain. After all, the other three great sees, and every smaller individual interest, had to come to Constantinople to win over the superpower, if that were needed.

This much and no more is said here on very large, complicated subjects, only to introduce the word *ecumenical*. Anything so described was "of the whole civilized world". Yet what a preposterous boast! first made for ecclesiastical matters in the AD 330s and subsequently competed for and valorously claimed for themselves by councils which certainly should have known better. As, for example, at Ephesus I. The party of the Alexandrian bishop met by itself but claimed to be doing so as a synod in obedience to the emperor's summons, which underlay the claim then to be ecumenical; but their opponents across town made the same claim with better reason, as the presiding official, Candidianus, all too accurately pointed out. To yield to the Egyptian church would, he said, incur the danger to church unity that always lay in "particular" synods, meaning such narrow and partisan groups as Cyril had brought together to do his will.[5] Though no clean determination of who was right could be arrived at, still, the view of the time was clear. The determinant of ecumenicity was imperial initiative, which in practice meant Constantinople. Given the realities of power, armed if needed, no other view could prevail.

Yet an additional factor of inclusiveness did have much weight. At Ephesus, the Egyptian party pointed to their having the participation not only of Rome's representatives but of Africa's as well (meaning themselves!) and "more than two hundred assembled from the entire civilized world, the *oikoumene*, all the West voting with us." Their arguments for their belief included — they really rested on — the democratic element within the whole of Christendom and Christian thinking. The fact was explored in my second chapter, above. This same element determined the beliefs arrived at within the council of Ephesus. It couldn't be ignored. Its enforcement, however, required much more: imperial participation, participation of wide areas and populations.

In my seventh chapter, below, the operation of these two determinants, secular-imperial and ecclesiastical-democratic, will appear more fully.

Ambition for ecumenicity might affect the nature of debate. Wherever there were two minds about a theological question, those two could talk it out between them. If the conversation didn't degenerate into a shouting match, the course of it would follow reason. Such conversations are in fact reported across the history of the third century church and later. Conducted in front of other people, they still spoke to reason because everyone in the audience had heard everything that was said. Everyone knew the flow of argument. As much could be claimed by the readers of imaginary written debates, of which several have survived, by Jerome or Nestorius or others.

When, however, two minds explained themselves to a huge audience whom they could reach only by catch-words, slogans, and name-calling, then a merely social element could determine the winner. The winner won by insisting that "everyone" believed this or that — everyone who was someone. Democracy seems to have been the determining force; but it was no longer rational, at least not strictly so. How could it be? — when participants in its processes had not been personally present, or able, or sufficiently interested, to follow the debate. They rather counted on being, as they insisted, "everyone". The determining force was the instinct of our species to conform to surrounding opinion.

Accordingly, in advocacy of any doctrine the words with weight are "general" or "standard", *katholikos* or *orthodoxos*. No further explanation or defense may be thought necessary.[6] All sides of a dispute will insist theirs is the really catholic one. Ambrose complains of the fact.[7] Today a scholar will occasionally put the two italicized words in quotation marks to avoid the appearance of retrospective partisanship in doctrinal history, but readers know what view is actually the only possible one, the one that is universal (within the particular universe they call their own).

To claim anything like ecumenicity, help from the court was essential. It was accordingly sought out all the time. To my knowledge, no one has studied the flow of ecclesiastical business into court circles, there to be (or never to be) placed before the emperor himself; so the questions, How did it all work and who talked to whom? remain to be answered. A little information, however, is easily to be had, to shed light on particular causes and moments. Perhaps nothing much more could be learned from a careful search.

As one would expect, their Highnesses, emperors and sometimes a wife or sister, could hardly show themselves in public without someone coming up to beg a favor; and among the reports of such little moments there is one that shows the possible complications. It takes the form of a petition handed in at Antioch in AD 363 to the visiting Jovian by supporters of a doctrine out of favor at the time, the Arian:[8]

> "We beg of Your Power, Your Emperorship, Your Piety, to hear us." The King said, "Who are you? Where are you from?" The Arians said, "We are Christians, Lord." The King said, "Where do you come from, what city?" The Arians said, "Alexandria." The King said, "What do you want?" The Arians said, "We beg Your Power, Your Emperorship, to give us a bishop." The King said, "I gave orders for the previous one, Athanasius whom you had previously, to be placed on the throne." The Arians said, "We beg Your Power, he has been in exile and under charges for many years." A soldier, suddenly inflamed, broke in, "I beg Your Emperorship myself to examine these men, and who they are and from where. For these are the dregs and offal of Cappadocia, the cast-offs from that impious [former Alexandrian bishop] George. They have made a waste of their city and the whole world." The King listened and put spurs to his horse and departed for the Square

— the matter being one he didn't care to get into at the moment; and he can hardly be blamed. It was in dispute. He had had enough of that.

Yet it was a dispute on a relatively small scale. It concerned the balance of representation of competing doctrines within one city, not the balance within a council. The former was a more common point of request; the latter, far more serious, because it involved cities and churches of all the participants. Consider the call for a council at Carthage in AD 411 (the issue, doctrinal but not theological) determining which of two parties would control literally hundreds of sees in Africa. The Caecilianists knew the meeting must be in their own hands; and through their envoy to the court they made sure that there would be a most friendly official to preside and only small, equal contingents assembled from each side, their own and the Donatists'.[9] To insure the emperor's acquiescence in their plan, they presented it in the form of a brief, roundly traducing their opponents as victims or purveyors of "vain error and sterile schism," of *superstitio* and cunning campaigns. This was all he was told about the situation; the document formed the basis for his decision in their favor — though, as the Donatists alleged, it was all "lies". Which was likely enough; but the Caecilianists refused to share with the Donatists the contents of the petition no matter how hard they were pressed. Not surprisingly they emerged the victors. Control of the man who controlled outcomes was demonstrated once more to be a great thing.

Those hundreds of sees at stake recall the hundreds of thousands of gold coins lavished by the Alexandrian bishop on his own interests at court, in turn to affect the hundred sees subordinate to him. He had been aware of the many persons who actually had or alleged their influence over important decisions, and who stretched out a hand to receive, not to give; or not to give until they had received. Contemporary church historians occasionally supply the names involved in the emperors' actions of state at various times in the fourth and fifth centuries: the presbyter said to be "the close companion of the emperor's wife and of the eunuchs in attendance on her bedchamber"; some particular bishops there "who had gotten in line the men powerful in the palace, to adopt their views," and "had brought round to their own views the influential persons in the palace"; still others who worked through or on Eusebius, Prefect of the Sacred Chamber, he, however, being besieged also by "many who were influential and were seeking Eusebius' favor." The outcome of a church council could be determined by having the right connections in the capital, as a bishop of a small see reports rather bitterly about his adversaries: "they won over the people of the imperial court and everyone else of chief influence and so could turn to their business from a position of great superiority. They themselves were both prosecutors and jurors and executioners and everything they chose."[10]

The existence of the quite obscure "Resident [ecclesiastical] Council" in Constantinople to which the emperors sometimes turned for a quick decision indicates a population of bishops always handy, two or three dozen detached from whatever sees they ought to have been serving. The general problem of such ambitious figures drawn to the capital had been addressed as early as the AD 340s; "for great numbers of bishops," so declared a conciliar canon of that date, "never cease from hanging about the imperial court . . . so that just one individual submits many and various petitions at court;" and, so warns the bishop who recommends the canon, "Our importunity, our constant crowding about, and our quite improper requests cost us the welcome and ready belief that we ought to have won." To which, at the authorizing council, "All present responded, 'So be it decided.' "[11] Obviously, however, the canon did nothing to solve the problem.

Bishops except in the most obscure corners would certainly be familiar with the realities of power just outlined. They would know the stories—a great many more stories and in much greater detail than have survived. It was, after all, in the interests of great courtiers and officials to be talked about and to advertise who they were; and among the people who sought them out, the excitement attending an approach to the King would be shared afterwards with constituents. More advertising. A few accounts were quoted in the previous chapter; some others in this one. Out of real experience and gossip in combination, thus widely known, the leaders of doctrinal parties must then plan how they might add secular weight to their ecclesiastical positions.

In AD 410 the process was indicated for the Carthage council of the following year. Get to power and bend it to your truth—which need not be everyone's truth.

We have information about another juncture with an equally successful outcome, a generation earlier (AD 381). The bishop second in authority in Italy, perhaps in the west, was Ambrose in Milan. His maiden venture into religious controversy had been opposed, one might say shown up, by an aged bishop in a backward region, Palladius, who presided over the lower Danube sees. Ambrose amended his tract and approached the emperor with the request for a council on it. His doughty septuagenarian adversary also but separately approached the emperor in person, he too suggesting (as he thought, the first to do so) that a council should be called to explore his theological differences with Milan. It should be a high-prestige big general meeting with an adequate representation from the east; and he got the promise of this, for a site, Aquileia, just north of the modern Trieste:[12]

> "Our emperor Gratian ordered the Oriental bishops to come; do you deny he ordered them? The emperor himself told us he had ordered the Oriental bishops to come.' Bishop Ambrose said: 'In any case, he ordered it so that whoever he did not prohibit could come here.' Palladius said: 'But your petition made it so that they didn't come. By an appearance of false intention you obtained this and narrowed the council . . . You got to the emperor, you got at him so there would be no full council . . . Without an Oriental council we won't reply to you."

Ambrose had thus narrowed the thing to a size he could totally control. Most of the bishops attending were subordinate to him; most, perhaps all, owed their past or future careers to his favor. It only remains unclear, whether his plan required him to have deceived the emperor or whether he and the emperor together joined in deceiving Palladius. The first explanation seems the more likely, given the evidence for such deception being tried and succeeding at other times. Absolute monarchs, walled in as they are, must submit to being misinformed so long as they insist on being absolute.[13]

The outcome at Aquileia shows how crucial it was to get one's friends in and keep one's enemies out. This strategy worked much more surely than persuasion in debate. All that a likely loser could do was to withhold his attendance lest he be condemned, as we can see happening at Carthage around AD 310, or again a generation later at Serdica: for, as a synodal letter says about Eusebius of Nicomedia and others of his mind at that time, "when they arrived at Serdica and saw our brethren Athanasius [of Alexandria, often deposed] and Marcellus [of Ancyra, at one point deposed] and Asclepius [of Gaza, at one point exiled] and the others, they were afraid to attend the trial [*krisis*, as it is called, truly]; and they were summoned to do so not once or twice but often. They didn't answer the summons."[14] The same response or lack of response will be seen often again at such major meetings as Ephesus I, II, and Chalcedon. To avoid being formally judged heretical was sometimes the best one could hope for; for judgement so often meant disaster.

Imperial calls to attend were naturally expressed in terms one shouldn't disregard. "We will not tolerate an excuse toward God or Ourselves for any failure to appear promptly and at the assigned time and place, with all zeal," so Theodosius II writes to Cyril of Alexandria before Ephesus I.[15] No doubt "regrets" were acceptable from the infirm and perhaps there was no follow-up against others who simply never replied. There is evidence for that. Yet at Serdica the "Orientals" as they were referred to — at the time, meaning Eusebius of Nicomedia and his party, above — "wouldn't assemble together with the Holy Synod, only turned up there at the assembly-point to demonstrate their attendance, and then promptly took off."[16] So they didn't want to seem openly defiant. A few years later a bishop speaks of participants at a council being "forced" to attend, meaning by the emperor, and specifying the high officials with alarming titles who circulated to insure compliance throughout the west provinces, while in the east likewise, officials "obeyed the general orders under which they were to compel all bishops to the council."[17] We hear of the summons being split between the imperial secretariat and some individual metropolitan.[18]

On occasion, the emperor specified exactly what participation he wanted. Theodosius II wanted only two or three bishops from each province for Ephesus I, a request honored by the Orientals but not by the Egyptians;[19] and in his letter to the bishop of Alexandria (Dioscurus) leading up to Ephesus II, he asked for attendance by the bishops of ten Egyptian cities of substance, metropolises, and ten more from smaller places in the province — "and no others but these that have been authorized shall trouble the Holy Synod." These "will join all the bishops . . . to whom We have written to assemble."[20]

From the beginning, meaning in AD 313, then in the next year, then at Nicaea, and off and on in subsequent mentions, the imperial post was put at the disposal of those attending, for sea travel as well as land.[21] It was also available to cart off wrong-headed bishops to exile in one or another part of the Roman Gulag, whether or not they were ever to finish their journey in good health. Nevertheless, from some points of north Africa to northern Italy or from Mesopotamia to the Mediterranean coast was a very long journey for men in their later years, and not all of those finished who started out.

On arrival, they might find imperial hospitality (or they might find none) to lodge and feed them. Councils called by the emperor sometimes met where he himself could lodge, himself with his court, though this was rare.[22] At Serdica, modern Sophia, the more welcome Orientals got rooms in the imperial palace (one of many grand great mansions scattered about in provincial cities for government use).[23] As there were some ninety such guests, the size of the building can be imagined. They remained only until all the stragglers had arrived and registered. We are told that on the way west "they had formed assemblies of their own at stopping points and extracted oaths not to attend the trial when they arrived at Serdica, nor even to join the holy great Synod." Instead — though not before a couple of their number had gone over to the other side — they withdrew to the next-door town to hold their own separate council. In the same fashion some years later a council at Seleuceia (AD 359) split apart, and one half called itself official and issued its credal decisions.

Pre-conciliar caucusing receives mention at another moment, too, at the little town Chalcedon, so convenient to the capital: "Everyone [aligned with the writer] assembled there and took counsel together, how to succeed in presenting their case," since it wouldn't do to go into action unprepared.[24] A party, *tagma*, had to act like one, after all, in a disciplined manner. Its members would be reminded of the fact when they first came together, early or later on their way to the point of assembly; they would learn what was going to happen as they traveled toward it together, by donkey along the rocky bits or on the smooth bits perhaps by ox-cart such as could still be enjoyed or endured fifty years ago in eastern Anatolia, ambling along at a pace that invited conversation as the long hours passed. Party plans no doubt were often discussed at the point of origin, too, in episcopal elections. These had doctrinal implications. A few details were mentioned in the second chapter, above; in the next, more will emerge within the context of councils actually at work.

Practice makes perfect. As the Christian community was drawn more deeply in doctrinal strife, ways to win were refined and elaborated. They very soon exceeded anything to be found in secular affairs. Available for a start were lists of occupants of sees kept up to date by metropolitan bishops for their individual provinces and, above them, by patriarchs. Antioch's lists would include well over 150 spread across an enormous area, constituting what opponents called *Orientales* after the title of their secular region, the *dioikesis Oriens*.[25] Within this there would rarely be perfect unity; rather, at most times, different theological positions taking their name from whoever was seen as their chief proponent: as for example "the Eusebians" to mean all clergy in agreement with the bishop of Nicomedia regarding Christ's substance, *ousia*. In ordinary Greek, they were "those around" or "with" So-and-So, which is how they would be seen at assemblies of any sort, physically clustering together.[26]

In contrast, the Egyptians. The nature of their organization was made clear at Chalcedon, when their contingent came under pressure to sign a statement under preparation at the moment, and they refused.[27]

> The Egyptian bishops said, "If anyone goes beyond what we said in the petitions we offered, whether Eutyches [accused of heresy] or some other, let him be accursed; but all our Holy Fathers [the other bishops in the council] know that, regarding the letter of Leo Most Holy and Most-a-Friend-to-God, the high bishop of Rome, on every question we wait on the opinion of our Most Blessed archbishop; and we beg your indulgence in awaiting the views of our president, because we follow him in all regards and the Most Holy Fathers, three hundred and eighteen, who assembled at Nicaea and gave the Rule that the whole Egypt region should follow the archbishop of Alexandria and do nothing apart from him at the will of some other subordinate bishop."
>
> Eusebius bishop of Dorylaeum [who was pressing the accusations that were the focus of the council's session, and would be balked by the Egyptians] said, "They're lying." Florentius bishop of Sardis said, "Let them prove what they say." All the Most Reverend Bishops shouted out, "Openly curse Eutyches' doctrines! Whoever doesn't sign the [Leo] Letter that the whole council agrees to is a heretic! Curses on Dioscorus [ex-archbishop of Alexandria, deposed a week earlier] and those who cling to him! If they're not of a right understanding, how can they choose a bishop [to replace Dioscorus]?"
>
> The Most Reverend Egyptian bishops shouted, "It's a battle over faith!..."
>
> The Most Reverend Cecropius bishop of Sebastopolis said, "These men don't know how to believe, and now they want to learn?" Photius the Most Reverend bishop of Tyre said, "Do you agree to the Letter or not?..." All the Most Reverend bishops shouted, "Whoever doesn't agree to the Letter of the Most Holy Leo is a heretic!..."
>
> [And, surrendering,] the Most Reverend Egyptian bishops shouted, "Curses on Eutyches and whoever agrees with him!"

The Most Reverend bishops [who wanted it in writing] said, "Let them sign on to Leo's Letter! Whoever doesn't sign on is a heretic!"

The Most Reverend Egyptian bishops shouted, "We can't sign without our archbishop's consent."

Acacius Most Reverend bishop of Ariarathea said, "It would be indeed peculiar, to disregard the whole council while waiting for some one person who at some future date will be bishop of the great city of Alexandria. The idea among these people here is to make chaos out of everything just as they did at [the council of] Ephesus and fill the whole world with disgraceful disorder."

And (he goes on) if they don't sign, let's depose them all.

To this, the whole council shouts its approval. In response, the Egyptians plead that they have made clear what their faith was, truly catholic. They call attention to how few they are, a mere sixteen or so unable to speak, or rather unable to sign, for so large a number as the Egyptian church includes. If they acted in contravention of ancient custom and canons, "everybody in the Egyptian region would be on our backs. Have mercy on our gray hair."

They may be imagined in great distress. The threat of deposition was of course no empty one; neither was the alternative, to be ostracized or perhaps beaten up on their return to their homes. Retaliation upon bishops could indeed be expected if they were seen to betray their constituents. There were well known instances.[28] So the Egyptians wept, perhaps, as speakers both at councils and while preaching are sometimes said to do. Handbooks of rhetoric recommended that one should not hold back one's tears as one spoke if it suited one's words, or should at least let one's emotions freely rise to the pathos of the subject. Celebrity performers set the style.[29] But there was shouting, too: a lot of that, from the majority who were not celebrities. The scene was an emotional one, with a full share of drama real or contrived.

We can follow its unfolding with the advantage of detailed knowledge: knowledge of how people went about group decision-making, about the routine for formal registration of one's vote at an ecclesiastical meeting or, for that matter, at a secular one. We know more than a little about the process of election determining the presence of these particular human beings at this particular assembly — all these things a part of the mental baggage of the Egyptians and their opponents. In their minds, too, was a "battle over faith," where faith broken would certainly bring down God's wrath upon his wretched servants. The unseen touched the seen everywhere, every day.

Yet to defy one's opponents was to join the parade of the deposed, visible to the mind's eye: the parade of the exiled, the frail aged driven off to some part of the Gulag or, if not that, at best destined for poverty and abuse in their home-towns.

If the participants in the scene have not left us a record of the thoughts determining their actions, we, even from our limited acquaintance with their world, can reconstitute those thoughts to make a composite being. He is, we can say, a person in his later years, his fifties up to a hundred (!like Ossius); devout, Bible-reading to a fault, if that be possible; no great logician, certainly no match for colleagues in higher stations who argue in such wonderful twists and terminology, not always readily understood. All the more reason to agree to their conclusions, to follow their lead, to fold one's self safely into the com-pany of the like-minded who carry some leader's name: "Eusebians" or such.

Thus in the composite being can be discerned a tumble of ideas at moments of danger, a mass of mixed motives and impulses such as agitate humans great and small and middle sized.

Councils in action

1. The stage

In picturing the past, a natural starting point is the physical setting. Nine out of ten councils — the diocesan or provincial ones, whether annual or semi-annual — would meet in the convener's church. For those others authorized by the emperor, there would be no difficulty in finding the right space for a few score of participants, even for several hundreds. They too might use a church or sometimes an imperial palace. Constantine offered his at Nicaea; Justinian his, the Hormisdas in the capital or the Rufinianum near Chalcedon. There were palaces everywhere. Their giant halls and lavish use of marble can be easily imagined.

Structures or complexes that deserved the name *palace* were not the emperors' monopoly. Architecture like most other arts of Roman civilization had always been in the hands of the very rich. They wanted show for their money and favored grandeur, whether by their gift to their cities or to themselves; so one could expect to find, in or close to any city, ample or positively gigantic structures well suited to a public meeting. Great personages seem generally to have had, and their position naturally required, an audience hall in their residence, a *secretarium* that might be blocked off by a curtain, where they could hold daily receptions, hear petitions, and settle business that was best kept from the public. Equally well, it might serve a council. Perhaps it was this sort of hall that a church patroness provided in the early fourth century for a council in Carthage. A governor would certainly have a *secretarium*. Bishops, too, with business of increasing importance, would need such a space. One would be built on to their church, where councils could meet.

Yet once, at Carthage, a thousand-plus of clergy had to look to the city's most commodious public-baths complex for anything big enough to hold them all.[1] Participant-numbers naturally determined how much room had to be provided. A sampling of these numbers was supplied in parentheses to the council-list in my first chapter. However, they indicate only the bishops attending, who usually brought along one or more of their lower clergy. They could anticipate, after all, a lot of writing and checking of documents to be done, as will appear later. Consequently from the mid-third century when we first can peer into the inner workings of a council, we find presbyters and deacons present for such duties, sometimes with exorcists and lectors added (the lectors explained by the occasional bishop who couldn't read).[2] At one meeting the ratio of bishops to lower clergy can be compared: about one to three. As a rule, then, in picturing the crowd, the total of bishops at a council should be at the very least, doubled. Small wonder that only the largest hall in the Gargilian Baths in Carthage could hold the participants of AD 411.

Clergy who were not bishops were not supposed to play an active part; but occasionally they did speak out or even subscribed to a decision in their own name. They joined in shouts which amounted to votes.[3] They were at times also joined by laity who could stand looking in at the door or perhaps in side aisles.[4] Reports of lay participation in informal church gatherings such as at Tyre (above, Chap. 5) were occasionally read aloud at councils, so that the popular and the conciliar made a seamless pair. Those shouting crowds, however, were not physically present at councils.

Bishops were provided with their individual chairs and, after they sat down, so did any representatives of the emperor who were present; but everybody else had to stand.[5] That meant that the front rows, the more visible, presented the white-bearded older clergy, a mass of Santa-Clauses, while to the rear were the younger black-beards. All wore wool, summer or winter. So far from cleanliness being next to godliness, they all shared a particular veneration for those who washed least.[6]

At Rome in AD 502, 76 (or 80) bishops, meaning no less than 150 clergy and probably over 200, met in the ecclesiastical part of the so-called Sessorian palace. This can only have been, by its modern name, Santa Croce in Gerusalemme.[7] Here the nave without the side aisles measured roughly 125 × 27 feet, large enough for both the standing and the seated — not without some crowding but allowing a clear sight of the action to everyone present.

On the other hand, at Ephesus, a much larger number assembled: some 200

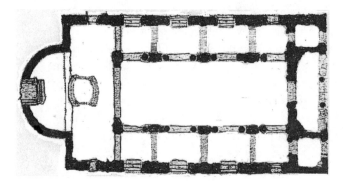

Fig. 5. Santa Croce, Rome

bishops for the first gathering under Cyril, bishop of Alexandria, meaning (by my reckoning) 400–550 clergy of all ranks. A stoa running along the south side of the Olympieion, near the harbor, was to accommodate them. It was open on one side and quite wide enough for them all (around 92 feet); certainly long enough, too — some 865 feet (of which 295 feet at the west end was later adapted for the so-called Mary church).[8] In the plan shown here, a dotted line indicates the eastern wall of the later Mary church; for perhaps this was in fact the line chosen earlier for both Ephesus I and II. Two rows of thrones could be set up along each side for the bishops, leaving lower clergy to stand

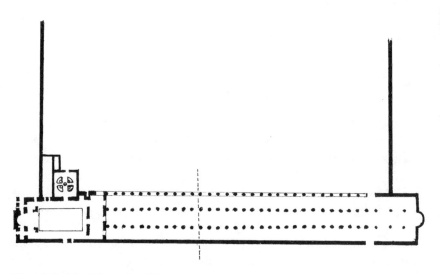

Fig. 6. A Hall for Ephesus I and II

behind them, while an area at the top was reserved for dignitaries and witnesses. It would have been difficult or impossible for some participants toward the rear to hear everything that was said or read aloud at the head of the meeting, but a speaker used to the pulpit could perhaps reach even those ears.[9]

The details of the setting are of only antiquarian interest, except as they affected the dynamics of assemblies. At times, however, they did just that; for it is not possible to picture any intelligent participation of a thousand persons in a discussion, that is, being able to hear what was said clearly enough to follow it and then to react, either by an appropriate acclamation or by inward agreement; nor could so large a mass of humanity be anything but intimidating to someone who might want to stand up and say something. Chalcedon is a specific case in point. Here were 350 bishops or more, with their attendants, hence a total of perhaps a thousand.[10] Working sessions went on and on for weeks, people came and went, it was a whole town on top of a town. Size and duration alike invited a strong lead from whoever was in charge. It had to be, and was inevitably, a meeting run from the top down. In fact, these were no fewer than nineteen imperial officers of very high rank sharing that responsibility.

Ordinary social uses were in agreement with the physical arrangements of any such meeting; that is, regard for rank pervaded the world of the fourth, fifth, and sixth centuries in all its individual acts and relationships. Yet there were the contrary habits of democratic assertion and of loud, very rough confrontational behavior. Much has been said of these, above. The flow of action at councils was therefore difficult to predict or control, and interesting to observe.

As to rank and deference: titles could be insultingly withheld at meetings, as at Aquileia by the person in charge and by his partisans also. There, every bishop was identified as such save the oldest among them, who should have been the most deferred to; but he and his one colleague were the targets of attack; so they were referred to only by their bare names. The colleague, too, was made to stand while others sat during his testimony and interrogation.[11] The insult to these two was all the more to be noticed, compared with conventional respect for the status, *bishop*, shown even in addressing (for example) "that impious madman, the Most Reverend and Beloved-of-God, Bishop So-and-So" — as also, with more wholehearted deference, "Your Sublimity", "Your Holiness and Wisdom", "Your Marvelousness", "In-All-Things-Most-Holy-to-God, Bishop So-and-So".[12] Such terms of compliment extended also to secular grandees, "So-and-So, Magnificent Man", the "Most Magnificent Esteemed Officials and the Supernatural Senate" — these, quite aside from the statutory designations for the Most Distinguished Most Perfect So-and-So (reserved for governors), The Godlike Summit (the emperor), or the Most Holy

Most Pious Most Christian Emperors (more fully named). To our own ears the forms of address in other times and among other peoples have sometimes the quality of comic opera. But it was not really comic at all.

Persons of the ranks just instanced sat up front. Of course they did, since theirs was the privilege of running the show. In their hand, notionally, or sometimes visible at their back, was the armed force they could bring to bear in support of their words. Of this, more later. Force of another sort, God-given, was in the hands of bishops toward whom the secular authorities generally felt or at least displayed a ritual respect and to whom, on credal questions, they deferred. On a raised platform which is sometimes mentioned, they all sat together, ecclesiastical and secular, if in fact any secular officials had been deputed to the job; otherwise, only the bishop or bishops, plural, to whom the control of business had been consigned by the emperor.[13] They generally spoke while seated. Others had to rise to do so.

Councils of particular interest, those twenty-five identified earlier as emperor-summoned, were adversarial affairs. They pitted personal ambitions and ideas about the Trinity against each other, each with their champions, each with their convictions, each louder than the other to prevail. At Constantinople in 381, the so-called second ecumenical, the man in the president's chair heard and later recalled how

> those very bishops that trumpet peace to all, in their calls to the cathedral nave, raged savagely against each other and as they shouted, gathering their allies, accused and were accused, and jumped about and almost out of their skins, seizing on anyone they could get to first, in a wild contest for supremacy and sole control . . .[14]

Where such passions were likely to be acted out, it was natural to divide the parties in the dispute, one to the more honored left of the president or administrative commission, the other to the right. The writer quoted just above described them as "two choruses" flanking persons whom he calls "the presiding officers" (as he himself had been), "teachers of the masses".[15] No doubt the exact placing of audience-members as well, whether up toward the front or not, along each side, took account of perceived rank. Certainly a sequence of speaking was observed toward the start of a session and then of subscribing at the end, giving first place to the occupant of the see where the council met, and next, to the heads of the greater churches before the lesser — though a strict logic seems not to have been enforced.[16] "The masses" would thus be removed some distance from where the action was, up front, so to be taught by that distance to respect their betters.

The lesson was taught also by the organization of the audience into voting blocs, such as the Egyptians already encountered, above. Egypt was more easily disciplined than other dioceses. Still, among the rest, notice the airy confidence of the more powerful who don't hesitate to sign for their suffragans: "Diogenes metropolitan bishop of Cyzicus on behalf of myself and absent bishops under me," one of them writes, giving six names; likewise 14 other metropolitans for 93 suffragans. This was how it worked at Chalcedon in AD 451. The suffragans had surrendered their minds and votes in advance of the council or they were assumed to be willing to do so, as a sort of blank check. Similarly when a bishop of the Oriental bloc explained his vote, he said he was, after all, just following the lead of his own metropolitan (this, in AD 449).[17]

Blocs of course could work too well. They could split the church forever. The point, taking me beyond the proper boundaries of my study, is still worth noting. It resulted not only in the division between the western and eastern, Latin and Greek churches; but within the latter, between Orthodox, Nestorian, and Monophysite.[18]

Above metropolitans rose three and eventually four patriarchs. Constantinople claimed on occasion even to rule over the independent churches of Greece and the central and western parts of modern Turkey, among which Ephesus was the most important. At times these latter acted as a mass just like churches under the patriarchs of the capital, or of Antioch with its "Orientals", Alexandria with its Egyptians, or Jerusalem.[19] And always, or at least much too frequently for the peace of Christendom, there was the complicating possibility of a coalition of quite small or middle-sized clusters of churches, each centered in a single name, each organized for battle: for example, the Jerusalem bishop "and many of the priests around him," meaning his party or bloc, joined to the Constantinopolitan bishop "with the bishops around him." A formidable mass!—then to be added to the council-president's party of Egyptians at Ephesus II in AD 449.[20] He was Dioscorus, bishop of Alexandria.

A fact of life, this need for blocs—which gained rapid recognition after Nicaea. Decisions to engage in a trial of strength increasingly involved planning and the careful massing of force. Anyone in a front seat, then, you could be sure was there for good reason; and, with much at stake, every person of influence must be given a part to play. At Nicaea, it had been the emperor himself as the conspicuous center of the assembly. True, a score of dissidents stood out against him for a time. It was only fear not persuasion that brought them around. No matter—once a majority was assured, then the decision of the council was assured as well. A lid had been, as it were, nailed down on dissidence; the true terms of the faith had been agreed on; and only this final fact, not the means of its attainment, need be remembered. The outcome of a council meeting thus made the occasion worth every risk.

Yet in fact the means could not really be forgotten. No, when Constantine's mighty Philoumenos stepped down from the dais in the front of the assembly, from among all "the teachers of the masses," and in his own hand carried the sign-sheet around from one bishop to another with the word *homoousios* almost visibly inscribed on it as its title, there at that moment could be seen that curious compromise with "democratic assertion" which was the Christian Church in Council.

Nicaea's constituent mass, like that of any other council, was made up of ordinary bishops from all sorts of provincial settings. As voters they were ultimately in charge. In a literal, numerical sense that was true. So too in charge was a second element, the more-than-ordinary, including the learned but unidentifiable prompter (Ossius?) who had drawn from decades prior that mysterious convenience, the Greek term *homoousios* meaning "of identical substance". It served ultimately as the key to resolving complicated, angry, and much too long debate. Imposing the term on all or almost all, ultimately, was the third element in the scene, the secular power in the person of some great lord, emperor or emperor's agent, able to represent him physically. The three together were needed to combine in the securing of victory, *nike*, at the meeting.

2. *Dioscorus*

Now to see the three actors at work in more detail, the one council of Chalcedon may serve very well; or rather, excerpts from a single session of that council may serve (from among fifteen sessions spread over a month and more). As a warning: detail is not naturally neat, and the chosen moments are not meant to prove any single point — rather, to show what sort of interplay of forces must be observed and understood by ordinary bishops, and what participation might be expected of them.

First: Chalcedon the town was very well known among residents of Constantinople for the miracles so frequently performed there at the tomb of the martyr, St. Euphemia. The site was convenient for the emperor, too, since her shrine lay only a few hundred yards from the Bosporus within sight of his palace. The complex of three buildings there was immense. Two of its parts each sufficed for sessions at different times, and besides, the distribution of the participants was untidy and required even more space than the total participation would suggest.[21] Only a small minority of them were seated on the right: fewer than a score of Egyptians joined by eight heads of churches around Jerusalem and scattered others. The left, the side of favor and honor, had to accommodate huge numbers: first, assorted independent churches, then some Orientals, then more independents, scores more Orientals, then a group from Pontus (northern and northwestern Turkey).

From the sequence in the attendance-sheet signed by all at the end of each session, it is clear that they presented themselves neatly by provinces (Isauria, Osrhoene, Cilicia, Euphratensis, Mesopotamia, Phoenicia, and so forth, according to the secular divisions of the empire); further, that they must have been seated in these same groups. The shouts that the secretaries noted down are identified thus. They had to be coordinated; therefore they were from a mass. For the Greek-speaking regions (only a few Roman delegates who spoke in Latin were present), the whole assembly represented a tremendous effort at inclusion, with the aim of smothering dissent beyond all doubt.

Dioscorus of Alexandria was the first and principal target of attack, though not the only one. He must have realized by rumor, to begin with, and then by sight of the crowds recruited for his demolition, that his time was up. As will be seen, he was deposed and sent in exile to the first of several uncomfortable little towns, till he died.

A word to explain what he had done requiring punishment. He had supported the monk, Eutyches, head of a large monastery in the eastern capital. Eutyches had been at war with his neighbor, the bishop Flavian of that city, who had had him deposed in AD 448 for propagating doctrine that Flavian rejected (it had to do with Christ's *ousia*). Eutyches appealed the decision to a friendly emperor and won the promise of a council to review the verdict, counting on the support of Dioscorus and his Egyptian subordinates. The council, Ephesus II, convened in August of AD 449. Dioscorus presided, duly restoring Eutyches and deposing Flavian. Flavian, however, being first held under guard and then hustled off to his place of exile, died on the road. Dioscorus was blamed. Not long afterward the emperor whose favor had been the key to all these events went out for his usual ride around the circuit of the city, was bucked off his horse, and died of his fall.[22] His sister, then, of entirely different doctrinal views, had everything in her hand. She took to husband a new emperor of her own views, while Eutyches' chief champion at court was executed. In these so-abruptly changed circumstances, the avengers of Flavian emerged to demand yet another council, and got it, for the autumn of AD 451.

The person there presiding was a grand civil officer chosen by the emperor, with a well thought-out agenda. It took a paper form, as was routine. Whoever had business with a council prepared in advance whatever supporting documents he would need, by which, as they were read into the record, his business would inch along. Thus, a little way into Chalcedon, the Flavianists very insistently asked of their opponents, Why, at Ephesus II, did you not read a crucial document, a letter from Leo of Rome some months prior, containing his credal Extract, his *tomos*? It was meant to support the Flavianist position against Eutyches, and its importance was so great that a Flavianist could say at the time of its original receipt, two years before Chalcedon, Whoever doesn't sign on to it doesn't belong in the Church.[23] How come, then, it was never read into the record at Chalcedon? "The Orientals and the Most Reverend Bishops with them shouted out, 'The letter wasn't read us! If it had been, it would have been recorded!' "

To which Dioscorus replied that he had indeed asked that it be read, and the *acta* of Ephesus II would show as much. His two colleagues in the presidency of Ephesus II would confirm the truth of this. But "Eusebius the Most Reverend Bishop of Dorylaeum said, 'He's lying.' "[24] The remark is hardly polite, but nothing exceptional. "He lied," says the Most Reverend Bassianus later in Chalcedon, in comment on someone else; and "Valerius the Bishop said, 'I too agree that the Most Reverend Bishop Athanasius taught lies' " which he attributed to other lofty teachers, including Cyril; and so said still others, detecting the same fraud: "the Most Reverend Bishop Athanasius lied." So again says Eusebius in regarding Dioscorus' supporters: " 'They're lying!' Florentius the Most Reverend Bishop of Sardis said, 'Let them demonstrate what they say.' All the Most Reverend Bishops shouted, 'Curse Eutyches' teachings openly! He is a heretic, whoever doesn't sign on to the letter [of Cyril] that the whole council agrees on!' " "It would have been better if they had never been born," declares an outraged participant at Ephesus II, speaking of Flavian and Eusebius, "but instead, better to have a donkey's millstone round their necks and toss them into the sea, since they drew simple souls into damnation."[25]

Familiar qualities of debate (if it deserves the term): rude, intemperate, and hate-filled—violence in words. Familiar also, the charges of forged or false documents. They will appear again (section 4, below). A familiar claim, that wrong ideas took hold not because they carried conviction in themselves but because innocent people didn't understand them aright. And a familiar tactic of pressure in moments of debate, to insist that "everyone" agrees—unless there should be some few who want to hold out and suffer the penalties. Finally, a practice to be noted as particularly relevant to my study: that of many persons speaking as one like a Greek chorus, in comment on, or interruption of, what the "teachers of the masses" had just said. It is natural to wonder, how could hundreds of one party or the whole council be quoted as if they were a single voice? What were the conventions governing this?

The answer is not simple, though some of the materials were laid out in my second chapter. People of those times and places when they were assembled as a group or audience commonly did utter unison shouts. They were used to it. The practice was illustrated earlier with many examples. Participants must have responded to dictation by some one member of the group, whether a leader accepted in advance or someone who made himself heard spontaneously. There was no trick to it, after all. "What do we want? Fair pay! What do we want?" shouted by one person and answered by all those marching with him in unison, "Fair pay!" — this is the sort of exchange that most people today have heard or engaged in. It was just a much more common experience in the later empire, turned to use at Chalcedon and other councils. Reporters took down what was said and quoted it to inform or influence a higher-up not present or to influence some later occasion or debate. That practice too has been described.

However, at church councils and only in these settings we are sometimes given impossibly strung-out acclamations. "The Holy Council said, 'From here as well, the words that Theodoret impiously wrote, the Holy Council of Chalcedon has extracted some remarkable subtleties, for in full knowledge of his blasphemies, first, they used a great number of acclamations against him'" and then went on to curse him! The statement made is too long, we can't believe anyone shouted this, and most particularly, a mass of people would never choose sarcasm for its style of comment.[26] Or as another instance, what of the charge that a document is forged? "The Holy Council said, 'The comparison that has been made shows for certain that the letter in every detail — the one Ibas is said to have written — is contrary to the *Definition* of faith which the Chalcedon Council declared to be the true correct belief.'" The argument offered is one of textual criticism! which cannot have been packaged as a chant. And we have other statements attributed to the entirety of the meeting which string together dozens of words, up to some 150 or more in a single breath — if it can be believed.[27]

But that is not credible. We must imagine instead that the same person, the coach, who was relied on to lead acclamations of normal length, three or four up to ten words, let's say — that same person was also entitled to make extended statements on behalf of all. The right was recognized by both his comrades and by reporters. The Greek chorus evidently had a director: some individual, almost never named, was noticed for his abilities, for his knack of seeing the kernel of what needed to be said and of serving it up in a neat little package; so he was singled out, made spokesman. Later no doubt he would be rewarded with higher responsibilities.[28]

The presiding board of nineteen at Chalcedon likewise had a single spokesman, unidentified; for they are said, all of them together, to speak as one. Following Eusebius' flat accusation against Dioscorus, "He's lying," they turn to the two bishops of Jerusalem and Caesarea-in-Cappadocia, colleagues of Dioscorus in the presidency of Ephesus II, asking: Can either of you two explain why the important *tomos* was not read at that council? One of the two bishops recalls that, when Dioscorus asked for its reading, "the Presbyter and Top-Wax Steno, John" — such being the titles borne by a high bureaucrat within the church — "said he had in his hand a letter from the emperor which I asked him to read." But then after that, the presidents persist, did he read the letter? "No, neither the Top-Wax Steno nor anyone else had the letter in his hands."[29] Evidently, then, the agenda had been prepared in a physical form, as a stack of documents to be fed to some special person among the high personages at the front of the meeting. For tidiness' sake, the stack might be all copied into a notebook, which in fact is referred to as the *codex* in the proceedings at Chalcedon and elsewhere; and other documents would also be neat and handy to be read out when their turn came.[30] It might be a copy of the proceedings at Nicaea, it might be a collection of Cyril's letters.

The presiding officials give up on this line of questioning, from which Dioscorus emerges a little damaged; for evidently he was anxious to have some company in defending himself for the actions taken at Ephesus II. As he insists, quoting the authorizing letter of the emperor in AD 449,[31]

> "... it was not myself alone to whom the Most Divine King entrusted the trial [of Flavian]. It also gave authority to the Most Pious Bishop Juvenal [of Jerusalem] and the Most Holy Bishop Thalassios [of Caesarea]. It was we, then, we who passed judgement and the entire council agreed with us. Why is it myself alone that these persons attack? — since the authority was entrusted equally to the three of us and, as I said, the entire council agreed with us and registered it with their own proper votes, *phonai*, and signed to it, and it was submitted to the Most Pious King of Holy Memory, the deceased Theodosius, and all the decisions were ratified by the Holy and Ecumenical Council by general law."

> The Orientals and the Most Reverend Bishops of their party yelled out, "Nobody agreed! It was by compulsion, compulsion by blows! We signed a blank sheet! We were threatened with deposition! We were threatened with exile! Soldiers with batons and swords were ranged against us and we were scared of the batons and swords! It was in fear that we signed! Batons and swords all around, and what sort of a council? That's why he had the soldiers! Throw out the murderer! It was soldiers that did for Flavian!"

> The Egyptians and the Most Reverend Bishops of their party yelled out, "They [the Orientals] were the very first to sign! And how come it's clergy who are shouting now? It's a council of bishops not of clergy! Throw out the extra people! The signers to the front and center! We signed with yourselves!"

Further complaints follow next from the frantically apologetic Orientals: they repeat, they had been outnumbered two to one, terrified, presented with only a blank page instead of the text of a decision to sign. Could they be blamed for what they had done? Counter-complaints follow from the Egyptians as well, against those vociferous non-bishops around them who shouldn't be heard from at all. The list of signatures of Ephesus II is then read aloud, all 135 names, to show what the situation had been two years earlier. Only 17 participants at that council had been Egyptian, the rest a mix of independents and Orientals.[32] The excuse of numbers, then, didn't really work for the Orientals. Yet terrification by soldiers sounds likely enough, given their frequent use by one doctrinal party or another, not least at Ephesus I twenty years prior, when the Egyptians under Cyril "took over the city square with the soldiers they had brought with them, filled the city with uproar, circled about our lodgings publicly, coming up to our caucus place to disturb it," and so forth. In these terms anyway the embattled bishop of Constantinople had written to the emperor and he added accusations of Cyril's mobilizing the local yokels and riffraff from the harbor to assault himself and his cowering comrades.[33] Their bed-and-breakfast doorways had been marked for easier identification by the mob.

There is nothing extraordinary in the fact of these angry dangerous people whirling about a council in the streets or into its very midst; nothing extraordinary, given the remarkable increase in the rate of homicides in the eastern regions associated with religious disputes over the whole period AD 325–553. That phenomenon was examined, earlier, simply as an indicator of rough-stuff of every kind in every province. Attainment of a majority of votes and consequently of a desired decision could not, on some occasions, represent anything but physical strength or the (quite believable) threat of its application. Indeed and truly, bishops did sign, as the Orientals tearfully confessed, out of fear. At Chalcedon "they say that Amphilochius [of Side] was beaten on his head by Aetius the deacon, to make him sign." Why should this not be believed? — since even that saintly centenarian, Ossius, a century earlier, had been made to sign, it was said, through torture, and since the harsh realities of disputes within living memory must have been known to anyone with eyes and ears, through scores and scores of incidents at episcopal elections, or in churches, or in any urban setting one cared to look at.[34]

It detracted, however, from the authority of a council if signatures were known to have been gained only or mostly by threats. For this reason, freedom of choice was sometimes stressed, as appears at the end of the following exchange at Chalcedon:[35]

> Dioscorus the Most Reverend Bishop of Alexandria said, "The Most Pious Bishop Basil in the *acta* attacks his own words where he said, 'That

wasn't what I said, that was recorded in error!' Now if Eutyches' position contradicted the teachings of the church, he shouldn't just be punished but be burnt alive. My concern is for the catholic apostolic faith, not for any man. I have my mind fixed on the divine, I'm not looking to any one person, I'm not worried about anyone but about my own soul and the right pure faith."

Basil the Most Reverend Bishop of Seleuceia said, "As you read the trial-record of Eutyches in the *acta*, my own words . . . fit with those of the Fathers who were met earlier at Ephesus [I], where I approve the letter of the Holy Cyril who presided at that council, . . . the words 'I worship our one Lord Jesus Christ, only begotten Son of God, God the Word made flesh and known through His two natures, *physeis*, after He was made man.' "

The Egyptians and the Most Reverend Bishops of their party shouted out, "Let no one divide the indivisible! No one says the one Son is two!"

The Orientals and the Most Reverend Bishops of their party shouted out, "Curses on whoever divides! Curses on the divider!"

The Egyptians . . . shouted out, "Report the votes, *phonai*, to the King! . . ."

Basil . . . said, "What I said [at Ephesus II] was 'known in two natures after union,' in perfect God-ness and perfect humanness . . ." [this, followed by much more of a theological nature].

The presidents said, "So, in offering such an orthodox profession, why did you sign on to the deposition of Flavian of Blessed Memory?"

Basil . . . said, "Because I was under the judgement of 120 or 130 bishops and had to conform to their decisions."

Dioscorus . . . said, "Now is fulfilled what was written, 'Out of your own mouth you will be acquitted and out of your own mouth you will be condemned' [Mt 12.37]. You have gone against what is right and abandoned your faith out of your fear of other men. . . ."

Basil . . . said . . . [answering with some biblical quotations of his own].

The Orientals . . . shouted out, "We have all sinned! Forgive us all!"

The presidents said, "But earlier you declared that you were compelled to sign on to a blank page out of force and necessity, for the deposition of Flavian of holy memory."

The Orientals . . . shouted out, "We have all sinned! Forgive us all!"

Question and answer thus ended in what the council wanted, a complete surrender. There should be no further pretense that the anti-Flavian vote was extracted by *force majeur* from signatories ignorant of what they were doing, and so they should be excused. That had been the best defense available but it wouldn't work. Neither would Basil's confident and complicated parsing of the Incarnation, and the attempt to shelter under the lee of Cyril's writings, which were in fact too many for ready comprehension and accommodated various positions. It is notable that the Orientals and Egyptians who are locked in such angry combat with each other both proclaim their veneration for Cyril. They proclaim it again and again, in competitive chants as if each side wanted to be the louder. It is only an isolated lecture delivered in the midst of these demonstrations that explains, in the most gingerly and genuflecting fashion: the blessed Cyril's venerable insights were occasionally expressed in ways that could be misunderstood. Thus, Eustathius of Berytus.[36]

In contrast, Dioscorus' statements, just above, are notable for the resounding assertion of personal faith that they offer. We look for this in someone who took such risks and suffered so much for his particular Christology (it is irrelevant that he always gave as good as he got).[37] "It's my soul I'm talking about," he bursts out a little later in explanation of his head-on argument at that moment, "I just have to speak four-square." His words recall his Egyptian colleagues (Chap. 6, above) protesting "it's a battle over faith" — before they give in. There could be no doubt about the deadly seriousness of Chalcedon or, for that matter, of any other council devoted to theological thrashing-out.

Such occasions had the words of the bible at their center, whatever other words, by the million, they might give rise to as well. So Dioscorus naturally has resort sometimes to scriptural citations, as we have seen. At Ephesus II he had declared, and the words are now read at Chalcedon from the *acta*,[38]

> "I hunt through them [scriptures], as I've said, but I don't change them; for our Savior taught us, saying, 'Search diligently in the Scriptures' [Jn 5.39]. Still, someone who searches doesn't change."
>
> Eusebius . . . said, "The Savior said, 'Seek and you shall find' [Mt 7.7]."
>
> Constantine Most Devoted Secretary of the Divine Consistory read aloud from the same document [*acta* of Ephesus II],
>
> Dioscorus . . . said, "Though there are two councils cited [Nicaea and Ephesus II] they come to a single faith."
>
> The Holy Council [Ephesus II] said, "The Fathers [of Nicaea] defined everything beyond any correction. Curses on anyone who departs from what they said! No one adds, no one takes away!"
>
> Dioscorus . . . said, "Both because God approves your acclamations and you yourselves say they are firm and pleasing to God, if anyone

rummages around or pries or invents in a way contrary to what has been settled on or contrary to the teachings determined by the Fathers at Nicaea or assembled here, let him be accursed."

The Holy Council said, "To the great guardian of the faith, Dioscorus, archbishop!"

Dioscorus . . . said, "Let me say one more thing, something fearful and awful: 'If a man sins against another man, God will intervene, but if a man sins against the Lord, who can intercede for him?' [I Sam 2.25]. If then the Holy Breath, the *Pneuma*, sits among the Fathers as they have been in session and has determined what has been determined, anyone who overturns them rejects the favor of the *Pneuma*."

The Holy Council said, "We all say the same! Curses on whoever overturns them! Cast him out!"

Dioscorus . . . said, "No one determines what has been already determined."

The Holy Council said, "These shouts are of the Holy Pneuma! To the guardian of the regulations, the *canon*! The Fathers live through you! To the guardian of the faith!"

And with these ringing praises to the Egyptian patriarch, a high point was reached in that council of which Dioscorus was chief and president. The moment is now recalled, only two years later at Chalcedon, in a setting as dissimilar as can be imagined. The difference is underlined by the sour protest of a hostile bishop who cannot credit the earlier praises: "Nobody said that."[39] To which Dioscorus rejoins, "They want to deny everything already settled. Maybe they'll say we weren't even there!"

Here at Chalcedon as we know, but no doubt also at Ephesus II, the physical expression of the Pneuma was reverently displayed before the circle of the presiding personages, its pages to be turned in search of guidance as that might be needed (yet there were very few verses in it that were not known by heart to at least some one among the bishops present). Awareness of the supernatural as a presence at council meetings is often mentioned in the proceedings. Reminders were hardly necessary — least, at Chalcedon. For, as the bishops gathered for their business, they had, and they well knew they had, a dramatic witness to divine powers in the person or relics of a martyr in whose very house they met: the relics of St. Euphemia, no more than a hundred feet from where they sat. From these, a supply of miracle-working blood was often drawn by the bishop of the see by means of a sponge inserted into the repository of the saint's remains — blood "known to all Christians," as our source tells us. It was saluted with shouts by all the worshippers summoned out from the capital by prior announcement of the wonder to be wrought, every time. So much of it would be drawn out, it could be shared not only with the emperor, the local bishop, and all great personages attending, but with the multitude also.[40]

Yet the beneficence of the supernatural no more than matched the terrors of it. Dioscorus has just been heard referring to them, using heavy words: *fearful* and *awful*. He and the bishops around him well knew of Arius' last moments, only a few miles away in the public latrine of the capital. They could not forget what they had often heard or read about. There, Arius' impious disturbance of Nicene certainties had been rightly punished — rightly and terribly. It was just such a fate that councils were forever calling down upon the impious by their shouted "anathemas". Many stormy moments in their sessions must thus have raised a shudder.

In the face of those Nicene certainties, outbursts of veneration at Ephesus II were heard, just above, as they could be heard at some moment in almost every council summoned by the emperor for doctrinal decisions. It was quite natural therefore to hear the monk Eutyches, also — the target of AD 448 and the salvage of Ephesus II — insisting in his defense that it was he that had affirmed Nicaea's words while Cyril had instead tried to force his own interpretations on others. To this view of things, Basil of Seleuceia objected when it was quoted from the *acta*: "He lied . . . ," says Basil; and to this in turn, after Basil has explained himself a little further, "the Egyptians reply with a shout, 'No one accepts any additions [to Nicaea]! No one shortens it! Let the Nicene words prevail! The orthodox King commands!' "[41]

Discussion now returns to the question about Christ's *physis* and what words Nicaea used to describe this. The Orientals insist that Nicaea needed, and from Cyril Nicaea received, interpretive words to exclude misunderstanding. His words amounted to saying that "Christ's was not two natures but one." To this, when Eustathius explains it and flings down his own copy of Cyril's very letters, all the Egyptians offer ecstatic assent. "Eustathius expressed it beautifully! The orthodox man expressed it beautifully! Here's to the praiseworthy and pious Cyril!"[42] Borne aloft by these shouts, Eustathius unwisely adds, "the blessed Flavian accepted exactly this" that Cyril declared, "and just this is what he wrote to the emperor."

Well, then, ask the presiding officials, if that's what Flavian said, why did you depose him? "I was wrong," says Eustathius; and he goes on before long to declare Flavian and Cyril of one mind, in the midst of many declarations that Flavian's deposition must be reversed.

"Not two natures but one" is, however, a statement to be carefully parsed. At what point and in what way did Christ's two natures become one? Cyril

and Flavian after him had said, Two after union in a fleshly human form; and
Eusebius of Dorylaeum, Eutyches' accuser, put it thus also in AD 448. Did
Eutyches agree? "Yes, from two natures." But "two natures after incarnation,
Sir Monk, and of the same *ousia* as we humans?"[43] At this very thought, read
out to them from the *acta* the following year at Ephesus II,

> The Holy Council [of AD 449] said, "Away with him, burn Eusebius!
> Burn him alive! Make two out of him! As he divided, let him be divided!"
>   Dioscorus . . . said, "Is this form of expression acceptable to you, to
> say, 'Two natures after being made man' "?
>   The Holy Council said, "Cursed be whoever says so."
>   Dioscorus . . . said, "Since I need your shouts, *phonai*, and hands, if
> you can't shout, hold up your hands."
>   The Holy Council said, "If anyone says Two, let him be cursed."
>   The above being read aloud [now at Chalcedon], the Orientals and
> the Most Reverend Bishops with them shouted, "No one said this! It was
> Dioscorus said this! It was the Egyptians said this!"
>   The Most Reverend Egyptian Bishops said, "This is what we said then
> and we say so now, too."

— so once again the frantic Orientals scramble out from under their words of
the previous year and the Egyptians stick to their guns.

At Chalcedon the recall of past proceedings turns once more to Ephesus II,
at which Dioscorus had endorsed Eutyches' belief in Christ made " 'completely man for our salvation. . . .' The Holy Council said, 'This is the faith of
the [Nicene] Fathers.' " The interrogation of Eutyches the year prior by Flavian himself had reduced the elderly monk (no logician) to penitent confusion;
but he had caught himself at the end and defied his interrogator (see below).
For this he later earned the applause of Dioscorus and the bishops of Ephesus
II — the latter at Chalcedon for a third time denying they ever said what is
contained in the *acta*. One of them (Basil) seeks to rewrite his own words in
particular. He is challenged: "Your speech, *phone*, was then forged?" "I don't
remember," he says, "and I'm not sure."[44]

Discussion and maneuvering at Chalcedon led to the vindication of Flavian
through a second condemnation of Eutyches; also, in time, to the deposing of
Dioscorus. A little under two hundred bishops gave in their voice-vote to this
outcome. When it was known, others came forward to a total of about 250
signatures.[45] Where had the extra fifty been when the trial was in progress?
There is no saying. People present at any council must have slipped out to
relieve themselves or to eat, but this final discrepancy remains puzzling, between the audience and the voters of record, still more between the audience

and the several hundreds who attended (above, note 10). In explanation, Roman lawyers would have asked, *cui bono?* Who stood to gain? To establish one's name among the winners, once it became clear who the winners were going to be, was obviously a good thing to do, and it was perhaps the rule rather than the exception in the wake of the larger imperially-summoned councils. On at least one occasion it was the only alternative to being deposed.[46]

For the deposition of Dioscorus, what counted was the initial gaining of a majority. Clearly this was achieved long in advance behind palace doors by those who sought the summoning of a grand assembly for AD 451. Set against its numbers from the start, Dioscorus' cause had no chance; but its members hung on to it and their leader for much of a long day, before the bishop of Jerusalem and the occupants of his dependent sees arose from their seats and crossed over to their opponents. They were applauded and welcomed, and joined by all the mainland and northern Greek bishops as well, rising and walking across the nave.[47] Dioscorus was left to insist with undiminished conviction that, contrary to the developing consensus, "Flavian was obviously deposed for saying 'after the union, a single nature' while I for my part have the witness of the Holy Fathers Athanasius, Gregory [of Nazianzus], and Cyril at many junctures, that one must not say 'two natures after union' but rather 'one single nature of the Logos made flesh'. I am driven out in the company of the Fathers."

The council didn't agree.[48]

3. Management

The theological questions at the center of this particular conflict, pitting the Flavianists against Dioscorus, recall those other scores of questions listed in my first chapter. Neither their substance nor their merits are my concern; yet their general *quality* is important to notice. They required the understanding of very abstract ideas: ideas about the differences within the whole, and among the individual parts, and in the constituent material or substance of a being, Christ — his *prosopon*, *hypostaseis*, and *ousia* — diachronically considered. Not a matter for Everyman, this! Such perplexities could only be shared among a general audience — it would be too generous to say they were enucleated or fairly represented — in much simplified phrases, of which specimens have been heard in excerpts from Chalcedon, above: "dividing Christ in two" or the like. More, too, was said about this in Chapter 3.

To parse such phrases was to invite disputes. The decades around Nicaea had taught the lesson; and disputes were exactly what no emperor desired, lest they roil the realm and draw down God's wrath. There was certainly no room for them in the management of Dioscorus' trial. True, it was his theology that first headed the formal charges against him; but it was not allowed to lead into a debate. Instead, it gave way almost immediately to charges of mere (though very serious) misconduct. These were relatively easy to handle, whereas questions of faith must certainly complicate proceedings. Faith, then, was left out; and none of Dioscorus' supporters were present to object.[49]

The handling of Dioscorus and the contentious issues he represented, along with his Egyptian sees, betrays the hand of a church leadership set apart from the mass of bishops. Mass and leadership (along with secular power) were seen, above, as the constituent parts of the Church in Council. How did these two interact? Who was in charge? If they differed in their concerns, how did one or the other prevail over the other?

Consider a certain moment in the fourth session of Chalcedon, when a charismatic monk of Syria, Barsumas, is introduced with his party to present a petition. It had been received at court. A eunuch is in the party as a sign of its reception and it is therefore approved by the presiding officials, all great courtiers themselves. The Flavianists oppose it. Their head, Anatolius, successor to Flavian on the throne of the capital, detects among the monks two priests who had been condemned.[50] He says they mustn't be admitted. When they object,

> Aetius archdeacon of the holy church of Constantinople going up to Calopodius the Eunuch said to him, "The archbishop through me the archdeacon has said to you that you have been condemned, so get out."
>
> Calopodius said, "Why?"
>
> Aetius the archdeacon said, "As a heretic."
>
> Calopodius said, "I suggest our petition be read."
>
> The Most Magnificent and Glorious Officials said, "Let it be read."
>
> [In part, it asks for a council to be called, "but without rioting or signatures obtained by force and the harassment which is forever being plotted against us" in our embattled monasteries . . .]
>
> Diogenes the Most Reverend Bishop of Cyzicus said, "Barsumas who came in with them killed the Blessed Flavian. He stood there and said, 'Kill him.' And if he is not named among the petitioners, why did he come in?"
>
> All the Most Reverend Bishops shouted out, "Barsumas subverted all Syria! He brought down a thousand monks on us!"
>
> The Most Magnificent and Glorious Officials . . . said to the monks, " . . . the emperor commands your entrance . . ."
>
> All the Most Reverend Bishops shouted out, "Kick out the murderer Barsumas! Send the murderer to the arena! A curse on Barsumas! Send Barsumas into exile!"

The Most Magnificent and Glorious Officials . . . said, "Read the document."

The management, as it may be called, evidently decided to ride right over the furious objections of the council, even though they and the council both knew that the petition was meant to initiate a reconsideration of Dioscorus' condemnation. This latter was a most inflammatory issue, of course.

Or again at the first session of Chalcedon the deposed bishop of Cyrrhus, an Oriental, was to be allowed a seat, whereupon,[51]

> The Most Reverend Bishops of Egypt, Illyricum, and Palestine shouted, "Mercy on us, the faith is stricken! Church rules ejected this man! Get rid of him! Get rid of the teacher of Nestorius! [heretic, anti-*theotokos*]."
>
> The Most Reverend Bishops, Orientals, and of Pontus, Asia, and Thrace, shouted, "We signed a blank sheet! We were beaten so we signed! Away with the Manichaeans! Away with the enemies of Flavian! Away with the enemies of the faith!"
>
> Dioscorus Most Reverend Bishop of Alexandria said, "Why was Cyril evicted who was cursed by this man?"
>
> The Orientals [and the rest], "Away with Dioscorus the murderer! . . ."
>
> The Most Glorious Officials . . . [admit Theodoret of Cyrrhus to be seated, to the applause of the Orientals].
>
> The Egyptians and their party shouted, "Don't call him a bishop, he's no bishop! . . ."
>
> The Orientals and their party shouted, "The orthodox man to the council! Away with the trouble-makers! Away with the murderers!"
>
> [The two parties trade shouts against each other and their champions, interspersed with loyal praises for the empress, emperor, and senate].
>
> The Egyptians and their party shouted, "Theodoret accused even Cyril! If we let Theodoret in, we throw out Cyril! Church rules ejected this man! God turned against this man!"
>
> The Most Glorious Officials . . . said, "These vulgar shouts are unsuited to bishops and don't help either party. So then, permit the reading of all the documents."
>
> The Egyptians . . . shouted, "Throw out the one man, and we'll all listen! It is from piety that we shout! We say what we do for the sake of the catholic faith."
>
> The Most Glorious Officials . . . said, "You should rather, with God, permit the hearing . . . ," [which now the bishops do, all together].

The scene recalls another two years earlier where Dioscorus presided and, ever ready with scripture, eventually quieted a tumultuous exchange with the reminder, " 'It is written, 'The words of the wise should be heard in silence.' [Eccl. 9.17] Let us have no uproar. Let us not give an opening to reproach from the unbelievers."[52]

At junctures of this sort the person in charge of the assembly balances atop crowd passions which he can barely control and must certainly have found alarming. The bloodshed they could lead to in less august settings, everyone well knew.

At other moments the determination of the council can be opposed by management apparently without trouble. "The Most Reverend bishops shouted, 'Justice calls for Bassianus, let church rules prevail!' The Most Glorious Officials said, 'However, to Ourselves it seems best . . . ,' " and they proceed to contradict the council and successfully impose their own decision, though they do so in conciliatory language: " 'We leave it to the council, how far to follow the opinion in this case which seemed best.' The Holy Council shouted, 'This is a just opinion! This is God's judgement!' "[53]

The moment is a little unusual, raising the question, how often the mass of a council changed its collective mind. It happened only rarely. At a session of Chalcedon "the Most Reverend Bishops shouted, 'Now cursed be Theodoret!' " [anti-Cyrillian bishop of Cyrrhus], as he entered the meeting; whereupon he proffered documents and explanations, asked that these be read aloud, heard his request rejected by the bishops with angry shouts, but after some further exchange succeeded in registering his change of mind to their satisfaction.[54] It was really a case of an accused person repenting rather than of a whole assembly yielding; and in that respect it is more typical, more in character. Whole assemblies came to their business with their minds set and generally obedient to their patriarchs and metropolitans.

As a rule, council presidents could manage to secure an orderly flow of business because their authority derived from the emperor or from established church procedures. At some level both were respected as divine. They not only prepared the agenda with attendant documents and living witnesses, as has been seen, but could intervene at any moment to incline a discussion in some chosen direction. Where one side was favored from the start, needless to say that side would be favored at each crucial point of debate, insuring the desired outcome. A case in illustration is the Carthage council of AD 411, initiated by a prominent bishop and then overseen by a close personal friend of his, whose bias appears in a string of procedural judgements.[55] Additional powers of control lay in a president's calling on speakers known to be reliable; also, in his freedom to change the subject when some awkward juncture was reached, and in the privilege he enjoyed of framing the summary of a statement or interrogation so as to dictate the council's terms of response. All of these devices were (it will be remembered) at the call of Ambrose in the council of Aquileia so that he got exactly what he wanted.[56]

At Serdica in illustration of this last device — the "indicative summary", as it may be called — we have the venerable Ossius inviting legislation with the words, "If it so please all of you, that an evil of this sort should be fiercely and rigorously punished, so that it may not enjoy communion for the laity, let everybody answer 'So be it!' " His audience oblige him as bidden with an acclamation or shout which was at the same time a vote. No doubt the same sort of summing up of discussion was in use at Nicaea and as far back as councils went, since such was also the practice in the Roman senate and by extension, in the town senates of the provinces.[57] It was still the practice at the end of the period studied here, that is, past the mid-sixth century. It was always for the president to define what was to be decided, and to add color in descriptive phrasing if he wished; "to frame the motion," as we would say today. In contrast, no statements or proposals seem to have arisen from the floor of councils. The mass of bishops therefore had nothing but their shouts to depend on when they wished to oppose or modify the course of the proceedings.

Since, however, shouts were reported up the line to a governor, high prefect, or the emperor himself, as is so often specified, there is no denying their formal authority. So long as they were permitted in councils, or rather, so long as they were the ordinary punctuation of proceedings, it must also be clear that persons presiding did pay attention to them. How otherwise could disputes be resolved? — such as had occasioned the council in the first place? The powers of "management" to run things were therefore by no means unlimited, and the proof of realities lies in the splits tolerated or unavoidable in a large number of actual meetings: for example, Nicaea with a hold-out minority of about 10% who yielded to reason in due course; or at Ariminum in AD 359, a minority of about 20 percent; a minority at Seleuceia, 20–25 percent who pulled out;[58] or a minority at Constantinople in AD 381, of about 25 percent, who saw how the land lay and retired after a time.[59] On other occasions, prior planning secured virtual unanimity of voters, Aquileia being one illustration, Arausio another, and Ephesus I, perhaps the best; for here, in violation of the terms set by the emperor, the Alexandrian patriarch brought along a great regimented mass of his suffragans, assembled them in an unauthorized session, expelled the proper president by main force, and designated the proceedings as the intended council — a coup d'état, as it is rightly called, but assuring a clear victory. For the moment.[60]

At Chalcedon the hold-outs in a complicated moment can't be well counted today since the *notarius* who wrote up the proceedings was too hasty in assigning the shouts of some participants to the whole assembly. The topic under consideration was the Roman bishop's *Extract*, hailed, so says the *notarius*, by everybody. It agreed with Cyril; why then was it never shared by Dioscorus with the sessions of Ephesus II? However, "the Most Reverend Bishops of Illyricum and Palestine still hesitated"; they wouldn't be satisfied with the reading of further passages from the document, despite repeated reassurances and a rhetorical protest from the presiding officials, "After all of this, who can still be in doubt?" It was all very well for others, whom the *notarius* took to be everyone, to "shout out, 'No one is in doubt.'" Doubters there were, in fact. To the pacific proposal that more time should be allowed them for study, "All the Most Reverend Bishops shouted, 'This is what we believe! None of us doubts! Now we sign on to it!'" Not so fast, again warned the officials: it's not essential that all should agree; the doubters should still be given a little extra instruction. No, no, shout the majority, we're calling for the Fathers. Dissent is, heard once more: yet "the Constantinopolitan Clergy shouted, 'It's a few only that are clamoring, it's not the whole council that speaks.'" So it went, back and forth, until the session was brought to a close.[61]

At the next session but one (the fifth), after a creed, the *Definition* of Chalcedon, had been agreed on, as it seemed, John bishop of Germanicia protested, "the *Definition* isn't good and should be recast from scratch."[62] His fellows around him, excepting only those of Rome and a few Orientals, protested, "The *Definition* suits everybody! This is the faith of the Fathers! Whoever holds to anything other than this is a heretic! Whoever thinks differently, let him be accursed! . . ." Despite cautionary remarks from the presiding bishop of Constantinople, they repeat, "Let Holy Mary *theotokos* be inscribed, let her be put into the creed!" Threats from the three western bishops to walk out are of no avail; "and when the Most Reverend Bishop John of Germanicia approached the Most Glorious Officials again, the Most Reverend Bishops shouted, "Away with the Nestorians! Away with God's enemies! Who they are, you can barely see them! The whole universe is orthodox!" They add no fewer than 28 more acclamations to the same effect, to make clear their stubborn insistence on the ground gained thus far through hearings and documents; their thunder fills the nave and a long loud interval; they threaten to walk out, themselves; and despite conciliatory suggestions by the bishop in charge, even proposing the referral of the confrontation to the emperor for some sort of way out, only a Blue-Ribbon conference finally brings the matter to an end. It presents its conclusions with the warning words, "Let the Holy Council listen in silence" to what is now presented. Whereupon, with maximum formality and flourishing of titles, the Constantinopolitan archbishop's spokesman announces, "The Holy and Great Council . . . has laid down the definition that follows in writing, below. . . ." Notice "*Has laid down*". It is a fait accompli. To preclude any further protest at this point, a very full assertion of the authority of that writing is rolled out in incontrovertible solemnity, to bring the session to its close.

In these various scenes of disagreement, more or less agreeably resolved, three points may be noticed. First, in that familiar democratic fashion by which the majority rules and the minority must submit, the greater number in church councils puts the heaviest possible psychological pressure on hold-outs by telling them they simply don't exist, they are too few to be counted, they are at odds with absolutely everyone else. "We" are "everyone" — such was the cry — and if you don't join actively in our acclamations, you are a heretic.[63] The device has been met with more than once in the previous chapters. Its effectiveness, readers today can easily feel within themselves.

Second, the majority could and did at times get its way against opposition of very great weight, being to this degree difficult or impossible to manage. Similar instances of crowds in other settings who overwhelm some contrary-minded official were noted in my second chapter.

And third (returning to the phenomenon noticed at the beginning of this present section), delicate theological distinctions and arguments could be brought before councils from out of much more disciplined, written, specialist discussion, and the management of them was claimed by the leadership without challenge. Division of labor, it might be called. Deep matters should be left to deep thinkers, as most bishops were content to agree. Anyone in doubt about the wisdom of this might learn better from the conduct of discussion in councils.

In illustration, notice some minutes of back-and-forth at the Constantinople council of AD 448, where the monk Eutyches was attacked by the patriarch Flavian and the ferocious Eusebius of Dorylaeum. The latter asked, first, referring to the monk,[64]

> Does he concur in what was just read aloud from the Blessed Cyril, and declare "There are two after the union into a single being, *prosopon*, and a single individuality, *hypostasis*?" Or does he disagree?
>
> (Flavian:) You heard, then, Priest Eutyches, what your accuser says. Say now if you agree, Union from two natures, *physeis*.
>
> (Eutyches:) Yes, from two natures.
>
> (Eusebius:) Do you declare Two natures after Incarnation, Sir Chief Monk, and do you say Christ is of the same substance, *ousia*, in the flesh as ourselves? Or do you disagree?
>
> (Eutyches:) I didn't come here for an argument, but to satisfy Your Holiness of my manner of thinking; and I wrote out my thoughts on this paper and you can have it read aloud.

(Flavian:) Read it yourself.

(Eutyches:) I can't.

(Flavian:) Why not? If it's yours, read it yourself.

(Eutyches:) It's of my dictation and it's the same as the exposition of the Holy Fathers.

(Flavian:) What Fathers? Speak for yourself. Why do you need any paper?

(Eutyches:) Here's my belief: I worship the Father with the Son and the Son with the Father, and the Holy Breath, the *Pneuma*, with the Father and the Son. I declare his coming to have been his Incarnation out of the flesh of the Holy Virgin and his being made wholly man for our salvation. This I declare before the Father and the Son and the Holy Pneuma and Your Holiness.

(Flavian:) Do you declare our Lord Jesus Christ to be his only Son, of the same substance as the Father in god-ness and of the same substance as his mother in his humanness?

(Eutyches:) Since I trusted myself to Your Holiness, I've said what I thought about the Father, the Son, and the Holy Pneuma. Why go on? Don't interrogate me.

(Flavian:) But do you agree, From two natures?

(Eutyches:) I declare my God and Lord is Lord of heaven and earth, but until today I didn't allow myself any disputation about "natures" though I do declare that up to now I have declined to say he is of the same substance as ourselves. . . . I have said the Holy Virgin was of the same substance as ourselves and that Our Lord was made flesh out of her.

(Flavian:) The Virgin is of the same substance from whom Our Master Christ was made flesh?

(Eutyches:) I said the Virgin was of the same substance as ourselves.

(Flavian:) If the mother is of the same substance as ourselves, so is he, for he is called the Son of man. If his mother then is of the same substance with ourselves, he is too, insofar as the flesh.

(Eutyches:) Since you're saying it now, I agree with all of you.

[The secular president intervenes at this point to repeat the lesson; and Eutyches repeats:] Until today, I didn't say . . .

(Flavian:) Then do you declare the true faith because you're forced to or of your own mind?

(Eutyches:) Take it as it is, Sire, now. Until this very hour I feared to say, because I knew our Lord was God and I was afraid of any disputating about "natures". But since Your Holiness does not fear to do so and to teach me, I do say so now.

(Flavian:) We're not proposing any novelties, but as the Fathers expounded the faith, and in the faith just as it was propounded by them, all
of us who believe want to stand fast and introduce no novelties.

The Most Magnificent and Most Glorious Nobleman Florentius said,
"Yes or no, do you say Our Lord Only-Begotten of the Virgin is of the
same substance with ourselves and of two natures after his Incarnation?"

(Eutyches:) I say Our Lord is of two natures before the union, but after
the union I say he was of one nature.

With this stubborn reply at the end, however, Eutyches has invited his own
deposition. What he or anyone said or didn't say in the face of such theological
perplexities was subject to ecclesiastical judgement or, for that matter, to
secular; for there were after all imperial laws against heresy. He would know
he was going to have a hard time of it: would be attacked from all quarters and
in a most public manner and with just such an outcome. His is a story with
some human interest, is it not? It sheds a little more light on the management
of councils, too, and of permitted thought. In particular, however, the length
of the excerpt is justified by what it tells us about the level of theological
sophistication among those whom the leaders wanted to manage.

We have at Chalcedon a second archimandrite (Carosus) speaking of Eutyches with reverence; being pressed to curse him publicly; protesting, "Judge
not that ye be not judged" [Mt. 7.1]; being again badgered and bullied; and in
self-defense professing his loyalty to Nicaea's bishops and the doctrine of the
318 — "otherwise I don't know what you're saying to me, but the power is in
your hands, you're bishops, if you want to send me into exile." A third monk,
Dorotheus, in just the same simple fashion, declares his conventionally Nicene
faith and recites it all as best he could, only adding, "bear with me and correct
me if I've left anything out." And twenty years earlier at Ephesus the mere
suggestion of re-working the creed of the Holy Fathers had been greeted with
horror by the whole council: "Anyone who engages in such disputation, let
him be cursed!"[65] Such views have been often heard, above, expressed by
various councils. All such scattered testimonies as these tell us how people
thought and how willing or able they were to engage in controversies that
required logical, analytical thinking. Still, what we have only makes us wish
we had a lot more.

A common agreement shielded the moment of Christ's conception from
analytical thought, even from the most reverent inquiry. This point of theology
was "beyond words," "beyond comprehension."[66] Nicaea too was sacrosanct.
Yes, but only among the mass of bishops. Among the leadership it was more
common to agree that Nicaea needed fencing around with curses aimed

against sundry misinterpretations, clause by clause. These curses, Flavian was trying to supply, or to get his monkish victims to do so with him, in the extended exchange just quoted. He was only following in the path of Cyril, who had insisted that a certain adversary not merely adhere to the Nicene creed but, in writing and on oath, subscribe to a defining set of anathemas. He himself would be glad to lay them out. Indeed, he did so, in the form of his notorious Twelve (AD 430).[67] They were only the most authoritative assemblage of such curses; many hundreds more could be combed out of conciliar *acta*, giving to long stretches of the proceedings a flavor of what Dioscorus would call the *awful* and *fearful*.

The difference in powers of thought between what may be described, very approximately, as a leadership stratum or class — Flavian, let us say, or Cyril — and the clerical masses, emerges further at the close of Chalcedon's first session. Dioscorus and a number of other bishops with him have been satisfactorily dealt with, to the applause of the Orientals. The Most Glorious Officials and Supernatural Senators go on to invite the Most Reverend Bishops, in the intermission, to set down in writing their own individual creeds. This they may do without any apprehension, since the Most Godly and Pious Emperor himself subscribes to all the proper forebears, doctrinally, especially the Holy Fathers of Nicaea. But it appears in the sequel that no one wants to accept the invitation. When business resumes, "the Most Reverend Bishops shouted, 'No one makes a new exposition of faith, we don't try to do it, we don't dare to propose one; for the Fathers taught, and what they expounded is safely preserved in writing, and beyond this we can't say anything.' "[68]

That's not good enough, the presiding personages retort. We'd like your representatives, carefully chosen, to draft a comprehensive statement of faith,

> removing all ambiguities; and if there are any persons who are not like-minded (which we don't think is the case), the wishes of these too can be established.
>
> The Most Reverend Bishops shouted out, "We don't do any expounding in writing. Church rules say what is preached serves well enough as expounding. As the rules indicate, there isn't supposed to be any other expounding; and what was taught by the [Nicene] Fathers is maintained."[69]

Just what was the cause of this fear of writing? Was Eutyches remembered, or Carosus or Dorotheus or others whose faith or innocence was so plainly greater than their understanding? Surely the reason nobody wanted to write down what he believed in was the fear of being caught as they had been, by recorded words, words never to be denied, plain to be read in the blackest ink and (as it might turn out) serving the most fatal purposes.

4. Exact words

Today's reader of conciliar *acta* must see them as a sort of Near Eastern *tel*, a mound built up by successive occupants upon the remains and reminders of past times, over a span of decades—eventually, of centuries. What happened in AD 325 was written down and soon drawn upon at Serdica, as the *acta* of Serdica were read aloud in 359, and so forth, through what has been seen, above, of councils in 431, 448, 449, and 451, all piled up and waiting to be rummaged into and retrieved word for word, a great heap of documents to which were added certain writings of certain bishops of one city or another, and certain additional pages brought in as *aides-mémoire* by witnesses, in great numbers, to be topped off by a more than ornamental copy of the bible.

In good Roman legal fashion, these all were the materials for a verdict. Many a throne, many a life depended on what they said. Their obvious significance asserted itself even against a council's heavy atmosphere, the tedium of a single voice droning on through pages and pages read aloud; it stirred to attention the rear-most rows of participants who could not hear clearly; to our disbelief it succeeded in keeping participants awake for hours on end.

The certainty of this is clearest in the century that runs from the mid–350s to the mid–450s. During this period the councils of concern to my study followed each other most closely; and participants more often than not attended more than a single council in a given decade (repeaters can be tracked through signature-lists). This meant that they would hear their very selves in the shouts they had joined in, in some previous session. One such experience, when it served as a reminder of a most horrible error, is reflected in an account quoted above. It suggests why, listening to read-aloud documents, the audience didn't nod off—even though the spoken words of living participants made up less than half of the proceedings of many councils.

As a further stimulus to an alert attention, the accusation has been heard in *acta*-excerpts above, that the record had been cooked. It allegedly included what wasn't said or it excluded what was. For such misrepresentations the audience had to listen carefully, and they evidently knew it. The trouble to begin with was the lack of any one single official copy, though some which were held in the largest churches enjoyed a special respect. Where there was controversy, as so often, the two sides (or more) had their own stenos, *notarii*, each, and transcribed the product into their own fair copy for their own archives, later. At Aquileia the presiding bishop denied his adversaries this safeguard, despite their repeated protests. There was no appeal possible. Without some control on truth, however, bias and mis-statement would naturally creep into the record and ordinary routines were thus an invitation to charges of falsification, against which the frequent practice of reading aloud the *acta* of one session before the next began, was not adequate. There could always be changes introduced thereafter; as much was sometimes proven.[70]

Perhaps the fullest challenge to the authenticity of a record was offered by Eutyches at Chalcedon, in the course of which his adversary's own stenos, no less than five of them, priests, are called in to testify, most unwillingly. It could only spell trouble for them or, in their own careful words, "It's not without its dangers". At first they stonewalled. Their archbishop Flavian required the support of the Most Magnificent Ex-Prefect of the Capital, Six Times Ex-Praetorian Prefect, Ex-Consul, Nobleman, Flavius, before the stenos complied — partially.[71] But first, they must know what the text was against which their own was to be checked (it was of course Eutyches' own, or rather, a copy of that). Further inquiry showed that certain words even of the supereminent Flavius had been mis-reported, at which he was quite upset. Participant bishops from the audience were called up to say what they had heard and said, and whether they had joined in a shout of "Curses on him [Eutyches]!" in the sessions being recalled (as to which, they didn't agree with each other). In the end, the spokesman for the *notarii* had to explain,

> In such Most Holy Councils, it often happens that one of the Most Reverend Bishops present will say something and what is said by one will be written down and understood as if by all together. This is what happened from the start, so that when one person speaks, we write, "The Holy Council said". If it's found, then, that now one or another person spoke, and that the Most-Dear-to-God Bishops spoke out, and the Most Holy Clergy concurred and so shouted, we do ask that this acclamation should not be absolutely excluded or set aside from the record, the *acta*, since all the Holy Bishops appear to have signed it and . . . [but here, the supereminent Flavius interrupts the speaker].

All this protracted discussion — attended by the greatest possible publicity like a show trial in some modern capital city, and involving dozens of persons, some of modest rank yet bishops, others of very high rank up to the absolute top — indicates the significance attaching to written testimony. By people's exact words they were established among the great and good, or they were cast down to some wretched depth. Hence the significance also of the keenest oversight over the making of the record which must become or be seen as the very truth; and indeed, before the next session is over, the chief of the five stenos serving the archbishop registers a complaint with one of the civil stenos about subordinates who had made changes in the record: "he himself was obliged to reveal this since he was afraid of their malignity — though he did so against his wishes."[72] His second-hand accusation is heard with the comment, "This testimony similarly will be entered in the *acta*. Let them be made public." Thus the layers of words were built up on the documentary *tel*.

Where so much depended on written words, naturally they were often falsified. Much forgery went on, both of the documents to be adduced in the flow of conciliar argument and in the production of the written proceedings themselves. Various mentions of the sort have been encountered, above.

As to these documents themselves, whether tracts or letters, the trick was to get them accepted as coming from some source widely respected. It might be the bishop of Rome of high authority, inviting a false attribution; or it might be Athanasius or Cyril or some earlier great teacher of the church. Faked or doctored texts were composed especially in service to suspect or minority credos which lacked genuine champions of weight.[73] Predictably, Nicaea was touched. Most notoriously and consequentially, an edition of its *acta* included in them a rule only voted into existence later by a very different council. Grafted on to the Nicene canons, it gave the bishop of Rome a general appellate jurisdiction over the whole church. The error or deceit of this originated in the Roman chancery and was not uncovered until the fifth century.[74]

Acta of less ancient, less awe-inspiring councils provoked challenge quite frequently.[75] One spectacular bit of improvement appears not to have been detected in Antiquity, though it was certainly meant to have an influence on current church struggles. In common fashion but on a grand scale, suited to the place of meeting of the council involved, in Rome, it inflated the number of participants not by a dozen or so but by the hundreds, borrowing their names from mostly African signature lists of other councils.[76]

With this scandal we have entered the sixth century, when ecclesiastical divisions provoked the pious attentions, or despotic meddling, of the emperor Justinian (AD 527–65). During a good part of his long reign, the western provinces were lost to him entirely. Their churches, many now heretical according to his lights, were beyond his influence. In the East, however, the fissures left by the disputes at Chalcedon remained still open and within his reach, to repair. The so-called Orientals of the previous century had retained their identity in Antioch and Syria, opposed by "Occidentals" in the terminology of the time. These latter occupied the sees of modern Turkey, Greece, and the lower Danube lands.[77] Between them, Christ's nature or natures, plural, continued to be a war zone; the Occidentals insisting on the full and simultaneous duality of Christ, both man and God, while the Orientals emphasized the perfection of his divinity in one individuality and earned the name of "One-Naturers", Monophysites.

Early in his reign (AD 531) Justinian agreed with the leaders whom he favored to summon a small council for the following year, with only six bishops on each side. In AD 532 when they did meet, a good crowd of additional clergy and monks attended, too, in a grand setting similar perhaps to Rome's Pantheon if a bit smaller. Hypatius of Ephesus spoke for the favored side, representing an eminent city and church, with Seleuceia as a second famous one also represented; and their colleagues no doubt could be trusted to support them. In contrast, the Orientals had to confess "on the grounds of age and weakness" that they could not exert themselves fully, and [we] "are insignificant bishops in small towns . . . , we do not speak for the [church] as a whole."[78]

A participant on each side later wrote up an account of the proceedings in the form of a letter, expecting it to get some publicity. To have the two to compare is most unusual. The Occidental version is twice as long as the Oriental and differently constituted, being more like a conventional *acta*-text. It incorporates quite a few quoted documents, mostly Cyrillian. The Occidental and Oriental reporters of course made quite different choices about what they should emphasize or even mention. The Occidentals spend some time accusing their adversaries of using forged documents and bring to bear contentious logic in which readers can almost hear "Gotcha!" from time to time. Readers of previous conciliar *acta* are prepared to find these various features.

No real *acta*, however, existed, ever. This fact too is most unusual, even unique. On the second of three days, when "they gathered together again and first of all the orthodox [Oriental] bishops asked that what was said might be taken down in writing, just as they had asked the previous day without success, the opposing bishops did not like this;" nor did the president chosen by the emperor, his Sacred Treasurer, allow it, since it wasn't specified in the call of the meeting.[79] A real explanation for this is not given; today, readers may speculate as they wish. All that is certain is that the two adversaries and the emperor, each of the three in the Seven-Apsed Hall of the Hormisdas Palace in Constantinople, made, each, their own assessment of their best interests.

The atmosphere is clear from the very start, introducing the Ephesus bishop as his adversary sees him:

> Hypatius began churning over his usual old inanities, blaming the Blessed Dioscorus for accepting the wicked Eutyches at the second synod of Ephesus. It is the custom of the upholders of the heresy of Nestorius to collect together empty complaints against the orthodox [= Oriental] Fathers: since they cannot make a defense for their own flimsy teachings, they hope to cover up their own wicked beliefs and not let them be examined, by means of calumnies against the Saints.[80]

The statement draws the reader in an instant to the center of ancient, complicated hostilities; or, to recall my metaphor of a *tel*, it reaches down into layer
after layer of rancorous debate, accumulated over a century and more earlier.
Cyril's name especially recurs. Debate requires the support of his exact words;
but since he had so effectively championed quite contradictory views about
Christ's nature, the Occidentals in his defense are obliged to dismiss a part of
his writings as fakes; they must somehow get rid of quotations of his thought,
too, that they don't want to appear in the record. And that introduces into
both accounts the person of Ibas.

Why Ibas? Enough to say that he had attended Chalcedon and there, in the
course of defending himself against charges of heresy, had adduced certain of
his own writings, especially a letter to bishop Mari, and certain passages from
Cyril. Being quoted, these all became part of the *acta* of Chalcedon and were
accepted as such by the council's hundreds of signatories.[81] Cyril's exact words
as Ibas chose to quote them were, however, heretical in the Occidentals' view,
despite the veneration the Occidentals expressed for the great patriarch of
Alexandria. A problem! to which this party addressed itself at the juncture
now being described.

Ibas' letter to Mari being now recalled along with its acceptance by Chalcedon, "despite its being full of every sort of wickedness" (as the Orientals say),
the Occidentals simply "renounced the Session, saying, 'This did not take
place at Chalcedon.' And they demanded that the orthodox [Oriental] bishops
demonstrate that it did. At this the orthodox bishops laughed, and said,
'whence else can you show it?'" [other than from the *acta* that had just been
read aloud].[82] Should a part of history be simply expunged? As the discussion
goes on and the Occidentals are challenged to put their views in writing, once
more they decline. They evidently had more to fear than to gain from a perma-
nent public record.

The two accounts move past the two opening sessions to the last. On that
day, Justinian himself presided. After counseling the Orientals against "excessive scruples" or over-emphasis on detail, in the end he dismissed them in
disgust. He had certainly not gained what he sought. Neither had his clients,
the Occidentals.

It has been pointed out that the two parties were not all that far apart—a
judgement perhaps anachronistic. Yet in common they did share a veneration
for Cyprian, Basil, Athanasius, the three Gregory's, Ambrose, and in particular, Cyril. These were also the names to be found most often, so it seems, in the
individual churches' honor rolls, those diptychs regularly recited at services.
Their choices might include someone unworthy, no doubt; so the Occidentals
at the meeting with Justinian insist on the need for the screening of names and

of statements of faith, too, through the major councils, thus certifying them as "synodical".[83] At this point the Orientals ask, "And what about Ibas and Theodoret [bêtes-noirs of the Monophysites] who were endorsed as orthodox by the council [Chalcedon] and are read off as orthodox in the diptychs?" The question was very awkward.

Of course, theological belief should be derived from scripture, in which the bishops in AD 532 or at any other date or place of meeting were well versed. They could quote it readily; they do so, in fact; they all had a very great amount of it by heart; and this would have been true of the few illiterate in the church's government as well as the more highly educated. Nothing added more weight to one's ideas or propositions. What need, then, of the approval of an interpretation by conciliar action?

The answer appears in the reaction to a moment's testimony at Chalcedon, in connection with the proceedings against Eutyches (they have been looked at, above). It was said that

> "he declared himself prepared to agree with the teachings of the Holy Fathers assembled at Nicaea and Ephesus, and promised to sign on to their interpretations, but if in fact they happened to have gone wrong or erred in anything they said, he didn't reproach them nor did he agree with them, but instead he looked carefully at Scripture alone, as being more trustworthy than the Holy Fathers' teaching."
>
> And as this was being read aloud [at Chalcedon], Constantine the Most Reverend Deacon and Monk [who was acting as agent for Eutyches] said, "Though the Holy Fathers spoke to different intent at different times and I agree with everything, still, in the rules of belief, I don't agree [with them]."
>
> Then there was some disturbance and murmuring . . .[84]

— "disturbance and murmuring" indeed, because, among the generality of bishops, the choice of scripture alone as a foundation for belief had become much too daunting, too dangerous. Luther's day lay far in the future. They wanted the comfort of interpretive authority — so long as it was short and simple. Nicaea they enthusiastically reaffirmed, as we have seen so often; but so often whole councils could be heard, too, exclaiming, in effect, "No fancy theorizing! Leave us alone with the Fathers! They are enough! Above all, leave it to the Fathers to intervene in the debate over Christ's *ousia*." The Greek term with its compound *homoousios*, the Fathers had approved. It lay at the very center of the doctrinal struggles from the early fourth century up to the present moment under Justinian. To toss it out, as the monks suggested in the moment just quoted, was quite impossible; in the same Chalcedonian debate at a later moment, even Eutyches himself gave a grudging approval to *homoousios*.[85] Better, then, the joint and *democratic* sorting out of the best opinions by the best judges assembled in the face of the church, beginning with the 318 of 325: better, synodical certification.

This could yet be found, so Justinian may have thought: certification of some unifying creed could be found, a creed somehow attainable through honest debate. But reality proved him wrong. Debate on the first day, as the Occidentals described it to him in a private evening audience, could only draw out familiar arguments and inflame old quarrels. These appeared again on the next day and, under Justinian's own eye, on the third as well. "Scruples" or "details" he called them — just as Constantine had once dismissed the arguments around Arius as "extremely trivial and quite unworthy of so much controversy," "small and quite minute points". By AD 532 they had a long history, in the course of which they had become even harder to form or force into a consensus.

So much for the ideas at work in AD 532. Twenty years later the emperor made his most serious attempt, another council prepared for by a long polemical tract of his own devising, *On the True Faith*. In the course of this document he returned to the problem of Ibas and Ibas' letter to Mari, bishop of Nisibis. What was at stake was still the establishing of Chalcedon as a certifying council, which could not be done if it certified any attack on Cyril; yet exactly this it had done. Justinian could be rightly confronted with that "awkward question" noticed above. Accordingly, Ibas' letter had better not be by Ibas. It could only be "the said-to-be-by-Ibas-Letter to the Persian heretic Mari" and "anyone who acquits the aforesaid impious letter or says it is right, or any part of it, and fails to curse it, is himself to be accursed." Someone, there could be no saying who, had cobbled together that wretched document "for the deceiving of the more simple-minded" (familiar charge). It might even be found "in certain codices," that is, in proper bound collections of documents.[86] However, let no one be deceived by it or by its defenders.

Since the emperor had been on a rampage in areas of Oriental strength to replace possible dissidents on their thrones and terrify those who were left sitting, and since he invited only a tiny handful of Egyptian bishops, the great assembly of 150-odd who gathered at Constantinople in AD 553 proved wonderfully well behaved. The whole thing had been meticulously planned, too: relevant documents all ready to hand, the sequence of topics determined in advance, and even "seemingly spontaneous interventions somehow 'stage-managed'."[87] The bishops obediently listened to Justinian's reminders of what his tract had taught and duly convicted unnamed heretics of forging the more offensive parts of certain impious documents.

The Holy Council said, ' "The comparison that has been made between the letter said to be Ibas' and the Chalcedonian *Definition* declared by the Holy Council as the true faith, finds the letter to be quite different in every detail."

All the bishops shouted, "That's what we all say. The letter is heretical! We condemn the Letter said to be Ibas'!"

— and they added twenty more shouts against it.[88]

With these, enough said of the matter. There was more, very much more business to occupy the council. The opposition of "the Most Holy Bishop Vigilius" of Rome, often resident in recent years in Constantinople but speaking for the western parts, had to be dealt with. So too the special targets of Justinian's theological publications, detested by those Monophysites in eastern parts whom he wished to conciliate. Ibas was only one; a troublesome second was Theodore of Mopsuestia, while Theodoret of Cyrrhus was surely the worst of the lot, the most influential and most quoted from his abundant writings. Selected texts of his were now read into the record. Their main points when arranged in a composite credo aroused horror:

"The Holy Council cried out, "Satan made up this credo! Curses on whoever made up this credo! . . . A curse on whoever doesn't curse him!"[89]

Heretical words like those thus quoted were all down in black and white, enough to destroy whoever wrote or so much as recited them; for words of course were things. Recited, they amounted to offerings. They had better be right. They therefore constituted the chief business of the church's most important assemblies.

Summary

Two subjects have occupied me in this essay: a certain sort of church council and a certain sort of participant.

The latter, my "ordinary bishop", of course never existed. He is a notional figure, like Sloan Wilson's "Man in the Gray Flannel Suit", once so useful in explaining the life and habits of American businessmen. Such constructs are quite everyday in political, sociological, or marketing discussions — and in the historical. Historians in generalizing will speak of "the Napoleonic soldier", let us say, or "the pioneer" or "the rural voter".

It's no use objecting that a chosen type in some points resembles other people in his society and so can't be strictly isolated or demarcated. Quite true. The definition is offered only as a convenient handle, in approximate terms. An "ordinary" bishop at a council is just one among a mass of many human beings who sit facing a few. The different positions indicate different roles. In a later moment of his life he may hope to find himself up front, just as his leaders once sat among the ordinary. He is not of some different species, no zebra among giraffes. Nevertheless, he is not up front. There are reasons, reasons of who he is and where he came from. He is himself, really distinguishable.

It must be added, that he is much more than the imagined type; he doesn't exist only in and for the one role. Like any notional figure, he comes to it with impulses, values, needs, and fears formed in other settings to which he will return. He and the other types instanced, pioneers and so on, are whole beings all the time, even if only a chosen part of them is under our observation at a particular moment. All the rest of their character, while it may not especially suit the analytical purposes of the *observer*, is not all that counts for *them*. They come from and hark back to a childhood, they have a future in their thoughts, a family, a town or a village to which in some sense they must render an account. All that they are, they bring to their actions as (more narrowly) a soldier, a pioneer, a voter — or a bishop.

Obvious remarks, these — offered only to explain the arrangement of my chapters. They are meant to show, first, what sort of experiences my bishops had had, before I go on to show how they behaved at councils.

Between the experiences and the behavior no one doubts that a connection existed. Yet so tangled are the roots of other people's actions, it can only be by exception that we can say for sure, "they acted in this way *because.* . . ." Knowing the difficulties, then, what is the political analyst to do? or the marketing adviser or social scientist, or the historian?

Each discipline has its own devices. Among historians, it is biography that is most likely to succeed, concentrating on some single figure; but even biography succeeds best when it serves up a "life and times", with the (usually unspoken) assumption that the times shape the life and will in some useful way explain the flow of actions to be studied. Would not the same device work also with the biography of a notional figure, an "ordinary bishop"? It is this hope that determines my approach, it explains my introductory chapters. They are meant to introduce the times, the background, and all the more likely ingredients that shaped the majority's decisions in church councils.

In the very first place, the persons coming together to vote about God did so according to certain accepted forms and expectations about group action. They knew they were entitled, all together, to arrive at authoritative decisions because that was simply how decisions were arrived at in the world as they knew it. It was common sense to do it this way; common usage had taught them so, in all sorts of civic and professional settings.

However, some bishops were by their own admission ill-equipped to follow the arguments they had to resolve — arguments in which some of their fellows seemed so adept and passionately involved. They therefore welcomed various simple tags and titles to hang on to, *Nestorian, Manichean, Cyrillian*, and so forth, helpful to their understanding. Often they ducked decisions on complicated questions, surely because they understood their own lack of understanding, at least at the required level. They can be heard calling for short, familiar formulations to accept or reject. They prefer old, well-hashed-out answers which others before them have approved in councils assembled.

So much for my second and third chapters, regarding the democratic and cognitive elements in the behavior of council-participants. A further common element across the two was the social: a life-experience that encouraged them to think in groups, to meet frequently together for business which was ordinarily not very contentious, to travel together to councils, lodge together, sit together in sessions, look to a common leader, and of course if necessary to suffer together.

They did all this, however, not as one whole. Secular divisions of the population, into first- or second-rank cities and into provinces and dioceses, reflected ancient realities of language, terrain, and patterns of trade and travel; and the same undeniable realities were in turn reflected among bishops and had obvious effects on the way they thought and voted. No other sector of the population was affected so deeply as bishops. No other could anywhere nearly match the degree of cohesion achieved in *their* lives and affiliations, over time; and the cohesion or compaction was both demonstrated and reinforced by the terms in which they came to speak of themselves and each other as "Occidentals" or "Orientals" or "Egyptians".

So much is clear. More difficult aspects of their behavior to explain are, first, the decision to debate and vote about God at all, and second, the strong feelings generated in the process (thus, my fourth and fifth chapters).

Let Justinian help us with the first, the need for debate. In AD 553, welcoming the council of that year, he invites participants all to join him in an exercise of right thinking and true belief, especially regarding the matters he had laid out for them in his summons:

> Discussing the aforesaid thus with all meticulous care as befits clergy, bearing in mind the fear of God and judgement to come, and counting nothing more important than piety and correct belief and truth and God's glory and honor, bearing in mind moreover the Apostle's pronouncement also which was directed against those who transmit anything contrary to right belief, as he so clearly said, that is, "if we ourselves, or an angel from heaven, should preach a gospel at variance with the gospel preached to you, he shall be held outcast. . . ."

—and the emperor goes on to quote more of the passage (Gal. 1.8ff.).[1]

His solemn warning fairly represents the general sense, across the foregoing three centuries, that theology had to be set right; that it was a very urgent matter, subject to dire penalties for any failure. His same words, however, invite attention to the feelings that energized debate. To understand these, observers must confront questions of motive which carry them well beyond anything the eye or ear may take in. The evidence to work with is, still and first, that of the eye and the ear, whatever can be seen or heard and so is easily set down in historical sources; but empathy and inference must come into play, too. Observers must reach into themselves to compare what can be seen and heard with whatever they can find to match it in their own past. How had they themselves felt at such similar moments?

As one single flow, this is the most familiar of analytical processes. We make use of it every day in our contacts with each other. Applying it to our understanding of bishops, then, we see and take note of their acts of submission and accents of awe toward copies of the bible in their midst. We reason, from awe and submission to anxious feelings that would account for such anxious behavior. Further, we see bishops, not inside councils but in other settings and in their writings, also accepting and promulgating reports of superhuman beings and forces as part of their thought-world — beings and forces very well able to make a mere mortal anxious. Whether they are agents in evil or punitive acts or in the good and beneficent, makes no difference. Of whatever sort, they are ubiquitous, as much a presence and taken for granted as the weather; and they are to be credited by everyone, high or low.

Low or *high*: a novelty, this certainly is, distinguishing the period studied. For, in earlier times, the educated elite had not subscribed to such beliefs. Now, however, bishops join the most humble in circulating miracle-reports and associated relics; in pointing to the works of God or of Satan. They believed, yes, but more than such a ridiculously obvious observation, they believed very strongly.

This conclusion too is forced on us through the eye and the ear. In discussions about faith, bishops in councils are reliably reported to clap, stamp, yell, spring from their seats, and wave their arms in transports of feeling. They may carry on for many minutes at a time, for as much as an hour or more of high-decibel expressions of religious conviction. As in their celebrating of reports about the active presence and ubiquity of the supernatural — and because of this, too — they manifest an entirely novel fervor about their religion. The evidence lies in their actions, which in worldly terms expose them to the heaviest costs. The fact is very significant, it amounts to proof: they risk every sort of suffering for the views they profess.

A particular proof of fervor lies also in the suffering they are as ready to inflict as to suffer, where differences in belief arise. This too, in its remarkable prevalence, is a novelty. In councils, bishops are at their most ceremonious and reverent; yet even in such a solemn setting they sometimes strike each other or restrain by force, muzzle or shove each other, throw about this or that object, and yell out the most savage cries for this or that adversary to be killed in this or that cruel manner. Outside of the council chamber, they directly incite or participate in physical acts against their adversaries, or witness such acts without protest; nor can they be heard often, or ever, calling for an end to all the death and destruction which darkened the streets around them.

Actions of this exaggerated sort (in my fifth chapter and elsewhere) could only arise out of passion or deeply felt resolve, nothing else. Emotions served as the engine of historical significance, as one might say; meaning that bishops not so moved to action, not so in the grip of convictions which absolutely had to be realized, never would have made changes of a significance sufficient to interest historians — changes that made headlines.

The *force* of feelings is therefore something quite essential to acknowledge among ordinary bishops, and to explain. The observer today must not only note what they said and did but in what state of mind. Otherwise there can be no useful understanding.[2] To that end, their every act must seem truly inevitable, something they were absolutely bound to do, in any right reading of the evidence; and this right reading can only be an empathetic one by which we today feel within ourselves what actors felt in the past.

In aid of empathy, in fact there is much to notice of an emotional nature in councils: sobbing, weeping, supplication; expressions of outrage at injustice or cruel interrogation; harsh sarcasm. On troubled questions the participants may en masse rise from their seats and surge forward to the front of the hall, there to fling themselves down before the session-president and clasp his knees or his feet, crying out to him.[3] It is often a dramatic scene, inviting us to call up the reserves of our own emotional experience. Where there is no specification of any emotion in the *acta* (certainly none to be expected from the stenographic report) then those *acta* can and should be read aloud like the script of a play to bring out what is really going on.

Who today will do this? The emotions of the past were indeed recognized by historians long ago. Their descendants, however, are more likely to favor the notion — the counterintuitive, not to say quite ridiculous, belief — that one can best understand a person, impersonally.

So much for "ordinary bishops". My other chief concern has been that "certain sort of church council", considered as a whole, which assembled at the emperor's invitation to consider doctrinal disputes and alternatives. The initiating force was usually, though not always, one of the eastern patriarchs. Thus, the trio was complete to which I have referred elsewhere, made up of ordinary bishops, church leaders, and the secular authority. Together they determined the outcome of conciliar proceedings.

Only the latter two of the three are generally treated as determinants of doctrine. It is certainly they who provide us with all that is individual drama and story, through their characters, intrigues, ambitions, alliances, bargains, or applications of force; through the sudden shifts in weight of influence when one of them dies, or when someone rams through a piece of what amounts to legislation. Thereby, overnight, some new article of faith determines who is a heretic, who is a hero. No doubt all this level and kind of activity is what Rowan Williams had in mind when he wrote, "Orthodoxy is constructed in the processes of both theological and political conflict; which means that understanding it fully should involve understanding these conflicts."[4]

Agreed. But when the broad flow of doctrinal development is considered, the forgotten third party in the forming of a creed sometimes displays its own power, its *kratos*. It is the ordinary bishops as a *demos* who came close to agreement, close enough for a successful vote at Nicaea. Nicaea laid a foundation. Still in AD 553 council participants could agree, but no longer with any hold-outs at all, "We believe, *credimus*, in one God, true God from true God, born not made, of the same substance as the Father, *homousion Patri, hoc est eiusdem cum Patre substantiae . . .*"[5] It was not they, the ordinary bishops, who still insisted on the further amplifying, parsing, and refining of these essential opening declarations. That was rather the work of church leaders and successive emperors, caught in irreconcilable disputes, forcing their will on council majorities, and successful only in alienating these latter from their own people. So it was in AD 359, 431, 451, or 553.

How different the course and outcome of church history might have been, in the period of my study, had the church's intellectual heroes been a little less heroic, had they more often deferred to those of their colleagues who were a little less intellectual! That transformation of the believing community on which contemporaries and near contemporaries commented (especially the Alexander quoted in Chap. 3, above — but not that witness alone) might never have taken place; the gulf there noted between the uppermost and the middling ranks need never have opened.

In the end, however, while the foundation endured and still endures today, the disputes endured as well, in a Christendom darkened and divided in six.[6]

Notes

Chapter 1: Introduction

1. No doubt five or ten meetings could be added and perhaps one or two should be deleted. There are of course indications of unspecified meetings, e.g. in Euseb., *HE* 10.3.1. My list expands substantially on Hefele (1907–09), passim, and on Constantelos (1982) 400, who draws on Hefele; more useful are *Prosopographie* 1 (1982) 1318ff. and 2 (2000) 2429f.; also Gaudemet (1977), passim. To illustrate many disagreements about numbers, notice the low estimate of Chalcedon's attendance in Camelot (1962) 120, a higher estimate in Honigman (1942–43) 52–58 (413 bishops' names), and the more traditional total of 500–600.

2. Gaul in 314: Pietri (1998) 677, though Rousselle (1977) 335 and LeGoff (1988) 1.66 and 69f., count only 11; in Gaul, 132 sees by the eighth century, in Gauthier and Picard (2002) 4, the same map shown in each volume of this topographic series; in north Africa, a total above the 400 sees which the Caecilianists and Donatists each claimed in AD 411, and without duplication in every town, cf. Shaw (1995) XI p. 27 and Lancel (1972–91) 1.119; and in the small but heavily populated Proconsularis alone, 164 sees, cf. Meyendorf (1989) 146; for Italy, Sotinel (1997) 194, and the total of populated centers in Morley (1996) 182. The sites shown in Talbert (2000) vol. 1 easily support the large figure in Morley.

3. For sees in Egypt, cf. Athanas., *Apol. c. Arianos* 71 (*PG* 25.373Dff.), Wipszycka (1983) 184, and Bagnall (1993) 285. In Tacoma (2004) 28 and 53, an estimate of a minimum population of 40–odd nome/district capitals at 5,000 each; but villages may have been occasionally larger; and, larger or smaller, they might merit a bishop, to yield the total of 100.

4. In a conversation reported to a crowd in a Constantinopolitan church in 431, the monk Dalmatius reminded Theodosius II that there were 6,000 bishops represented at the First Ephesus council (Mansi 4.1429Cf.); and the figure is accepted by Hefele (1907–09) 2.1050 n. 2, "on comptait dans le chrétienté environ six milles évêques." But Dalmatius had spent the 40 years previous immured in his monastery, and was offering a rounded-off figure intended to impress. Ill-informed hyperbole! Similarly, a certain Rusticus' claim that, by AD 518, 2,500 bishops *catholicam probasse*. Cf. the note by the Severini brothers in Mansi 8.578, taken by Hefele loc. cit. to mean, they had signed assent to Chalcedon. A figure of one thousand might be credible, but spread across three generations. The Egyptian total pointing to modest numbers elsewhere is supported by the count of sees represented at Chalcedon itself from the regions east and north of Egypt up to the Taurus mountains (so, including Cilicia and Isauria; total, 137 for the Antiochene patriarchate), in Devreesse (1945) 136–40, adding a few other names scattered among his lists of other councils, and showing many other sites in the area with one or more churches not attested in his conciliar lists, where sometimes there must have been a bishop. Frend (1972) 84 at the start of the fifth century sees a total of 141 in the same patriarchate, with another 60 under the Jerusalem patriarch. In Jones (1971) the maps of Syria, Mesopotamia, Armenia, and Cilicia show over 230 cities, which is not at odds with Devreesse and Frend. Turning to the region above the Taurus mountains, we have "Asia Minor, the land of 500 cities" (thus, some overlap with the area covered by Devreesse) in Jos., *BJ* 216.4, cited but largely discounted by Mitchell (1993) 1.80, and ca. 450 sites located on the map of "Asia" = Turkey in Jones (1971). Using these figures, it would be safe to add for this region a total of 150+ sees. To the 100 of Egypt, the 200+ of the Antiochene and Jerusalem patriarchates, and the 150+ for what is now Turkey above the Taurus range, we can add another 150+ for the Aegean and Greece and 50 more for the lower Danube provinces. The grand total: 650. But the low estimates used throughout this reasoning point to a better estimate somewhat higher. Fedalto (1988) can't be used to good effect, but is not in conflict.

5. Alberigo et al. (1991) 8 and 96 (at Chalcedon, mention of the routine being sometimes disregarded); Devreesse (1945) 120, Antioch; Basil, *Epp.* 95, 100, 142, in Barnes (1993) 171 and 294 n. 25; Hilary, *Ep.* 8.4, Thiel (2004) 144, and again, *Ep.* 11.2, *congregationes annuas* (not semiannual); Munier (1974) 34, annual regional meetings commanded by the Hippo council of 397, assuming also local meetings; but ten years later this is recognized as burdensome and discontinued, Hefele 2.157. On re-convening, cf. R. Williams (2001) 73f.

6. Provinces were brought up to just over 100 by Diocletian and to 117 by Constantine; then under his successors, to 120, cf. Stein (1949–59) 1.70 (62 provinces in the East alone in the late Empire, cf. Jones [1966] 1450). Division of a province might or might not produce an extra see, cf. Chadwick (2001) 341f., and 503.

7. The dozen best preserved are Aquileia (381), Carthage 411 and 419, Ephesus 431 and 449, Chalcedon 451, Constantinople 448/9, 518, and 532/3, Mopsuestia 550, and Constantinople 553, with substantial remains of the record from Ariminum 359, Diospolis 415, and others—almost all to be found in Mansi vols. 1–9 (1759–63); ecumenical councils I-V in Schwartz (1914–40), Greek and Latin; canons alone in Joannou (1962) and (Latin only) Alberigo et al. (1991). Mansi must still be used for some docu-

ments and may even (rarely) be preferred over more recent editions, see e.g., 5.296, *seauton*, over Schwartz (1914–40) 1, 1, 4, p. 12 *emauton*.

8. Arian marginalia to the *acta* of Aquileia in Zelzer (1982) 315–68; "not edifying," Moorehead (1999) 119; other texts, Brock (1981); Bardy (1923) 15, the Alexandrian bishop's tract of the 470s, only in Armenian, bits of Syriac; Flemming (1914–17); Severus' letters, cf. Brooks (1903); Dioscorus' letters, cf. Sellers (1961); and Philostorgius, e.g. *HE* 1.3, in Bidez (1913) 6.

9. Meyendorff (1989) 168 would have it that Nicaea "left no formal minutes" and it is true that there was no official edition of the *acta* of the first two ecumenical councils, only their canons tacked on to a collection of those of Ancyra, Neocaesarea, Gangra, etc., cf. Gribomont (1988) 289; but in fact Gelasius of Rome had a copy of Nicaea, Haase (1920) 10 and Marasco (2003) 285f.; and Schwartz (1914–40) 2, 1, p. 214, illustrates the general familiarity with the creed, which at Chalcedon "is preserved in writing as set out by them", the Fathers of 325. The taking of minutes, known by the early fourth century, Hess (1958) 26 would carry back possibly to the 250s; but actually first attested around AD 240, cf. Fischer and Lumpe (1999) 126 citing Euseb., *HE* 6.33 (Bostra); later, in Africa, p. 153 (Carthage, AD 255/6); and so forth, thereafter.

10. Greg. Naz., *De se ipso et de episcopis* 156ff. (*PG* 37.1177f.).

11. Illiterates common among the fourth/fifth/sixth-century Egyptian clergy and notoriously among ascetics, Gray (1979) 20 and Wipszycka (1984) 291f.and n. 27, much Egyptian evidence (unpersuasively minimized); illiterates elsewhere, in Honigman (1942–43) passim, where bishops are signed for by their lower clergy, mostly presbyters; among the 150 at Ephesus II, three evident illiterates (pp. 35ff.), while of 413 bishops present at Chalcedon to sign, 27 were signed for, ibid. pp. 52–58; further, MacMullen (1990) 321 n. 59 and (2003) 472 n. 19 with much bibliography; and on bishops of very humble origins, see e.g. Chadwick (1958) 295 or Sotinel (1997) 198.

12. The Ephesian bishop's house, setting for Ephesus I, Camelot (1962) 55; salary, in Jones (1964) 905; in Rome, Meyendorff (1989) 48; gigantic ordination-fees, ibid. 49 and Justinian, *Nov.* 123.3 (546); rewards as guest speaker, Soc., *HE* 6.11.1f. (*PG* 67.697A); bribe, below, Chap. 5 at n. 31.

13. Earlier, Euseb., *HE* 7.30.8 (later third century); in the fourth century, Greg. Naz., *Or.* 42.24 (*PG* 36.488Af.); held in honor (quoted), Joh. Chrysos., *In acta apost.* 3.5 (*PG* 60.40); and, in Alexandria, "some [clergy] who were ready and eloquent and of great wealth and dignity and of high birth as well, who had been called to the clerical orders by Cyril," Zach. Rhet. in Hamilton and Brooks (1899) 67f.

14. Ex-lawyer bishops: Amphilochius (Iconium, AD 373f.), *PLRE* 1; Severus of Antioch, Zach. Scholasticus, *Vita Severi*, in Kugener (1907) 52; Eusebius of Dorylaeum, in May (1989) 8; Hedde and Amann (1933) 682; and Lancel (1972–91) 1.234; Alypius (Thagaste, AD 394f.), *PLRE* 1; and Evagrius the historian also a lawyer, not a bishop. To show bishops as students of philosophy (a large subject indeed), see a sampling of the evidence in Basil, *Ep.* 9.4, in Forlin Patrucco (1983), Greg. Naz., *Peri kosmou* lines 67ff. (*PG* 37.421A), Marius Victorinus in Clark (1978) 4f., and Barnard (1978) 289, 293; hundreds of reff. to Philo and Clement of Alexandria in Ambrose, Lucchesi (1977); Hier., *Altercatio Luciferiani* 11 (*CCSL* 79b. 31f.), recruits drawn to the episcopal ranks from the midst of training in Aristotle and Plato; and Optimus a rhetor (bp. Agdamis in

Phrygia, AD 384f., then Antioch in Pisidia), *PLRE* 1. Episcopal ranks from the AD 370s on received a number of ex-imperial officials ordinarily in their latter years and not from the highest positions (except in Cple), e.g. Evagrius (Antioch 370s f.), Ambrose (Milan 374f.), Nectarius (Cple 381f.), Ablabius (Nicaea ca. 400f.), Paulinus (Nola ca. 400f.), Cyrrhus (Cotyaeum in Phrygia 443f.), Sidonius Apollinaris (Clermont 469f.), and later, Conon (Apamea), Abraham (Amida), and Gregory Attalus (Langres) — all these in *PLRE*.

15. MacMullen (2001) 10 n. 29; Batiffol (1913) 13; and Lancel (1972–91) 1.313ff., 327.

16. Lancel (1972–91) 3.936ff.

Chapter 2: The democratic element

1. Matthews (2000) 35f. offers a good sample of evidence; much more in Colin (1965) 111ff. and MacMullen (1966) 340f.

2. Theod., *HE* 2.17.4; similarly in Rome in AD 551, the Roman crowd intervenes successfully in support of the local bishop and against the urban prefect and the emperor's commands, cf. Sotinel (2000) 283.

3. In the AD 460s, the *Chron. pasch.* 467 in Dindorf (1832) 1.596; Malal., *Chron.* 14.38; cf. Anastasius forced to back down over a theological question in AD 510 in the capital, through rioting, Gray (1979) 39, and again backed down in 512 in the hippodrome, Malal., *Chron.* 16.19. On these and similar shows of monks' political power, later, see Bacht (1953) 278ff.

4. Malal., *Chron.* 14.2, AD 400.

5. The usurper-emperor Basiliscus in the *Vita S. Danielis Stylitae* 83, Delehaye (1923) 78, AD 475.

6. *Chron. pasch.* for AD 532 in Dindorf (1832) 1.620f., leading to a further dialogue before the palace and the emperor's dismissal of three high officials who were complained about by "the mob," *ta plethe*; 623f., more chants in the hippodrome, these hailing a rebel; a fuller dialogue in Theophanes, *Chron.* 181.32ff., cf. Bury (1958) 2.72 and Evans (1996) 119ff. A later date (AD 540s) was proposed by Baldwin (1981) 306. Cameron (1976) 327 supposes the record derives from a faction-archive; but as no such thing is known while imperial stenographers were evidently a practice in the imperial box, the *akta* must go back to these latter.

7. *Chron. pasch.* 532 in Dindorf (1832) 1.629; in Constantinople in 491, the acclamations of the *demos* to the empress, "Ariadne Augusta, thou conquerest!", Bury (1958) 2.430 from *De caerimoniis* 1.92 of Const. Porphyrogenitus; cf. Dittenberger (1903–05) 2.164 no. 515, glory and honor to the emperor, *succlamatum est* ,"Forever!" at Mylasa; earlier (AD 321) because it's a trial before a Roman authority, minutes which begin with a Latin protocol (date and place, PRyl 653).

8. Philo, *In Flaccum* 41, "the mob, *ochlos*, . . . shouted out at a single word of command," *synthema*; Dio 72 [73].20.2, where Dio recalls in the senate, besides "Lord", *kyrios* in the author's Greek but *dominus* in reality,"we shouted out many other similar things just as we were told, *hosa ekeleuometha*"; generally on claques, Cameron (1976) 234–49 passim; and Hamilton and Brooks (1899) 67, AD 450s.

9. MacMullen (1966) 338f.

10. *Chron. pasch.* 454 in Dindorf (1832) 1.464; Philo, *In Flaccum* 43; Ulpian in *Dig.* 49.1.12, cited by Colin (1965) 144.

11. POxy. 2407 (ca. 270?), with a little uncertainty whether it is a usual council meeting.

12. POxy. 2110 (370), concluding, *echei he pistis ton hypomnematon*; and individual signatures added in an Oxyrhynchus papyrus, each followed by *edoxe*, "so he opined," in Bowman (1971) 37.

13. *Année épigraphique* 1996 p. 466, in Chersonesus, cf. ibid. 2000 p. 479 with revisions.

14. MacMullen (1990) 20f. (John Chrysostom in Antioch); cf. Liebeschuetz (1972) 218.

15. POxy. 41 (toward AD 300); cf. Coles (1966) 22f., with a good though not complete list of council-*acta* in papyri, all of the later third century into the fourth, and Blume (1989) 272ff. Wilcken (1908) 115ff. discusses the relatively early *acta* of Antinoopolis (AD 258), surviving in more than one copy, as an illustration of the safe-keeping of the record. For "Ocean!" once again in a council meeting, POxy. 1413 (270–75). Notice Colin (1965) 122, "les acclamations approbatives . . . constituent un véritable vote . . . *ex(eboesan)*." Compare Bowman (1971) 104 on elections, where, after "an acclamation . . . , the acclamation seems to mark the fact that the man has actually been elected" (*SB* 7696). Colin (1965) 124 notices "they shouted" in texts of other Egyptian cities (Heracleopolis, etc.) and in other areas (Chalcis in Euboea, much earlier).

16. Roueché (1989) 98, 116, 120 at Aphrodisias, noting (p. 131) the "typical syllabic structure" of the recorded acclamations; eadem (1999) 162; *Supplementum epigraphicum graecum* 50 (2000) 449 no. 1344 at Perge; Queyrel (1992) 341ff.; Nollé (1998) 324 n. 4 (more on painted texts) and 325ff., passim (coins of many Greek cities from 190s AD with acclamatory legends); inscribed texts, Colin (1965) 21f., Roueché (1999) 1.163 and Engelmann (2000) 88 (Ephesus); Kolb (1999) 104f.; Lewin (1995) 111f. (Miletus); beginnings of the practice of inscribed acclamatory texts in the third century, Roueché (1997) 356, but in fact they can be found a little earlier, as Kolb points out (examples from Termessus ca. AD 200; Stratoniceia). For acclamations on stone in Italy, cf. Arval meetings, Kantorowicz (1946) 17 n. 9; Blume (1989) 289 on texts like *expostulatione populi, postulante plebe*; or *Année épigraphique* 1998 p. 272, in Ostia, honors voted AD 253/60, *postulantibus omnibus civibus*.

17. Trans. Pharr (1952) 4f., cf. Hirschfeld (1905) 937–40 with analogies including the Hippo-scene that produced Augustine's coadjutor in AD 426; and Matthews (2000) 39ff., 44, 46f. For another great list of acclamations in a church setting, see Mommsen (1894) 402f., 18 of them hailing an archdeacon of Rome in AD 499, another 52 and then 33 and then 90 hailing the bishop.

18. Blume (1989) 277 on POxy. 2435, Germanicus; Liebeschuetz (1972) 209, Antioch, every time the governor entered or left the city or the theater; *Chron. pasch.* 444 in Dindorf (1832) 1.596, Eudocia; at Edessa, Flemming (1914–17) 15, 19f., and 21 (Chaereas' report to Constantinopolitan officialdom); cf. Schwartz (1914–40) 1, 4, p. 201, the governor of an eastern province writes a letter in AD 434 "reporting to the Count of the East the shouts, *acclamationes*, of the people to him, and reporting to Count Titus those

made to himself as governor at Antioch," and subjoins a copy to another great official, "though we think it needless to supply the actual shouts since they are impossibly numerous and contain many blasphemous statements against certain persons," ibid. p. 202.

19. Pharr (1952) 28, *CT* 1.16.6.1 (Cple. AD 331); Liebeschuetz (1972) 218, concluding from the Antioch evidence that "acclamations were in fact a highly effective way of influencing the imperial representatives."

20. Schwartz (1914–40) 3 pp. 102f.

21. Hirschfeld (1905) 941, "it is safe to assume that the [Roman] senate's protocols in its Proceedings provided the model taken up in the ecclesiastical *acta*"; and surely law courts supplied the model of verbatim transcripts from the late third century on, of increasing importance and elaborateness, as seen in the valuable pages of Meyer (2004) 243ff. For the rising use of stenographers, see Marrou (1965) 449, 614f. Batiffol (1913) 6–9 shows the usages, *cogere* the *relatio, sententiae,* etc.; Haase (1920) 92, standing to vote; Hess (1958) 26, *acta* from mid-third century, and decision by majority and acclamation (pp. 30f.); Barnard (1983) 102f., the Roman civil model in various details, including majority rule; May (1989) 60, the three-witnesses rule and use of written evidence; Sieben (1992) 193, majority rule; Fischer and Lumpe (1997) 296, *sententiae* and other procedures, usages, and terminology: *censere, decernere, vindicare,* etc.

22. The fact pointed out by Shaw (1995) XI p. 15.

23. MacMullen (1988) 67f. with notes.

24. Bowman (1971) 38, instancing POxy. 1415 (late third century), exactly similar to a number of other records in Coles (1966) 22 n. 3.

25. Batiffol (1913) 14 on probable preparing for consensus before synods; Lanne (1971) 206f., concern for unanimity; also Sieben (1992) 192.

26. *Chron. pasch.* in Dindorf (1832) 1. 670f.

27. Cypr., *Ep.* 59, quoted in Sieben (1992) 193 (*Ep.* 67.1 is misunderstood by S.).

28. Hansen (2002) 41f., 85 (Gelasius, *HE*), where the account appears to exclude the recalcitrants from the council-total; Theodoret, *HE* 1.7.15, the *thorubos pleistos*; 1.8.10, hypocrites; Ortiz de Urbina (1963) 60, 63, punishments for the hold-outs; and for Philumenus, Master of Offices (so, with a question mark, *Prosopography of the Later Roman Empire*), cf. Bidez (1913) 10, in the variant MS of Philostorgius' *HE*.

29. In secular contexts, a very early example of *cheirotonia* in Colin (1965) 124; Lewin (1995) 24f., 31, examples into the third century AD; the practice in church councils, Mansi (1759–63) 4.1290, Ephesus I, or Schwartz (1914–40) 2, 1, p. 456, AD 451 and 2, 3, 1, p. 123, AD 449.

30. Specification of the electoral role of *nobiles* along with the *plebs* of Ephesus, Schwartz (1914–40) 2, 3, 3, p. 55; Mansi (1759–63) 9.276, specification of local *laudabiles* at a meeting; in the diocese Oriens under Antioch at least by AD 500, Devreesse (1945) 120; of *viri illustres* at Arausio in AD 529, Guarnieri (1983) 87f.; of *honoratiores* and *plebs,* in Pietri et al. (1992) 376; in Rome in AD 419, Pietri et al. (1992) 386 and around AD 500, Pietri and Pietri (1990) 294f. and Aimone (2000) 69ff., the split unclear; generally, Gaudemet (1974) 313ff. citing Theodoret, *HE* 4.20, etc., Guarnieri (1980) 352f. for the West, Meyendorff (1989) 44, and Gryson (1979) 343.

31. Meyendorff (1989) 44, the norms of nomination; Athanasius appoints his successor, Gryson (1979) 326 citing Soc., Soz, etc.; also Augustine, *Ep.* 213.1 (*CSEL* 57.372f.);

Hilary hurried the death of a bishop in order to appoint a favorite, cf. Leo magnus, *Ep.* 10.4 (*PL* 54.632Af.); further instances in Soc., *HE* 5.21.1 (*PG* 67.621A) and Gaudemet (1974) 313; nepotism by Cyril, Evagrius, *HE* 2.18 (ed. Bidez-Parmentier p. 86); Frend (1972) 25, John of Antioch appoints Domnus; also Ibas, two nephews, Frend (1972) 42; Soz., *HE* 8.16.4, kinsman; similarly involved, kin-ties in Basil's election, Gryson (1979) 337; episcopal "dynasties" not uncommon in the fifth century and later, Sotinel (1997) 199f.

32. Meyendorff (1989) 44; agreement in Gryson (1979) 304ff. and passim; vigorous role for the populace in second and third century, Gryson (1973) 356, 359, 371, 375, 379f.; Soc., *HE* 4.6.6, AD 364, the Cyzicus bishop sees the election as initiated by the people, *laos*; similarly, 5.8.12, AD 381; Aug., *Ep.* 213.3, Augustine's emphatic deference to popular opinion, asking for their acclamation, and getting it, dozens of times over; Hilary, *Ep.* 13.2 (p. 156 Thiel) in AD 463/4, a bishop shouldn't be imposed but rather solicited by the *populus*; similarly, the Hippo council (*CCL* 149 p. 39) of AD 393, in Sabw Kanyang (2000) 55; also, Lancel (1972–91) 2.743, Africa towards AD 400; similarly, Gelasius, *Ep.* frg. 4 (p. 485 Thiel), but adding a role for the *clerus* and calling the people a *turba*; similar, but noting slow changes over the course of the third to fifth century, Jones (1964) 918, Chadwick (2001) 314, 316, and 340, and Pietri et al. (1992) 373, summing up other scholars' views and (pp. 375–81) seeing the politicization of episcopal elections, in the terminology applied to them (in the West — for the East, Gryson [1980] 342ff.); the recommendations of the Antioch patriarch for three candidates to be forthcoming from the people and local clergy, in Brooks (1903) 66f., 91f., 94, 126. But as late as AD 552, the sense that a bishop should represent the *vota cleri simulque et populi*, Victor Tunnunensis, *Chron.* in Placanica (1997) 50.

33. Written accounts of the election must be signed by both parties to an episcopal election in Antioch in the AD 330s, Gryson (1979) 331; "votes controlled by Arius for the archbishopric [of Alexandria] he managed to transfer to him, Alexander, valuing Alexander above himself" and so assuring the eventual winner ca. AD 312, Philostorgius, *HE* 1.3 in Bidez (1913) 6.

34. *Axios*, the usual shout at ordination, underlying a scene at Ephesus AD 431, cf. Bell (1983) 79; for the scene of AD 390, cf. Philostorgius, *HE* 9.10, 9.13; further, Leo magnus, *Ep.* 12.1 (*PL* 54.646Af.), bishops have been pressured by the *populus* into bad choices for ordination.

35. For example, by a Nicene canon (18), deacons must know their place and never sit among presbyters; "subdeacons have no right to a place in the Diaconicum," says the Laodicean canon 21; utter silence commanded among lower clergy (which is excessive), Hier., *Ep.* 52.7.5 (*PL* 22.534); *ut lectores populum non salutent*, Sabw Kanyang (2000) 127, in the Hippo canon, 1a (*CCL* 149 p. 33); standing, at Aquileia, Gryson (1980a) 141, *impar stans*; *adstantibus diaconibus* as a common descriptive detail at meetings, Sabw Kanyang (2000) 163f.; restriction on communion, Turner (1899–1939) 1.453.

36. Sabw Kanyang (2000) 314ff.; Llewellyn (1977) 250; Mathisen (1987) 2; Hier., *Altercatio Luciferiani* 18 (*CCSL* 79b.44), *cui propter aetatem primatus ab omnibus deferabatur*; an instance of presbyters in a series speaking according as they declare their years in office, Mansi (1759–63) 9.279–86; and the higher-up laity in an ecclesiastical setting follow the same rule, testifying *aetate priores*, p. 284 (at Mopsuestia, AD 550).

Chapter 3: The cognitive element

1. Ignatius, *Ep.* 7.2 (*PG* 5.668), let the churches have one altar, one bishop, one Son born of one God the Father; later, the emperors and bishops together, below, n. 13.

2. Thomassen (2004) 249, citing NT, Justin, et al.

3. Alexander of Lycopolis, *Contra Manichaeos* 1f., Brinkman (1989) 3; for date, cf. p. xiv and Horst and Mansfeld (1974) 48. There is some unwillingness to accept the statement by our only source, that Alexander ended as a bishop; but the treatise doesn't make that at all unthinkable. As to the progress or development in Chistendom, from ethical emphasis to theological as the fourth century gets under way, see Kreider (2005) 61, 64, and passim.

4. Soc., *HE* 1.6.35; cf. a bishop's public letter a half-century later, reporting the results of sectarian quarreling, "the cause, this, of a lot of insulting remarks by both pagans and heretics," in Mansi (1759–63) 7.245; an emperor AD 452 fearing the same damage to the church, ibid. 6.494C; and another bishop on another occasion trying to calm down his colleagues' impassioned shouts for vengeance on an opponent, "Let's not give opening for reproach to the unbelievers," Flemming (1914–17) 57 lines 31ff.; cf. Constantine remarking on "not only the leaders of the churches [in the east] sparring with words, but the masses also divided into parts, some inclining to one side, some to the other. The spectacle of these events became so ridiculous that sacred aspects of divine doctrine were now subjected to disgraceful public mockery in the theaters of the unbelievers" (Euseb., *Vita Const.* 2.62.4f.).

5. Themistius, *Or.* 5.70a, in Maisano (1995).

6. Ammianus Marcellinus 21.16.18, writing in ? the 380s.

7. Soz., *HE* 3.13.4f.; cf. Mansi (1759–63) 7.245, the consciousness within the church of its continual disputes being "an occasion for much calumny, *loidoriai pollai*, from both pagans and heretics".

8. Bardy (1923) 27 and passim and Navascues (2004) 58, 90f., 437, 440, 449f., and passim, showing the term *homoousios* in Paul's teachings as recalled by the best sources, Hilary, Athanasius, and Basil, and elsewhere too; and Navascues also supplies careful discussion of his scholarly predecessors, of whom the chief concur with his findings; see also R. Williams (2001) 159. Euseb., *HE* 7.29 is the main source, with 7.30.19 on the appeal to Aurelian.

9. Suggested by Eusebius of Caesarea? As to *homoousios*, among other scholars, Chadwick (2001) 199 sees it as an invention of 325, which is unlikely (whether the emperor's or eastern bishops'); it "surfaced" (to use his word) in the AD 260s, prominently, cf. the preceding note, G. Jouassard in the *Lexikon für Theologie und Kirche*, ed. 2 (Freiburg 1963) 8.213, R. Hanig, ibid. ed. 3 (1998) 7.1527, or R. Williams (2001) 69; and it could be found subsequently but pre-325 in use among learned bishops known to Eusebius, *PG* 67.1541C. For discussions of God's nature, *hypostaseis*, and *ousia* a few years before Paul from Samosata, see Fischer and Lumpe (1997) 343f. on Dionysius of Rome.

10. Chadwick p. 271, Sirmium; Schwartz (1914–40) 2, 3, p. 117, " 'It does not occur in scripture, but in fact it is found in the Fathers' teachings.' To this, the Most Reverend presbyter Mamas [of Cple] said in reply, 'In just the same way that *homoousios* is not

found in scripture but is taught by the Holy Fathers, so the Fathers have taught about the two natures . . .' ", and so forth.

11. Soc., *HE* 1.7.3 (*PG* 67.56Aff.). I am not persuaded by the suggestion that the letter was addressed to Antioch, not Alexandria, in Hall (1998) 87.

12. Soc., *HE* 1.8.4 (*PG* 67. 1540A), discussion should only be framed in *aporrhetoi*; Euseb., *Vita Const.* 2.69.3, "we must therefore avoid being talkative in such matters, where the slower minds of the audience" may prevent comprehension; ibid. 2.68.2, "trivial"; *Vita Const.* 2.71.1, "minute".

13. Heim (1978) 61, cf. Kelly (1950) 254 — a common (not the only) interpretation to which I subscribed in *Constantine* (1969) 165f., and various other writers, more recently; cf. statements such as Theodosius', "The firm standing, *katastasis*, of our government depends upon piety toward God and what is natural and fitting and closely connects these two; for each advances through the increase of the other . . . We have been assigned to our rule by God, and as the link between the piety of Our subjects and their sharing in prosperity; so therefore we are ever vigilant to secure their joint action . . ." (Schwartz [1914–40] 1, 1, p. 115); an extended statement at Ephesus II, that Satan plots the splitting of the church and emperors must oppose him or endanger themselves and their realm, Schwartz (1914–40) 2, 2, 1, p. 85; or again in AD 449, Flemming (1914–17) 3.

14. "Legal necessity" in the Socrates-passage, above; Sabw Kanyang (2000) 65f., insistence in western church canons of AD 393 and 419 on the training of clerics in church law.

15. Cf. the statement of 356 by Hilary, so much discussed (*De synodis* 91), "I never heard the Nicene creed until I was exiled," with discussion by Moreschini (2001) 248f., and add to the same effect, what I think anyone would conclude from a general reading in the Latin as well as the Greek sources of the fourth and fifth centuries; cf. e.g. Chadwick (2001) 284, of a bishop in AD 359 from Africa, "a region little involved in the Greek debate, probably finding much of the debate almost incomprehensible."

16. MacMullen (2003) 472 on provision for bishops quite ignorant of doctrine, in fourth century canons.

17. Hier., *Altercatio Luciferiani* 11 (*CCSL* 79b.31f. = Canellis [2003] 126f.), written in the 370s by someone who knew the region from years of residence; the same thought elsewhere, e.g. Greg. Nyss., *Contra Eunomium* 1 (*PG* 45.265B), "it was the wicked cleverness, *kakotechnia*, of Aristotle that afforded to Aetius his impiety."

18. Epiphanius, *Panarion* 69.15.3, "a manner *arrhetos, akataleptos, achrantos*"; cf. *Adv. haer.* 13 (*PG* 42.429), Christ's flesh is *achronon* and *akatalepton*; or again and authoritatively by Cyril in his Fourth Letter to Nestorius (*PG* 77.45B), *aphrastos kai aperinoetos*, "beyond words, beyond thought". It is tempting to quote Augustine to much the same effect as Epiphanius in a well known effort to educate a simple audience about Arianism and its correction, the very finely didactic *Serm.* 117.2–7, sympathetically rendered in English by Hill (1992), especially pp. 212f.

19. Kelly (1950) 95f., 100ff., 172, 194, 324f.

20. Cf. Ambros., *De paradiso* 12.58 (*PL* 14.304C), and as later observed by Vincentius, *Commonitorium* 25 (*PL* 50.672): "Here, perhaps the question may be posed, whether heretics use the testimony of sacred scripture. Yes, they use it — in truth, a great deal, *vehementer*. For you see them flitting about among all the books of holy writ, Moses, Kings, Psalms, Apostles, Evangels, Prophets . . . They never propose anything

without trying to suggest it through the words of scripture. . . . Read the shorter works of Paul from Samosata, Priscillian, Eunomius, Jovinian, and the other plagues. There you will find a great mountain of citations. Almost every page is tinted and colored by passages from the Old Testament or the New" (*PL* 50.672).

21. As to the education of bishops, see above, Chap. 1 nn. 10 and 13; regarding Emeritus, above in Chap. 1, his rejoinder drawn from a quite obscure, extra-canonical text; an example of recall of a useful Cyril-letter by a bishop on the instant, Schwartz (1914–40) 2, 3, 2, p. 92; and in the accounts of monks and ascetics there are dozens of illustrations of memorized scripture.

22. Use but misunderstanding of technical terms is easily observed in the controversial literature and councils. See instances in Chap. 7, below, or in Hanson (1989) 144 on people using *ousia* and *hypostasis* differently from their interlocutors without realizing it (let alone, problems in Latin translation!); 146, Hanson himself at a loss "to know just what these two terms meant at the time," at Nicaea; and still more problems with Syriac! Cf. Brock (1996) 26ff.

23. An early instance in Hilary, *De synodis* 11 (*PL* 10.488B); and he breaks out in Latin at Ephesus, *kontradikitour, ho estin, antilegetai,* Schwartz (1914–40) 2, 1, 1, p. 191; occasional costs through mis-translation, Chadwick (2001) 560; Serdican proceedings and minutes in Latin, Hess (1958) 47; but normally, councils in east speak Greek and translate Latin, cf. Schwartz (1914–40) 2, 3, 2, p. 106, at Chalcedon.

24. Quoted, Kelly (1950) 205, on the meaning of Nicaea.

25. Schwartz (1914–40) 2, 1, 3, pp. 124ff. Just after the ref. to *physis*, I follow the MS that reads *peridechetai* and *dicitis*, with Mansi 7.491C. On the murdered bishop Severian, see Smith and Wace (1877–87) 4.626 and below, Chap. 5 n. 4, the rival being bishop Theodosius of Jerusalem (AD 451–57).

26. Schwartz (1914–40) 2, 1, 3, p. 130; and Marcian was joined by the empress, a match for him in her influence. She too in identical words and phrases touched the same main points for explanation and correction, and adds a passing threat of "such penalties as the laws prescribe".

27. The East Syrian or Assyrian Church called by the west "Nestorian", hounded out of the empire after Ephesus I and again by Zeno in the 480s, Adeney (1932) 97, Devreesse (1945) 50, 67, Roberson (1988) 1, and (the best) Brock (1996) 23, 33; and the Coptic Orthodox church in effect created by Egypt's refusal of Chalcedon, Roberson p. 4, Atiya (1967) 58, Meyendorff (1981) 30, Griggs (1990) 1, and S. J. Davis (2004) 84.

28. "The situation [post-Chalcedon] required great minds, capable of solving problems in the manner in which the great Cappadocian fathers — St Basil, St Gregory of Nazianzus — had in the late fourth century solved the dilemma" centered in *homoousios*, so says Meyendorff (1989) 193 — though I am not sure the possibilities for reconciliation by anyone at all were to be found, in the wording of Cyril, Chalcedon, and later controversy.

29. Sermons distributed in copies routinely, e.g. by Augustine, Sabw Kanyang (2000) 196; the "spider's web" in R. Williams (1989) 14; Brooks (1903) p. ix on the more than 3,759 letters written by one bishop over the span of a quarter-century; the several hundred surviving from Augustine or Basil, of unknown larger totals; examples of bishops' letters of advocacy or defense, Mouterde (1930) 46, from Rome "to all the faithful"; Schwartz (1914–40) 1, 1, 3, p. 46 (the bishop of Ephesus to all the *cleroi* of Cple); 1, 1, 3, p. 14, the

Cple clergy to the Ephesus clergy; reference there to an imperial letter to be read aloud "with the whole people assembled"; Soc., *HE* 4.22.1f. (bishop of Alexandria writes "to churches everywhere"); Ibas' famous letter to Mari bishop of Adashir (Schwartz 2, 1, 3, pp. 32ff.), often quoted or read into the record, itself to be disseminated; the bishop of Rome writes to a synod, Tyana AD 367, Soz., *HE* 6.12.2; a synod writes a letter to various other bishops of two provinces, Chadwick (2001) 276.

30. Epiphanius, *Panarion* 80.1.8.

31. On bishops as lobbyists at court, see the next chapter; for the quotation, Hier., *Ep.* 17.2 (*PL* 22.360), the fear of a *scisma* in the backcountry where Syriac was as much spoken as Greek; and notice the scenes indicated in canon 18 of the Ancyra council, Gryson (1979) 302.

32. The quotation from Chadwick (2001) 234, referring to Marcellus of Ancyra and Eusebius of Caesarea; Schwartz (1914–40) 4, 2, p. 122, Pelagius' letter of the 580s to the bishops of Histria, quoting a much earlier letter to the Cple bishop Proclus (434–436).

33. Barnes (1993) 230f.; Soc., *HE* 2.30.47, recall after Sirmium, in vain; 3.25.9f., creed in a synodal letter, AD 363.

34. Epiphanius, *Panarion* 69.4.3; R. Williams (2001) 48–58 passim; recognition of the routine of letters read aloud, and the effectiveness of the routine, in Flemming (1914–17) 141ff.

35. Cyril, *Ep.* 82 (*PG* 77.376Af.), on the deviant *ouk echonta pollen akribeian eis noun . . . idiotai gar eisin hoi polloi*; cf. a synodal letter from Ancyra warning against the spread of wrong beliefs "among simpler-minded folk," *tais ton haplousteron psychais*, Epiphanius, *Panarion* 73.2.5.

36. Evagrius, *HE* 2.5 (Bidez-Parmentier p. 53); for wrestling with these two prepositions, see among much evidence the *expositio Patricii et Aetii* in the *Hist. acephala* 4.6, *imago enim Dei factus est [Christus] et non ex Deo, et a Deo*, etc., in A. Martin (1985) 156.

37. Schwartz (1914–40) 1, 1, 1, p. 56, on *enanthroposis*; cf. the Antioch council of AD 325 preceding Nicaea which declared Christ "begotten in an ineffable, indescribable manner," Kelly (1950) 209; Eusebius of Caesarea criticized for a similar wording, "considering God to be beyond our knowledge and comprehension," *agnoston kai akatalepton*; Eusebius of Nicomedia quoted to the same effect (*PL* 8.1038A, Candidus' letter to Victorinus), "the origin of him [Christ] cannot be expressed in words nor even in thought, for not of human beings only but of those above them, we believe it to be beyond comprehension," in Victorinus, *De generatione* 3.2 (*PL* 8.1036B), inquiry in itself is a sin; Epiphanius presenting a creed of some circulation, "of which I myself don't understand all the subtleties," *Panarion* 72.10.4; Gregory Nazianzenus' impatience at *mikrologein*, "Let's not quibble about the existence of the Pneuma from before time" (*PG* 36.437D); Cyril quoted above in n. 18; and the request of the Armenian metropolitan in AD 451 that he and his flock should be excused from an understanding of difficult theology, since "we are in a remote corner of the world . . . , not speaking good Greek (or Latin) . . . we cannot deliver long sermons. We uphold the Nicene creed but avoid difficult questions beyond human grasp" (quoted in Chadwick [2001] 591). It is not uncommon to find the rationality, "the 'Greekness' ", of theological explanation itself objectionable, e.g. Duval (1981) 95.

38. E.g. Hilary, *De synodis* 11 (*PL* 10.488Af.), where he explains how the council of Sirmium avoided the term *homoousios*; Hilary, *De synodis* 11 (*PL* 10.488), "but the term 'substance', *ousia*, was settled on by the Fathers for its simplicity, *dia to haplousteron*, but aroused outrage among the people, *ho laos*, as unknown." The scriptural text, Isaiah 53.8, had in fact no relevance at all, but a canonical mis-translation persisted until recent decades.

39. *The Decline and Fall . . .* , near the beginning of the 27th chapter, and with a note to explain that the source of the picture was unknown to Gibbon yet attested by "a correct and liberal scholar." It has long since been traced to Gregory, cf. e.g. MacMullen (1989) 508 and (1990) 391 with similar passages; also in Cple, Greg. Naz., discovering the prevalence of confusion among the populace, *De vita sua* 1118f. (*PG* 37.1106f.).

40. Pitcher (1994) 101f.

41. The terms *haplousteroi, simpliciores*, or the like are scattered liberally through the relevant sources, with examples in texts cited above; also Mansi (1759–63) 9.250; 4.1031D; and *CT* 16.4.1 (AD 386) *de his qui super religione contendunt*, and 2 (AD 388), Pharr (1952) 449, "there shall be no opportunity for any man to go out to the public and to argue about religion. . . . ;" and the edict of Marcian AD 452, decreeing the burning of heretical texts lest *innocentium vel infirmorum animi decipiantur*, Schwartz (1914–40) 2, 3, p. 351. More bans on debate followed in the seventh century, Treadgold (1997) 305, 312f.

42. MacMullen (1989) 504ff.

43. Lact., *De mort. persecut.* 46; Kantorowicz (1946) 20; Creed (1984) 66f. with (p. 121) proper dismissal of Euseb., *Vita Const.* 4.19f. and the arguments of Moreau et al. to attribute the song to Constantine; similarly unpersuasive, Heim (1976) 66f., requiring Constantine to dictate the song to Licinius at Milan, AD 312, or that Lactantius' work was doctored at Trier (AD 314? or up to 323?) to include the song at Constantine's suggestion. On liturgical acclamations derived from secular, cf. Hirschfeld (1905) 940, instancing Aug., *Ep.* 213 (*PL* 33.966f.), Mommsen (1894) 402, the scene being Rome in AD 499, and Kantorowicz pp. 17f., 24, and passim.

44. Philostorgius, *HE* 2.2; Ambros., *Ep.* 85a (21a).34 (*CSEL* 82, 3 p. 105); Soz., *HE* 3.20.8, Antioch in AD 346, Arians and Anti-Arians ("*in* the Son"); Schwartz (1914–40) 1, 1, 2, p. 65, Nestorius' monks and Mansi (1759–63) 4. 1428C and 8.1065, all in Cple, see Chap. 5; much other material in MacMullen (1966a) 109ff.; (1990) 272f. with notes, p. 391 (including the little town of Cottiaeum).

45. MacMullen (1984) 135 and (1989), passim; above, Chap. 3 n. 18.

46. "Dissimilarian" in Prestige (1956) 3 ("dyophysitism" etc. being more familiar); Dovere (1998) 6f., *CT.* 16.5.66, on the *portentuosa superstitiosa*; Fotiniani from Photinus, in Zelzer (1982) 356; "Eutychian" in Zach. Rhet., Hamilton and Brooks (1899) 112; "Manichaean" as mere vituperation, e.g. Mansi (1959–63) 8.1084f.

47. Shaw (1995) XI 11f. (it is the 16th book of the *Theod. Code* that gathers anti-heretical law); cf. Brock (1996) 29, " 'Nestorian' was a convenient word with which to tar any of one's theological opponents".

48. Schwartz (1914–40) 1, 1, 5, p. 121; similar omnium-gatherum fulminations of the mid-sixth century from the emperor, Dindorf (1832) 1.662, or the bishop of Rome, Günther (1895–98) 295.

49. See e.g. Mansi (1979–63) 5.731–1022; 9.279ff.
50. MacMullen (2003a) passim.

Chapter 4: The "supernaturalist" element

1. A total of 162 names, but more than 185 by my count with allowance for gaps in Haase (1920) 25–28; a total of 194 to 203, Honigman (1942–43) 25, cf. Aubineau (1966) 6; or "not more than about 200" names, with more present but not voting, R. Williams (2001) 67; or Chadwick (1972) 132 and (2001) 198, "about 220 bishops *attended*" (my italics); a second stage of numbering, at 250 (Eusebius) or 260, Haase p. 82 and Aubineau p. 7; 270+ in Eustathius, and about 300 in Constantine (as quoted) in Soc., *HE* 1.9.31, and Athanasius, Haase p. 82, R. Williams p. 67, and Chadwick (2001) 281, the source for this latter figure also in an anon. fourth-century historian, Hansen (1902) 86, and Chrysostom, Aubineau pp. 9f.; 310 and more, in Epiphanius, *Ancoratus* 118, Kelly (1950) 310; thereafter, 318, e.g. in Sulp. Sev., *Chron.* 2.35.2, sometimes with more added; for Gen. 14.14 and Hilary in his *De synodis*, Chadwick (2001) 198, 280; tau-iota-eta as "Cross-Jesus", Aubineau p. 12; to mean Nicaea, Schwartz (1914–40) 2, 1, p. 274, at Chalcedon.

2. Tyana's boast, Soz., *HE* 6.12.2; representation at Aquileia, Savon (1997) 121; cf. the charge that impious opponents "thought to confirm their impiety [at Chalcedon] by their great numbers, making themselves double those of the holy council of Nicaea, as if to produce the belief in their greatness thereby," the speaker being an Alexandrian bishop in the AD 450s, Nau (1919) 285; at Carthage, elaborate devices of competition in counting, Mandouze (1982) 59; boast of numbers earlier, Euseb., *HE* 6.43.2; 7.7.5; emphasis on numbers to support validity, Cypr., *Ep.* 56.2; and Cyprian, *Ep.* 71, stress on numbers.

3. Sulp. Sev., *Chron.* 2.44.1, *auctoritas ex numero*; cf. again, Schwartz (1914–40) 2, 3, 2, p. 118, a bishop declares, "This universal synod is greater than the Egyptian region and deserves more authority to be believed, and it's not right to listen to ten heretics and disregard 1200 bishops" (the latter figure, ridiculously inflated, as appears further in the dialogue, where it is reduced to the still ridiculous number of 600).

4. Soz., *HE* 8.20.5, deposition of the Cple bishop John; Schwartz (1914–40) 1, 1, 3, pp. 12, 14, comparison of numbers voting for a deposition; a bishop in his bill of complaints argues at Ephesus I against his deposition by a trifling number of enemies, a mere 30 against the 200 that deposed their leader, Schwartz (1914–40) 1, 1, 3, p. 16; p. 20, again called "those few", *euarithmetoi*; the 200 inflated to 210, p. 30; appeal only to a larger council, Council of Nicaea, can. 6, and of Cple AD 381, can. 6; the appeal for the convening of an extra-large council on the grounds that "only the decision of a larger synod could displace that of a smaller," Horn (1982) 80; and the concession to the importance of numbers by a party who knew they were few and only "bishops in small towns," Sotinel (2000) 289, AD 532, cf. p. 292, *numerus parvus*.

5. Schwartz (1914–40) 2, 3, p. 252, *tantorum episcoporum, praesente eis et sancto spiritu*; Leo, *Ep.* 145.1 (*PL* 54.1114A), Chalcedon council "assembled through the Holy Spirit," cf. 155.2 (*PL* 54.1126C).

6. Mansi (1759–63) 4.1230 and Acts 2.1–4.

7. A synodal letter of Arles AD 314 explains its own decisions, *praesente spiritu*

sancto et angelis eiusdem, Maier (1987–89) 1.163; Evagrius, *HE* 2.18, Bidez and Parmentier (1964) 88; Schwartz (1914–40) 1, 1, 2, p. 70, Nestorius, according to a synodal letter, was punished "by the divinely inspired judgement of the bishops"; cf. in Ephesus AD 449, the acclamations, "Many years to the holy synod! Through you God has spoken! The Holy Spirit has spoken through you!" (Flemming [1914–17] 123 lines 22f.); cf. at Ephesus I, Schwartz (1914–40) 1, 1, 3, p. 11, "Christ, lord of all, present to show us"; a church historian of ca. AD 480 in Hansen (1902) 47 describing Nicaea's creed as the work of "these men [the 318] or rather the Holy Spirit speaking through them" (repeated at p. 86); a Coptic source declaring the 318 at Nicaea to have been counted as 319 because the Holy Spirit was present, Haase (1920) 45; "all the decisions taken in the great city of Ephesus as in a council directed, *kinetheises*, by the Holy Spirit," Schwartz (1914–40) 2, 1, p. 374.

8. Rufinus, *HE* 2.11, Ambrose; Euseb., *HE* 6.29.4; cf. a few years later the perceived role of *dei iudicium* or *divinum iudicium* in episcopal elections in Africa, which Granfield (1976) 43 finds in Cyprian's letters; election, says Cyprian, is *secundum vestra divina suffragia*, *Ep.* 43.1.3, in Gryson (1973) 380. Notice Sozomen's personal opinion of the unusual election of a Cple bishop, *HE* 7.8.8, "I believe this was not brought about through other than a divine impulse."

9. Ortiz de Urbina (1963) 160f.; Walter (1970) 34ff. In the lower left, identified by writing, the desperate suppliant, Macedonius heresiarch; (lost) in the right corner, perhaps Apollinaris.

10. A council meeting "in the presence of God's bishop and the sight of the altar" (where perhaps the bible might have been displayed), Cypr., *Ep.* 45.2.2f., cf. *Sententiae episcoporum de haereticis baptizandis* (*CSEL* 3.433–61), in a council of 256 at Carthage, many bishops in their voting opinions quote the bible, in up to a half dozen passages, perhaps from a copy at hand? A bible at hand at Ephesus I, Schwartz (1914–40) 1, 1, 3, p. 11; in AD 448 in Cple, Schwartz (1914–40) 2, 1, 1, p. 137; at Chalcedon, Mansi (1759–63) 9.276, *divinis igitur in medium prolatis scripturis*; ibid. 8 p. 1084, some reading from scripture; the bible at hand as a witness at Chalcedon, Schwartz (1914–40) 2, 3, 2, p. 131; again, p. 103; and in AD 550, Mansi (1759–63) 9.276, where, p. 279, witnesses speak while touching the bible (as often elsewhere); and the scriptures described as *phriktos*, "fearful", Schwartz (1914–40) 2, 1, 1, p. 166, cf. below, Chap. 7 n. 35. For attribution of conciliar decisions to the holy Pneuma, see e.g. Schwartz (1914–40) 2, 1, 1, p. 121, said of Nicaea at Cple AD 448.

11. *Collectanea antiariana parisina* (*CSEL* 65): *Gesta Nicaena* 5 p. 86.6, a bishop reminds the meeting that "at Ariminum there was discord injected by the Devil"; Nau (1919) 205, on Chalcedon; cf. the shouts at Chalcedon, "Don't give Satan an opening! Don't give Satan a chance!" (Schwartz [1914–40] 2, 3, 1, p. 91).

12. Early attribution of heresy to the Devil in Euseb., *HE* 5.14.1; 5.16.7; 5.16.9; 6.43.14; 7.31.1 (Manichaeism) — sometimes resulting in the need for conciliar action, Kretschmar (1961) 16. Diabolical origins of heresy, also in Soc., *HE* 1.9.18 and 21 and Opitz (1935) 19; Epiphanius, *Panarion* 69.2.1 and 69.12.1, "Arius, inspired by a diabolical energy"; Schwartz (1914–40) 2, 3, 2, p.134, assertion that the Devil sows weeds, *zizania* = "heresies" (Mt 13.25); also the Ebionites are Devil-inspired, Epiphanius, *Panarion* 3.27.1, as are other "heresies," 4.7.1ff., 4.7.9; 5.14.1; 5.16.9; 8.1.7; 8.16.3f.; Gelasius, *HE* 2.13.4, confusing eristics at Nicaea, *diabolike eutechnia*, but God inter-

venes to silence the Devil; Constantine echoes, ibid.; Euseb., *HE* 7.31.1, Mani's was "the Devil's heresy"; Serdica AD 343 declares "the coiling Devil poured out his poison of blasphemies", in vain, *Collectio antiariana parisina* (*CSEL* 65), this in the synodal letter I(9) p. 126; ibid., Frg. A §1 p. 43 at Paris AD 360, "the Devil's deceit" at work for the Arians; Evagrius, *HE* 1.1, *ho misokalos daimon* was responsible for the controversy over "in" and "from" in the 360s, cf. 2. 5 (Bidez and Parmentier [1964] 52) and above, Chap. 3 n. 31; "Satan stimulated schisms and divisions, troubles and disputes" in the church, Nau (1932) 185; the African church's split attributed in AD 411 to Satan, Lancel (1972–91) 2.562; "the evil scheming of some devil has brought war" into the church ranks, so says the emperor Theodosius, Schwartz (1914–40) 1, 1, 4, p. 5; toward the time of Ephesus I, the Messalians' beliefs are blamed on the Devil, Theodoret, *HE* 4.11.1, and Messalians' beliefs infected by *daimonos tinos energeia*, in Parmentier (1954) 229, cf. Sillett (2000) 271; Theodosius II refers to *dissidium diaboli technis injectum*, Mansi (1759–63) 5.282D; Cyril on the Devil's plots to disrupt the Christian community, *Ep.* 21 (*PG* 77.129D), with ref. to 1 Peter 5.8; Cyril again, Mansi (1759–63) 4.1012C; *stasis* in the Edessene church due to "an evil demon," Flemming (1914–17) 33, 35; in the sixth century, blame on the Devil for perceived heresy, Brooks (1903) 51; the view that the Devil, at work from the beginning, "thrust thorns of dispute deep into the midst of them (the Apostles)", Theodoret, *Haereticorum fabularum compendium* (*PG* 83.341B); and in general, Aug., *Civ. dei* 4.32.

13. Much source-material on baptismal exorcism, etc., cited in MacMullen (1997) 208f.; as active agent, notice how Satan drives persecutions in Euseb., *HE* 5 praef.; 5.1.5; 5.1.16; 5.1.35; 5.2.6; and 6.39.5; also in Maier (1987–89) 1.202; the Devil attacks the bishop of Rome, as Leo magnus explains, *Ep.* 21.1 or 102.4 (*PL* 54.715A or 987ff.); and beyond and following Athanasius' biography of Saint Antony, see, e.g., Lavenant (1963) 853ff. or Stewart (1991) 39; the Antioch riots of AD 387 caused by demons, Libanius, *Or.* 19.7 and 30ff.; Cple beset by disturbances, demonically instigated, Malalas, *Chron.* 18.71 AD 531, Thurn (2000) 394; at Edessa in the mid-fifth century, riot twice caused by a devil, as Chaereas the presiding official explains, Flemming (1914–17) 33 and 35; civil wars so caused, in Menas' sixth century dialogue on philosophy, Mazzuchi (2002) 105; epidemics, in Greg. Nyss., *De vita Greg. thaumat.*, *PG* 46.921Cf., 956f.; and Chrysostom's sermons to combat the view that demons govern all, *Adv. eos qui dicunt daemones gubernare* 6 (*PG* 49.254) and passim. For the earlier run-up to these views, cf. D. B. Martin (2004) 193ff., 204f.

14. Second-century instances in MacMullen (1984) 27 and 133 and (1997) 209; in the third century, e.g. the bishop of Neocaesarea, Greg. Nyss., *De vita Greg. Thaumat.*, *PG* 46.904C or 941D, with scholarly acceptance of the Gregorian authorship of the work by Mateo Seco (1984) 197 and other contributors to the same volume, pp. 16, 33, 37, 44f., 80f., 93, and 227; in the fourth century, MacMullen (1997) 209f.; Lact., *De mort. persecut.* 10.2; Günther (1895–98) 28, Rome in the 380s; Paulinus Mediolanensis, *Vita S. Ambrosii* 14, 16, 21, 28, 33, 43, and 48; Soc., *HE* 4.27.5; 4.24.14, exorcism by ascetics is "the routine activity", *synethe*; Soz., *HE* 3.14.29; 4.3.2; 4.16.12; and 5.10.2; Sulp. Sev., *Vita Martini* 17.1f.; and Delehaye (1923) 29 §29; 34 §37; and 75.

15. By ascetics, Delehaye p. 16 §16 or Soc., *HE* 4.24.14; by the bishop of Caesarea, Nau (1932) 290; and later, in Boulhol (1994) 257f. and MacMullen (1997) 210.

16. Notably by Antony, MacMullen (1997) 136; by others, Soc., *HE* 7.4.4f. (by

bishop of Cple); Theodoret, *HE* 4.16.1 (bishop of Edessa); 4.18.9, 4.23.5, and 4.27.2 (by ascetics); Soz., *HE* 1.14.9; 2.3.11; 2.7.2f.; 2.24.11; 3.14.29; 4.3.2; 6.20.6; 6.28.4; Philostorgius, *HE* 4.7; Paulinus Mediolanensis, *Vita S. Ambrosii* 10 and 14; in Eustathius' *Vita Eutychii*, sixth-century cures by bishops of Cple and Heracleopolis, in MacMullen (1997) 210, and by the bishop of Caesarea in Evagrius, *HE* 4.7.

17. Theodoret, *HE* 1.7.4 (a bishop at Nicaea); Soz., *HE* 3.14.40 (ascetic); Paulinus Mediolanensis, *Vita S. Ambrosii* 28 (bishop of Milan); Delehaye (1923) 35 §38 (ascetic cures infertility), 71f. §74, and 83 §89; and many instances in the Syriac life of Symeon Stylites, Lietzmann (1908) 36ff., as in Theodoret's version, Canivet and Leroy-Molinghen (1977–79) 2.195f.

18. On the miraculous controlling of natural phenomena, attested ubiquitously, see many examples in MacMullen (1997) 208f., 235f., adding Greg. Nyss., *Vita Greg. Thaumat.*, *PG* 46.929ff., 932B; *Peregrinatio S. Silvae* 19.10 (*CSEL* 39.62f.); the Syriac *Life* of Symeon Stylites, in Lietzmann (1908) 113 (drought cured); Vogûé (1994) 149, drought cured and on another occasion, rain is turned off; Soz., *HE* 7.26.4; or attacking armies sent packing, Evagrius, *HE* 4.27 and 28 (Bidez and Parmentier [1964] 175, 177). For an instructive contrast, cf. [Caesar], *Bell. Gall.* 8.43, a well among the besieged dries up because the Romans knew how to cut the supply, but "this, they" (the ignorant barbarians) "supposed was done by the will of the gods, not by the devising of men" (the actual author, Hirtius, being an intimate and so, representative of the intelligentsia like Caesar himself and Cicero).

19. Jones (1964) 957, in a section entitled "The growth of superstition" (my quantification of his feat is obviously a guess, but indeed there would have been 150 vols. of *PG* and *PL*).

20. Dindorf (1832) 1.629; comment in Whitby and Whitby (1989) 128n.; compare the sack of Rome seen by Timothy Ailouros as a punishment for Chalcedon's false dogma, Nau (1919) 215f.; Theodoret, *HE* 5.34.5f. (AD 403? — but not in other sources) with Soc., *HE* 6.19; Philostorgius, *HE* 12.10, quakes can't occur of natural causes, only by God's act; further discussion in Marasco (2003) 275f. on every sort of great event, divinely caused and understandable through scripture; and Malal., *Chron*, passim, quakes are always "by God's anger", e.g. 14.20, 14.21, 15.11, 16.18 (Thurn [2000] 281ff., etc.). Storms yield to prayer, Soc., *HE* 7.22.18; famine follows wicked deeds by the ruler, 4.16.7f. Cf. the supernatural shakiness of temple-construction by a nonbeliever in defiance of God, Soz., *HE* 5.2.13, and Philostorgius, *HE* 7.9.

21. To the sources on Arius' death in MacMullen (2003) 486, add Rufinus, *HE* 1.4, Nau (1932) 215 and Athanasius, *Ep. ad Serapionem de morte Arrii* 2 (*PL* 25.685ff.); Ambrose in *Gesta concilii Aquil.* 15, Zelzer (1982) 334, quoted, exactly similar to Athanasius' reasoning in *PG* 25.688Df. and especially his saying elsewhere about Arius' death, "Who will not at last learn from the occurrence of so great a sign that the heresy is hated by God?" (trans. Brakke [1995] 132). On Nestorius, add Euseb., *HE* 1.7, and Hamilton and Brooks (1899) 42; on Maximin's death, Lact., *De mort. persecut.* 33.1–10, Eusebius, *HE* 9.10.13–15, and Gelasius, *HE* in Hansen (1902) 12; various wicked souls whose teeth and tongues rot out, Theodoret, *HE* 3.7.4, or are eaten by worms, Philostorgius, *HE* 7.10; Günther (1895–98) 24; Valens is burnt alive, in Orosius, *Hist. libri sept.* 7.33; and bishops of Rome, consorting with Photinians and Acacians or otherwise

at fault, *Liber pont.* 63.2 and 75.2, Duchesne (1955) 1.232, 258 (the interpretation of the victim's death belongs to the AD 440s, R. Davis [2000] p. xiii). For the explanation of barbarian ravages as the consequence of heretic views, see Nau (1919) 216, in Chadwick (2001) 589, and Gryson (1980a) 214.

22. The punishment inflicted by or on behalf of bishops and ascetics who have suffered insult is a common theme in hagiography: e.g. Greg. Nyss., *Vita Greg. Thaumat.*, PG 46.940f.; by Basil, his *Epp.* 104, 110f., Rufinus, *HE* 2.9, and Nau (1932) 298f., 301f.; by Ambrose, Paulinus Mediolanensis, *Vita Ambrosii* 11, 43, and 54; Soc., *HE* 4.26.24; Soz., *HE* 6.16.2f.; Delehaye (1923) 58 §58; Philostorgius, *HE* 4.7; Theodoret, 4.16; and by Chrysostom in Palladius, *Dial. de vita S. Ioannis* 17 (*PG* 47.58f.); by Symeon Stylites, Lietzmann (1908) 103, 135f., etc., the Syriac translated by H. Hilgenfeld; and in the west, fear of a bishop's vengeance is general, Aug., *Ep.* 11*.13.4 (*CSEL* 88.61); for more instances, cf. MacMullen (1997) 168.

23. MacMullen (1997) 93–97.

24. Notice the revealing incident reported by Aug., *Ep.* 11*.13.4 (*CSEL* 88.61), where a sudden death is explained as chance, *casualiter*, only by "a few *infideles*".

25. The *teratodes* as Zosimus heard it, *Hist. nova* 4.21.2f., AD 367/8.

26. *Moralia* 664Bff., Loeb Library translation, the italics of *supernatural* being my own; and on Plutarch's position in life, Lamberton (2001) 52f.

27. Plutarch's tendencies show up well in *Moralia* 911ff.; further passages in MacMullen (1997) 202 and Veyne (1999) 390 and passim; on *deisidaemonia*, *Moralia* 548ff. and especially the essay at 164ff.; Battegazzore (1992) 20; Pott (1992) 36; *deisidaemonia* given to the continual detection of portents, *Moralia* 168C, cf. also Veyne pp. 393f.; discussion in Desiderio (1992) 78, 80ff. My definition of the word "nature" is meant to accord with what Jones had in mind, underlying "super-natural"; but a formal philosophical discussion is not my intent.

28. Plutarch's position along the scale, Veyne p. 387, going on (p. 413) to list "the greatest minds of the next three centuries — Origen, Plotinus, Porphyry, Augustine — who entertained no doubts about demonology. It was not a matter of [merely] popular belief." On the religiosity of the decades on both sides of the turn of the era, see e.g. Champeaux (1998) 148, "un crise" in Rome (but not a good discussion); better, Attridge (1978) 45f., 48; much on Cicero and Bk. II of his *De divinatione*, where the sceptical speaker is correctly taken as himself, cf. Linderski (1982) 37 and passim or Schofield (1986) 56 (Beard [1986] being unpersuasive). For an illustrative personality, Hirtius, see above, n. 18.

29. MacMullen (1997) 205f. (with a misprint in the 6th line of note 27, "17–29" where "117–29" is correct). Ibid. Chap. 3 and notes for context. My 1970 essay was then perhaps the longest discussion given to the change and perhaps remains so (updated, 1990, Chap. 11), with no more than Momigliano (1972) for company; and Momigliano's essay, at first praised though not profited from, soon sank out of sight (never quoted by the dozen or more scholars describing historiography of the late period, in the volume of Marasco [2003]).

30. The relation between the Christian elite and their heritage of non-Christian knowledge has been a hundred times explored; for the hostile side of the relation and its effects, see MacMullen (1997) 88ff. with notes; and a suggestive bit of evidence, that in the

province best attested, Egypt, the learned become "a niche-group" and " 'the output of papyri shows a dramatic falling-off after A.D. 300 which presumably reflects the general decay of Hellenism.' From the fourth century on the level of illiteracy becomes very high" — so, Messeri and Pintaudi (1998) 50, quoting other scholars.

31. *Civ. dei* 15.22, the *filii dei* and *illae seductae feminae* in Gen. 6.2; then (15.23, *CSEL* 40, 2.110) on Silvanuses and Pans (the one, common Gallic deities; the other, mainland Greek). Cf. Just., *Apol.* 2.5, anticipating Augustine. But Augustine is unhappy with Genesis and suggests ways of getting around its words, pp. 110f. (and he has much to say about demons in this work and elsewhere).

32. Gelasius, *HE* 2.13.1–7; Greg. Nyss., *Vita S. Macrinae*, *PG* 46.968C; Lavenant (1963) 811, 813; Hansen (1902) 48f.; Wipszycka (1992) 96; above, Chap. 1 n. 11; for the warning that ascetics should not do much reading, not even of the bible, to insure the simplicity of their thought, cf. Lavenant (1963) 811, 813; and many other references in MacMullen (1990) chap. 11 passim with notes (on anti-intellectualism, esp. pp. 124ff.) and (1997) 212f.; on the new meaning of "philosophize", *philosophein*, ibid. and (1984) 149.

33. Soz., *HE* 8.11.1f., most monks' reasoning very crude "from their simple-minded-ness"; their *simplicitas* noted in emperor Marcian's letter, Schwartz (1914–40) 2, 5, pp. 3f.; Bacht (1953) 233 on monks as links to "the people" and (248) their "Anti-Intellektual-ismus"; they are forbidden to read, part of the "marked anti-intellectualism" among them noted by Wipszycka (1992) 96. Eutyches' illiteracy is brought out by an accuser, below, Chap. 7 §3. He is described as not very bright, "un esprit médiocre", Hefele (1907–09) 2.504, along the lines of Leo, *Ep.* 35 and 88, *impudentissimus senex* and *stultissimus homo*, quoted in Vries (1975) 360.

34. Guy (1993) passim.

35. Guy (1993) 1.149–81 passim; *phobos tou Theou*, there throughout and at 118, 204, and passim.

36. Practices to eat little, often competitive among monks (and competition itself to be controlled), were universal in the ascetic/monastic movement, as everyone knows, cf. e.g. Butler (1904) 48, 71f.; Lietzmann (1908) 3; Delehaye (1923) 58 §58f.; or Canivet and Leroy-Molinghen (1977–79) 1.251 and 2.167f.

37. *Apophthegmata patrum* of Macarius the Egyptian, *PG* 65.268C, 288B, 293B, and 260Df.

38. Lietzmann (1908) 30.

39. Reff. to the ill-repute of monks and their rioting in MacMullen (1997) 16 with notes, and 171; further, Aug., *De opere monachorum* 28 (*PL* 40.575), *tam multos hypo-critas sub habitu monachorum*, etc.; a coercive force at Ephesus II, Schwartz (1914–40) 2, 3, 1, p. 50, and Chadwick (2001) 561; at Edessa the same year, Sellers (1961) 55; effective in riots in Jerusalem AD 451, Evagrius, *HE* 2.5, and Hamilton and Brooks (1899) 50, 53; bloody riots in Cple AD 512, ibid. 180; riots in 518–20, Baus et al. (1981) 435; in Cple AD 536, Mansi (1759–63) 8.927Ef. and their pressure on the emperor (quoted), Schwartz (1914–40) 1, 1, 2, p. 65.

40. Hamilton and Brooks (1899) 72, on Timothy Ailouros; ibid. 114, on Peter the Iberian; and A. Martin (1985) 237 and (quoted, regarding Anthony) 286. For the ability to work miracles as a sure sign of the possession of the Pneuma within one, see e.g. Günther (1895–98) 28, or Nagel (1966) 71.

41. Mansi (1759–63) 5.284; 282D, quoted; above, Chap. 3 n. 13 for similar views.

42. Mansi (1759–63) 7.23 (the ascetic monk Jacob addressed as well, among sixty-odd metropolitans); Marcian and Juvenal of Jerusalem write to monks, Schwartz (1914–40) 2, 5, pp. 4f, 9; and Evagrius, *HE* 2.10, where Symeon supporting Chalcedon argues only from numbers: so many bishops couldn't be wrong! On the belief that extreme ascetics could claim inspiration by the Pneuma, see Bacht (1953) 258; more broadly, their reporting that their access to God, who shares his thoughts in a conversation with them or a vision, gives them authority (Rousseau [1978] 27, 29, 42, 101; authority even in doctrinal questions, p. 30).

43. Gain (1985) 35f., 65f., monks as *chorespiscopi* in Anatolia; Nestorius once a monk, Moffett (1998) 172; Egyptian monks as bishops, Brakke (1995) 199ff.; on Dioscorus, S. J. Davis (2004) 68ff.; Barsumas invited to Chalcedon with nearly 100 of the city's monks, their names duly tallied, Schwartz (1914–40) 2, 3, 1, pp. 46, 169, and below, Chap. 7 at n. 50; monks present in council, AD 532, ibid. 4, 2, p. 170; one particular monastery at Cple termed "the dominant theological influence" on the court from the AD 440s, Gray (1979) 24f.; and prominence for Gerontius, archimandrite, the almoner and biographer of Melania, Kidd (1927) 5; Euthymius, archimandrite in Jerusalem, consulted on doctrine by the empress Eudoxia in AD 451, Smith and Wace (1877–87) 2.398f.; as bishops, such better-known figures as Sergius and James Baradaeus, ibid. 1.329; the great Severus of Antioch, ibid. 4.637, and his predecessor Flavian (AD 498–512), Evagrius, *HE* 3.32; early ones in *PG* 25.524–33, cited by Chadwick (1993) 49; many post-Chalcedon ex-monk bishops in Bacht (1953) passim, esp. 302f.; ibid. 283, ref. to "the obligatory year of ascetic practice [in a monastery, here, in the first decade of the sixth century] for one who would be a bishop, later," and (303) anticipating Meyendorff (1981) 27, "the episcopate reserved exclusively to monks"; for the western empire, some examples in Chadwick cit. p. 60 n. 21.

Chapter 5: The violent element

1. My primary-source dossier is in four parts: MacMullen (1990) 388f., (1997) 170, (2003) 492f., and the further items collected in this note. First, the general lament of a bishop in the AD 450s, Nau (1919) 214, 217, "How many thousands in the wake of [Chalcedon] have been killed for Christ in Alexandria, Egypt, Jerusalem. . . . What country, what city does not recall the deaths inflicted since then, to the present day, among the lambs of Christ, and the sentences of exile and confiscation of property" among bishops? Then, in more specific contexts, in **Egypt**, "deaths even of bishops" in the AD 330s, *Coll. antiariana parisina, Decretum sinodi orientalium apud Serdicam* 6 (*CSEL* 65.53), Athanasius' doing; more deaths in custody, *CSEL* 65.128; in **Alexandria** in AD 347, the bishop killed, Theodoret, *HE* 2.4; many victims of a ferocious bishop in AD 350s, Theodoret, *HE* 2.14.8f.; AD 457, a soldier kills the bishop in his church, Schwartz (1914–40) 2, 5, pp. 61, 78, and 124; AD 450s, many burnt to death, Evagr., *HE* 2.5 (Bidez and Parmentier [1964] 51), and "slaughters were matters of daily occurrence", Hamilton and Brooks (1899) 65; thousands of victims of General Narses in AD 536, Stein (1949–59) 2.384; "massacres" in the province generally in AD 530s, Pietri (1998) 408; at **Ephesus** in the 430s, *Mandatum gestum ab orientalibus* (to Cple), Schwartz (1914–40) 1, 3, p. 178, "bishops and clergy died"; in the AD 440s, Mansi (1759–63)

7.274, "many" killed; again, in Schwartz (1914–40) 2, 1, p. 404; again, Schwartz 2, 3, 3, p. 61; in **Antioch**, bishop Stephen accused of Nestorianism, exonerated at a council, cruelly killed for it at mass along with clergy, see Günther (1895–98) 148, Simplicius pope, *Ep.* 15.1 (Thiel [2004] 203), and Placanica (1997) 20; later, Victor Tunnunensis, *Chron.*, AD 479; "many" deaths AD 531, Malal., *Chron.* 18.64 (Thurn [2000] 391), cf. Stein (1949–59) 377; priest killed by patriarch, AD 538, Brooks (1924) 523; in other parts of the **East**, monks killed by troops at Neapolis (Palestine), Hamilton and Brooks (1899) 53, AD 450s; in the 2nd decade of the sixth century in **Syria**, attacks on monasteries, many monks slain, and some local civilian or official "Faustus committed all the murders, he killed tens of thousands", Schwartz (1914–40) 3, pp. 103 and 107 with Devreesse (1945) 70 and Pietri (1998) 135; priests and monks burnt alive in Amida, AD 537, Brooks (1924) 524; in mid-fifth century, a presbyter killed, Mansi (1759–63) 236; report of "many drowned" in Syria, Soc., *HE* 4.2.7; a bishop of Mopsuestia dies in imprisonment in the mid-fifth century, Chadwick (2001) 547; those seen as heretics in AD 530s burnt alive, Pietri (1998) 408; in **Constantinople** in AD 340s, "many killed", Soz., *HE* 3.9.3; at sea, 80 clergy drowned, Greg., Naz., *Or.* 33.4 (*PG* 36.220Af.); in AD 401/2, "some on both sides" killed in rioting, Soc., *HE* 6.8 (*PG* 67.689C); a monk beheaded in AD 516 (518?), Evagr., *HE* 3.44 (Bidez and Parmentier [1964] 146) and Malal., *Chron.* 16.19 (Thurn [2000] 334), along with the repression of the disorders, some of the rioters drowned, others executed, "a number beyond counting"; in **Italy**, bishop killed by a mob in Aquileia in the AD 330s, *Ep. synodi Sardiacensis ad Julium papam* 4 (*PL* 8.921); a presbyter killed in a riot in Ostia in the AD 370s, *Günther* (1895–98) 29; deaths in rioting in Rome AD 502, Mommsen (1894) 429, cf. Duchesne (1955) 1.49, *quanta homicidia*, and p. 99, "slaughter and killings among the clergy"; clergy killed in southern Italy in the AD 490s, Gelasius pope, *Ep.* 37, Thiel (2004) 450; in **Gaul**, clergy killed at Tolosa in the AD 350s, Hilary, *Contra Constantium* 11; church servant beaten to death in **Spain**, and by a bishop's act an imprisoned senator dies, Günther (1895–98) 27, AD 370s; many killed in AD 347/8 by a troop commander in north **Africa** (Numidia), *Passio Marculi* (*PL* 8.760) and *Passio Maximiani et Isaac* (*PL* 8.770); victims of massacres, Maier (1987–89) 1.199f.; and "the killings of the martyrs," *quantus sanguis christianus effusus* at the hands of a string of fourth century persecuting officials, Lancel (1972–91) 3.1216f.

2. Quoted, Liebeschuetz (1972) 126 and Cameron (1976) 185, 192. On killings in Antioch, cf. above, note 1, and Euseb., *Vita Const.* 3.59ff.; Soc. *HE* 1.24.5f.; 4.17; Soz., *HE* 6.18.1; Evagr., *HE* 3.10; 3.32; later, Palladius, *Dial.* 16. 113, 124f., and Victor Tunnunensis, *Chron.*, Placanica (1997) 20.

3. McLynn (1992) addressed by MacMullen (2003) 493ff. Compare Chadwick (2001) 588, "lives were lost" in a collision in Alexandria that sounds rather tame, and the brutal truth in Meyendorff (1989) 190, "troops put down the opposition at the cost of 10,000 victims" (the source is Zach. Rhet., in Hamilton and Brooks [1899] 76, where I prefer the variant reading, note 7, that shows the losses were suffered among the unarmed). For the name-calling that violence gave rise to — "violators of virgins" or "of holy shrines", "barbarians", "brigands", etc., if reference is to doctrinal antagonists, or most commonly "martyrs" and "champions of true religion" if one's friends — see Gaddis (1999) in a basically philological treatment.

4. Army units in towns and cities, MacMullen (1988) 145f.; instances showing how a local bishop had the local troop commander in his pocket, in *Collectanea antiariana parisina, Decretum sinodi apud Serdicam 6* (*CSEL* 65.53) and *Ep. synodi Sardicensis 3* (*CSEL* 65.111) concerning Athanasius and again in Theodoret, *HE* 2.14.8f. (Alexandria AD 357); AD 420s, Antioch's bishop directs the local commander to clear the city of a sect seen as undesirable, Stoop (1911) 690; Leo magnus, *Ep.* 10.6 (*PL* 54.633C, 637Af.), Hilary's use of troops; in AD 434 an army commander writes to an eastern bishop telling him to enforce credal conformity by use of "the most devoted troops in that same city", Schwartz (1914–40) 1, 4, p. 200; bishops throughout the east must anathematize Nestorian teachings, enforced methodically by the government in AD 435, Schwartz (1914–40) 1, 4, pp. 204f., 206; or Hamilton and Brooks (1899) 48 (Alexandria in the AD 450s) and 52f., the bishop of Jerusalem has an army at his beck (AD 453?); cf. Schwartz (1914–40) 1, 1, 3, p. 23, "we [bishops] greeted the soldiers in civil fashion, since in fact they were acquainted with bishop Commodus, In-All-Things-Holy-to-God, through their being barracked in the city, and they restrained all the clergy who were in a rage against us." For denial of army role, but tons of counter-evidence, cf. P. Brown's views addressed in MacMullen (2003) 480, to which much more can be added: e.g., Theodoret, *HE* 2.8.14; Hilary, *Contra Constantium* 11, "after you [Constantius] had brought to bear all your arms against the faith of the West, you turned your armies against the lambs of Christ"; Alexandrian city leaders call in troops against a bishop, AD 367, *Hist. acephala* 5.12 in A. Martin (1985) 167; Schwartz (1914–40) 1, 1, 2, pp. 10 and 17 and ibid. 1, 1, 5, p. 14, Ephesus AD 431; ibid. 2, 3, 2, p. 20, Chalcedon AD 451; Evagr., *HE* 2.5 (Bidez and Parmentier [1964] 51), AD 451; and general Narses sent with 6,000 men to secure a bishop on his throne, but killing 3,000 supporters of his rival in the process, AD 535, Meyendorf (1989) 225.

5. Chadwick (1980) 8 (the italics my own), repeating Socrates' opinion; Augustine and Chrysostom to the same effect, in MacMullen (2003) 487; Soz., *HE* 6.24.2, Milan AD 370s, where the defeated party "threatened to do whatever *usually* happens in such disorders" (my italics); Schwartz (1914–40) 2, 1, 3, p. 478, throughout much of the eastern empire, the death of a bishop is the occasion for "rioting, often"; and Jones (1964) 918, balancing the attested bloodshed at episcopal elections with orderly ones "more usually".

6. Sources for Rome (*caedes* etc.) in MacMullen (1990) 388 n. 32; disputed thrones, ibid. 390 nn. 41, 44, with incidents of violent conflict in Cyzicus, Cple, Antioch, Jerusalem, Edessa, Nicomedia, and Alexandria; instances in Chadwick (2001) 492f., 543, 547, 552 (but some references don't check); A. Martin (1985) 160 and 167 and Evagr., *HE* 2.5 and 8, various incidents in Alexandria; Hamilton and Brooks (1899) 65, Alexandria; Soz., *HE* 3.9.3, Cple; and from the western provinces, *Ep. synodi Sardiacensis ad Julium papam 4* (*PL* 8.921); Leo magnus, *Ep.* 10.6 and 12.1 (*PL* 54.633C and 646Af.), with "hideous tumult and savage disorders" (*Ep.* 12.7, 653B); Mommsen (1894) 429, Pietri (1998) 293, and Duchesne (1955) 1.46; and Pietri et al. (1992) 386ff. (north Africa and Gaul of fifth century).

7. Hier., *Altercatio Luciferiani* 19 (*CCSL* 79b.50).

8. Many instances of cruel treatment of uncooperative bishops and repeated exiles in MacMullen (2003) 482.

9. As illustrative, the exiling of 70 bishops through lobbying of the emperor by the bishop of Ancyra, Philostorgius, *HE* 4.8.

10. Basil, *Contra Eunomium* 1 (*PG* 45.288Df.); cf. Soc., *HE* 4.2.6.

11. Meyendorff (1989) 146.

12. Schwartz (1914–40) 1, 4, pp. 203f., in AD 435; Gray (1979) 47, quoting Michael the Syrian.

13. *Hist. acephala* 4.5 in A. Martin (1985) 154, the Cple bishop deposed 18 bishops; cf. Theodoret, *HE* 2.14.11, AD 357 in Alexandria; the Serdica council deposes ten bishops, *Coll. Antiariana Parisina. Ep. synodi Sardicensis* 7 (*CSEL* 65.119); John Chrysostom packs off 15 Asian bishops on his visit there, Schwartz (1914–40) 2, 3, 3, p. 62; Chalcedon deposes six very great bishops, Schwartz 2, 3, 1, p. 258; and the Alexandrian bishop asserts his powers through mass exiles, AD 452, Hamilton and Brooks (1899) 48.

14. Epiphanius, *Panarion* 72.7.2, bishop of Caesarea writes to Basil of Ancyra, "You should have your tongue cut out"; actual punishments of the sort, Victor Tunnunensis, *Chron.* a. 479, and others in MacMullen (2003) 479.

15. *Collectanea antiariana parisina. Ep. synodi Sardicensis* 6 (*CSEL* 65.111); Theodoret, *HE* 2.8.13; Schwartz (1914–40) 1, 3, p. 47.

16. Schwartz (1914–40) 2, 1, p. 404 and ibid. 2, 3, 3, pp. 53f., Bassianus accusing Stephen; his reply, ibid. pp. 54f. (*eranarii*, more commonly *arenarii*).

17. MacMullen (1990) 390 n. 41.

18. Soc., *HE* 6.8.7f.

19. To sample, skim *Cod. Theod.* 16.5 plus *Sirm.* 12 and 14, *Nov. Theod.* 3, and *Nov. Val.* 18, which all together carry the thunder through a century, with terms like *monstrous, pernicious, depraved, perverse, impious, abominable, execrable, noxious,* and *nefarious*; nouns like *madness, pestilence, poison, perfidy, insanity,* and *contagion*; and cf. above, Chap. 3 n. 47.

20. Joh. Chrysos., *PG* 60.225f. or 63.512; many other references in MacMullen (1990) 271 with nn. 46f.

21. Soz., *HE* 4.28.6f.

22. Flemming (1914–17) 131–133, acclamations read aloud at Ephesus II.

23. Schwartz (1914–40) 1, 1, 4, p. 10; more the next day, pp. 11f.

24. MacMullen (2003) 483, Chrysostom's words; pp. 479, 482, more clergy in physical violence; the assumption of violence and sectarian murderers among those attending a council, or the credibility of the charge, at Serdica AD 341, *Collectanea antiariana parisina* 19.1 (*CSEL* 65.60); Schwartz (1914–40) 1, 1, 5, p. 119, at Ephesus I, Cyril's party physically shove the presiding official out of the meeting *meth'hybreos*; ibid. 2, 3, 3, p. 36 (Ibas is the bishop).

25. Chalcedon in the fall of 431, after Ephesus I, Schwartz (1914–40) 1, 1, 7, p. 80, the writer Theodoret, the historian, being bishop of the little Syrian town Cyrrhus — a moderate and so attacked as a trimmer in the dispute between Nestorius and Cyril. He and other Easterners of the Antiochene party were there under a sort of house arrest. His application of bribes, *multa pecunia . . . multae auri librae*, to the pleading of his case at court outraged a fellow bishop, Acacius, ibid. 1, 4, p. 85. For a vivid scene exactly similar to the one quoted, in Cple after Ephesus I, where a great crowd of chanting monks approach the palace, a deputation is let in, it emerges soon to report on the audience, and then all repair to a church to hear read aloud the council reports in the emperor's hands, and the

deputation's comments, see Mansi (1759–63) 4.1428C–1429D = Schwartz (1914–40) 1, 1, 2, p. 68.

26. *Voces, phonai*, Schwartz (1914–40) 3, pp. 85ff.

27. Arson examples in *Collectanea antiariana parisina. Ep. synodi Sardicensis* 3 (*CSEL* 65.111), churches burnt in Egypt, and *Decretum sinodi apud Serdicam* 9 (*CSEL* 65.54), homes burnt in Ancyra; Soc., *HE* 4.22.6, "unspeakable devastation" in Egypt; of Cple churches, Soz., *HE* 4.20.3; Theodoret, *HE* 4.11.3; Evagrius, *HE* 3.44 (Bidez and Parmentier [1964] 146), AD 518 in Cple; more examples in MacMullen (1990) 393 n. 56 and (2003) 491; but destruction in what amounted to warfare against monasteries, Schwartz 3, p. 107.

28. *Stasis* with or without its brother-term "riot", *tarache*, in Soc., *HE* 1.24.5, Antioch AD 328; 2.6.1f.; Soz., *HE* 3.20.8, Antioch AD 340s; 4.15.5, Rome AD 350s; 5.13.2, Antioch AD 362; 8.6.6, Cple; Soc., *HE* 2.44.5f., Cple 350s; Basil, *Epp.* 230 and 240.2 (Nicopolis), 240, 258, Caesarea; Philostorgius, *HE* 9.13, Cyzicus AD 370s; Chadwick (2001) 351, 353, 368, Milan AD 370s; p. 417, Laodicea AD 362; p. 418, Antioch with four competing bishops in place in the 370s; D. H. Williams (1995) 74, Parma AD 378; Schwartz (1914–40) 1, 1, 3, p. 47; Hamilton and Brooks (1899) 67, Alexandria AD 450s; p. 50, Jerusalem AD 450s; Malal., *Chron* 16.19, Cple AD 512; Victor Tunnunensis, *Chron.* a. 539, Placanica (1997) 42, Alexandria; and above, in the references for violence amounting to death, and at episcopal elections.

29. Greg. Naz., *De vita sua* 1325ff. (*PG* 37.1120f.), AD 380 in Cple.

30. Quoted on the Roman bishop's *Tomos*, the *Chron. paschale*, Dindorf (1832) 1.629. To the many laws and actions instanced in MacMullen (1984) 124 and 164 and (1997) 162, add R. Williams (2001) 78, Constantine's edict for the burning of Arian documents and execution of owners of them; *Collectio antiarana parisina Frg. A* 27 (*CSEL* 65.66), vs. synodal letters in AD 360; Schwartz (1914–40) 1, 4, p. 204, vs. Nestorius' bks; Flemming (1914–17) 155, AD 449 vs. Dioscorus; Soz., *HE* 1.21.4; Mansi (1759–63) 9.250 vs. Nestorius; Schwartz (1914–40) 1, 1, 3, p. 69 AD 435 vs. Nestorius; ibid. 4, 2, p. 68, AD 520s vs. Nestorius; Mansi (1759–63) 8.1153; and Günther (1895–98) 292, vs. Nestorius.

31. Ecclesiastical bribes in the *Collectio Casinensis: Ep. Melketii*, Schwartz (1914–40) 1, 4, p. 155, "a thoroughly theatrical demonstration in support of John [bishop of Antioch, at Cple] in return for money paid down"; Ps.-Zach., Hamilton and Brooks (1899) 169, the bishop of Cple bribes the Master of Offices, AD 511; other examples and Cyril's in MacMullen (1988) 165f.; add, as not a secret, the mention in a contemporary sermon, Schwartz (1914–40) 1, 5, p. 43, the injured bishop saying to Cyril, "don't wound me with golden arrows, I have no golden arrows." Hefele (1907–09) 2.377 explains, "these presents [to Theodosius II] would not constitute any corrupt inducement; they are no more than a recommendation, entirely justified, in favor of a cause that might be just" (an interpretation of a sort offered by other scholars in those pages where the "presents" receive mention at all).

Chapter 6: Preliminaries

1. On Aurelian, cf. Chap. 3 n. 8 (not a doctrinal matter); for councils summoned by emperors (underlined in the list in Chap. 1, above) I draw only on Hefele. There may be

one or two more emperor-summoned councils that I've missed. Diospolis (Lydda, AD 415) has left some *acta*, but was not theological nor emperor-summoned.

2. At Nicaea, one or possibly three western bishops, Kretschmar (1961) 45; Ortiz de Urbina (1963) 139 or Chadwick (2001) 472, none at Cple AD 381; Kelly (1950) 281 and 309f., Sirmium II and Cple AD 381 wholly eastern; on the latter council, Taylor (1981) 48; Chadwick (2001) 534, Ephesus I "certainly not ecumenical", cf. the list containing only one westerner, a deacon, Schwartz (1914–40) 1, 1, 1, pp. 1–9; Camelot (1962) 120 on the fourth-century western paucity, with only two western bishops at Chalcedon present by accident; Evans (1996) 293 n. 20 on Chalcedon; on the eastern domination in AD 533, Treadgold (1997) 210; Justinian's manhandling of the western church, see e.g. Meyendorff (1989) 237–41, and the mere 3 (or 6) western bishops among some 150 at the council AD 553, Rome unrepresented, Hefele (1907–09) 3.65 and Gray (1979) 68. It is rare for emperor and pope to propose or discuss doctrine in concert, as in Coleman Norton (1966) 1149f. — though emperors of course legislated a great deal against perceived heresies. On western councils' reception of easterners, aside from the clear hostility in AD 359, see AD 345 at Milan, Alzati (1993) 61.

3. Mansi (1759–63) 8.969B; but notice from even the earliest years of my period of study how Eusebius "treats Constantine and the Logos as relatively equal coordinates", H. A. Drake cited in D. B. Martin (2004) 220.

4. Soc., *HE* 1.6.33 — so bishops of many other churches paid court to Eusebius of Nicomedia.

5. First description of councils as *ecumenical*, Chadwick (2001) 205, who (1972) explains the usage, not in terms of common speech (as I think is most likely) but in terms of a certain vaunting theatrical association of earlier times; and claims might not be accepted, as e.g. the ecumenicity of the council of Cple AD 381, self-proclaimed, Mansi (1759–63) 3.557, but still denied by the popes of the later fifth century, Konstantinidis (1982) 84, and recognized only in the sixth, Duval (1981) 69. Ephesus I (the Egyptian party of Cyril) claims to be ecumenical, Schwartz (1914–40) 1, 1, 3, p. 12, the synodal letter making quite untrue claims of representation from "the whole West"; 1, 3, p. 47, which Candidianus denies in a letter to Cyril, ibid. 1, 4, p. 32, *particularis . . . [ne] particularis quasdam synodos fieri, quod maxime in haereses et schismata convertere religionem nostram . . .* , lines 3, 9; in other letters, p. 33 lines 2 and 20; in contrast, the self-description by the Antiochene party "meeting by God's grace in Ephesus according to the letters/summons of our Emperors Most Pious and Beloved-of-Christ," ibid. 1, 4, pp. 36f.; cf. Nestorius' contesting of the Egyptian claim, Driver and Hodgson (1925) 129, 167. There is of course the dispute to the present day, whether the Egyptian group was "ecumenical", cf. e.g. Camelot (1962) 62 defining the word in terms of Rome's support, vs. Chadwick (2001) 534.

6. *Catholic* doctrine prescribed in laws from AD 326, *CT* 16.5.1, 4, etc., but rare in the *Code* after AD 383; claimed at Serdica AD 343, Athanasius, *De synodis* 26 (*PG* 26.728); but only falsely claimed by those whom "heretics" condemn, Günther (1895–98) 36 (Luciferians AD 384); discussion à propos AD 411 Carthage, Lancel (1972–91) 1.228f. and Shaw (1995) XI pp. 11f. *Orthodoxy* is claimed for the church represented at a council of the AD 340s, Athanasius, *De synodis* 26 (*PG* 26.728C); by the bishops of AD 381 at Cple, Theodoret, *HE* 5.8 (*PG* 82.1212B); for Chalcedon, Schwartz (1914–40) 2,

3, 2, pp. 6f., 17, and by its opponents, a bishop of Moesia, ibid. 1, 4, p. 114, and of Alexandria (Timothy), Nau (1919) 202f., 211, 237, 241; Dindorf (1832) 632, 636, imperial edict AD 523; claimed by the bishop of Antioch and fellow Monophysites, AD 530s, Brooks (1903) 8, 13, 51; and claimed in mutual name-calling, AD 532, Brock (1981) 94ff.

7. Humfress (2000) 144.

8. Soz., *HE* 2.28.5, Constantine on horseback near Cple where "suddenly in mid-highway Athanasius approached me [the emperor explains in a letter] with his retinue"; ibid. 8.13.4 (cf. Soc., *HE* 6.8), "the empress in her progress one day . . . in her royal chariot" was accosted on behalf of a church dispute; and, quoted, *First Arian Petition to Jovian* (*PG* 26.820). Add to this last Soc., *HE* 3.24.2, Jovian besieged by bishops' lobbying; similarly, Valens a little later, 4.2.2. Petitions for a balance of representation, i. e. a bishop to be appointed, were frequent, e.g. at Cple from monks in the AD 430s against a ban in local churches on the preaching of a creed opposed by the emperor, Schwartz (1914–40) 1, 1, 5, p. 8.

9. Brown (1970) 332; Lancel (1972–91) 1.25, 29; 2.564; the term *Caecilianist* used by Donatists of their opponents, ibid. 3.1005, 1078; refusal of the latter to share their petition, 3.1018–28, 1034, 1108f.; Donatist suspicions of their opponents' *mendacia* and *quod clementissimo imperatori mentiti sunt*, 3.1052, 1104; and the division a "heresy", Caecilianists *haeretici*, as the Donatists make plain, 3.1168. I don't assume a Donatist petition would have been more fair and even-handed than the Caecilianists'.

10. Basil, *Contra Eunomium* 1 (*PG* 29.505A), of the Cple council of AD 360.

11. MacMullen (1988) 241, with the Serdican can. 7.

12. D. H. Williams (1995) 176; Ambrose, *Ep.* 1 *extra collectionem, CSEL* 82 = Zelzer [1982] 330 §8, 352 §10, describing what Williams rightly calls "the trap"; 359 §54, *sine concilio orientali vobis non respondemus*; Gryson (1981a) 138; Gryson(1980a) 304, Ambrose dominant with his dozen local Italian bishops, and (p. 81) Palladius in his late seventies, writing (p. 83) his refutation of Ambrose's *De fide* in AD 379; on the trap and the nature of the attendance, pp. 130ff.; mis-reading by Savon (1997) 120 (supposing Palladius was the first to speak to Gratian); further, on the pliability of the participants, pp. 121, 124.

13. Examples of emperors deceived on church matters (as on others), MacMullen (1988) 147 with nn. 71–73; Lancel (1972–91) 2.675; 3.1032, "adversaries are always eager to twist into the emperor's ears unproven charges against their adversaries;" Mansi 4.1429C, the emperor amazed at mis-information about Ephesus I; Soc., *HE* 4.2.3, 4.4.3, and 4.6.4, Valens misled; or Justinian, see Liberatus, *Breviarium causae Nestorianorum et Eutychianorum* 24 (*PL* 68.1049Bf.), on the *dolum dolosorum*, "the trick of all tricks".

14. Carthage, the Donatists get no attendance from Caecilian, Fischer and Lumpe (1999) 416f.; at Cple (AD 335/6), only anti-Athanasian participants, Ortiz de Urbina (1963) 125; at Seleuceia AD 359, Soc., *HE* 2.39.20, the minority secede and lose out; Serdica, Theodoret, *HE* 2.8.7f., quoted; at The Oak AD 403, 29 out of 36 participants are Egyptian and so hostile to the target of the meeting, who defies it, Chadwick (2001) 494; or again at Cple AD 536, the bishop of Trapezus won't respond to a summons and is deposed, Mansi 8.929, 936–48.

15. Schwartz (1914–40) 1, 1, p. 116.

16. *Collectanea antiariana parisina. Ep. Synodi Sardicensis* 7 (*CSEL* 65.120) = Theodoret, *HE* 2.8.30.

17. At Sirmium AD 359, Sulpicius Sev., *Chron.* 2.41.1 (*acciti aut coacti*) and 2.42.1.

18. Soz., *HE* 8.16.3, for judgement on Chrysostom.

19. Schwartz (1914–40) 1, 1, 1, p. 115, Theodosius' letter to Cyril saying he should bring "a few, *oligous*, such as seems good to you from the province under your authority"; and Chadwick (2001) 534. Compare the specification of only three delegates from each see to annual provincial synods, Munier (1974) 34, Hippo can. 5a. The importance of the imperially authorized invitation list was understood, cf. e.g. Hilary, *Contra Constantium* 12, on the council of Seleuceia AD 359, "where there were as many blasphemers as Constantius chose", cf. Sulpicius Sev., *Chron.* 2.41.1, equal imperial control over the council of Ariminum of the same year.

20. Flemming (1914–17) 3, the Egyptian contingent being clear as nos. 92–113.

21. Fischer and Lumpe (1999) 433, to Rome; Turner (1899–1939) 1.377; Sulpicius Sev., *Chron.* 2.41f. (*PL* 20.152Cf.); and Theodoret, *HE* 1.7.2.

22. Bishops meet in a palace at Nicaea (Theodoret, *HE* 1.7.7) and lodge in one at Serdica (the eastern), with a fancy banquet, Barnard (1983) 48, and Hamilton and Brooks (1899) 49.

23. I offer a survey of provincial government palaces in *Athenaeum* 54 (1976) 30–36; at Serdica, Athanasius, *Hist. Arian.* 15 (*PG* 25.709D); for the attendance, Chadwick (2001) 242 (with about 75 eastern bishops); a split also at Seleuceia, ibid. 288 and Devreesse (1945) 14; one part of the Orientals cut off the other from attendance, Theodoret, *HE* 2.8.29.

24. Soz., *HE* 8.17.4, AD 402; the term *tagma* for a church faction in, e.g., Epiphanius, *Panarion* 73.27.6, or in Latin, *pars*, Sulpicius Sev., *Chron.* 2.41.3, 2.43.3, etc., or *factio*, Hilary, *Contra Const.* 2. Notice at Edessa (Chap. 2, above, at n. 18) the town's laity caucused in little groups to decide on the wording of their shouts, *psephismata*, which they had written out for presentation to the presiding official, cf. Flemming (1914–17) 21.

25. For a rough estimate of Oriental sees, cf. Chap. 1 n. 4; references to "Orientals" appear at least as early as AD 345 at Milan, Alzati (1993) 59; Hilary, *Contra Const.* 12, AD 359; Damasus, *Ep.* 2 frg. 2 (*PL* 13.353) on the council at Antioch of AD 376 with signatures of 152 *Orientales episcopi*; Zelzer (1982) 331; Epiphan., *Adv. haer.* 16 (*PG* 42.433); Schwartz (1914–40) 1, 1, 3, p. 51; 1, 1, 4, p. 35; 1, 1, 5, p. 119; 2, 3, 2, p. 17; 4, 2, pp. 184, etc.; Evagr., *HE* (Bidez and Parmentier [1964] 85); and so on, later.

26. For example, Athanasius, *De synodis* 15 (*PG* 26.705C), *hoi peri Eusebion*; Evagrius, *HE* 1.3, 1.10, etc., *amph'auton*.

27. Schwartz (1914–40) 2, 3, 2, pp. 116f., concluding, *omnes Aegyptiacae regionis insurgunt in nos. Ergo miseremini nostrae senectutis.*

28. Sulpicius Sev., *Chron.* 2.43.2, AD 359; Soc., *HE* 4.6.6, and Soz., *HE* 6.8.5, AD 364 at Cyzicus; or Hamilton and Brooks (1899) 52, AD 451.

29. MacMullen (2003) 140f.; Brooks (1903) 51; Hamilton and Brooks (1899) 47, "and he wept much, as did also others" at Chalcedon, being terrified into denying their faith.

Chapter 7: Councils in action

1. *Secretarium* = hearings-hall in Arsinoë, PRyl 653, AD 321, with explanation of the term in Lancel (1972–91) 1.52; a council meeting of 70 in an obviously very grand private house in Carthage, in AD 309/10, Fischer and Lumpe (1997) 416f.; at Serdica in the parish church of St. Vitus, Barnard (1983) 33; at Ariminum AD 359, meeting in the local church, Hier., *Altercatio Luciferiani* 18 (*CCSL* 79b.44); at Aquileia in AD 381 "in the church in the *secretarium*," Gryson (1980a) 274 and Cuscito (1982) 206; at Cple AD 381, the sessions begin in the palace, Ortiz de Urbina (1963) 169; at Cple in the baptistery of St. Sophia for smaller groups in AD 394 and 450, Mouterde (1930) 38; at Carthage AD 411 in the *secretarium* of the Gargilian Baths, Lancel (1972–91) 2.558; at Carthage AD 419 in the *secretarium basilicae Fausti*, Turner (1899–1939) 1.566; at Berytus AD 448 in "the New Church", Mansi (1759–63) 7.211; at Cple AD 448 in the *secretarium* of the bishop's residence, Schwartz (1914–40) 2, 1, 1, pp. 123 and 137 and 2, 3, 1, p. 116; in the patriarch's *secretarium* or the baptistery of the main church, May (1989) 9 or Pietri (1998) 47; at Arles in AD 449, the *secretarium basilicae, Institutio SS. episcoporum in causa insulae Lerinensis, CCSL* 148.133; at Cple in AD 449, a meeting "in the Great Portico of the Holy Church", Schwartz 2, 3, 1, p. 131; at Ephesus I under Cyril, 100+ in St. Mary's church, Schwartz 2, 3, 2, p. 3, called *theotokos,* ibid. 1, 1, 1, p. 8, and then moved to the patriarch's residence, Chadwick (2001) 532 and Camelot (1962) 55; at Rome AD 499, meeting in St. Peter's, Mommsen (1894) 399; at Rome AD 502 in the Sessorian palace, *Acta synhodorum habitarum Romae a. DI, MGH AA* 12.428 (see below); a dozen invited meet with Justinian in the Hormisdas Palace of Cple, AD 532, Brock (1981) 92 or Evans (1996) 111, and in the "heptaconch triclinium", Schwartz (1914–40) 4, 2, p. 169; at Chalcedon in St. Euphemia, Camelot (1962) 121; at Cple council AD 536 in the *mesaulus dytticus* of St. Mary's, Mansi (1759–63) 8.873; and AD 553 in the *secretarium* of St. Sophia, with 150+, Meyendorff (1989) 241.

2. Fischer and Lumpe (1999) 168, AD 251; 264f., AD 256, with "a great part of the populace present as well", Soden (1909) 248; Eusebius, *HE* 7.28.1, ca. AD 264; at Elvira AD 305 (? ca. 310), presbyters and deacons present, Batiffol (1913) 7; Arles AD 314, adding exorcists and lectors, a total of 77 lower clergy serving 26 bishops, Turner (1899– 1939) 1.398–414; ca. AD 319 at Alexandria, a synod where 65 deacons and presbyters subscribe, Hansen (1902) 24, 28f.; Aquileia AD 381, Gryson (1980) 282, Gryson (1981a) 138 and Zelzer (1982) 353f.; at Nemausis, AD 394, presbyters and deacons, Hefele (1907–09) 2.92f.; at Carthage AD 411, each bishop with 2 *notarii*, Lancel (1972– 91) 2.576; AD 495, Rome, Gelasius, *Ep.* 30, Thiel (2004) 437; at Cple AD 536, Mansi (1759–63) 8.880 (deacons, subdeacons, *notarii, procuratores et ceteri clerici*), 925, and 968; and attendance by lower clergy a routine, Honigman (1942–43) passim and Sabw Kanyang (2000) 163.

3. A deacon shouts, "I object", Schwartz (1914–40) 2, 1, 1, p. 191 (Hilary); *clerici* shout with others, Mansi 8.968, AD 536.

4. Laity present in mid-third century Carthage, Batiffol (1913) 6; at Nicaea, some lay presence, Guarnieri (1983) 85f., perhaps not during deliberations; at Ariminum AD 359, "crowds of laity", Hier., *Altercatio Luciferiani* 18 (*CCSL* 79b.44); at Ephesus II, "a great throng of seditious folk" drawn in by the president, according to his accuser, Schwartz

(1914–40) 2, 3, 1, p. 41; at Chalcedon, as witnesses only, Evagrius, *HE* 2.18, Bidez and Parmentier (1964) 76; and at western councils of the fifth century, but only magnates, *illustres*, Guarnieri 87f.

5. No one sits if bishops don't, Lancel (1972–91) 1.51; 2.797; 3.924f.; the seats called *thronoi*, Haase (1920) 45, at Nicaea, or at Cple AD 381, Greg. Naz., *De vita sua* 1509ff. (*PG* 37.1134f.), or at Chalcedon, Schwartz (1914–40) 2, 1, p. 369; seated, bishops *considentes*, deacons, etc., *adstantes*, Mansi 8.925, AD 536; other references in Sabw Kanyang (2000) 163f.; yet notice both bishops and presbyters *surgentes in synodo acclamaverunt*, Mansi (1759–63) 8.184.

6. White hair often appealed to, e.g. Schwartz (1914–40) 2, 3, 2, p. 118; and Mansi (1759–63) 8.229, in praise of a truly pious man, "fifty years a catholic and never washing once after his conversion".

7. Krautheimer (1937–77) 1.182 Fig. 108, as the site was in 1756; p. 177 on transformation of part of the palace complex into a church.

8. Hefele (1907–09) 2.298f., 198 bishops after an initial session of 160; on the church, Karwiese (1989) 27f. showing the wrongly accepted Mary-church to postdate both Ephesus I and II, but accepting the stoa as the place of meeting of the fifth century councils and as the shell of the later church, therefore as giving the lateral dimensions; ibid. for the meeting place being open on one side — so I have shown the columns, not a wall, along the north side of the meeting place, and added details from Fig. 14, p. 53, of Foss (1979) and Scherrer (1995) 165.

9. Acoustic difficulties in St. Peter's, preventing "any real discussion" in 1870, Will (2000) 251 (reference courtesy of P. Kiernan).

10. I agree with Camelot (1962) 120 who sets the Chalcedon council numbers at 350–360, without explanation. He must be subtracting the 95 absent signatories (below, at n. 15) from the 452 total. Honigman (1942–43) 43 indicates a total of no more than 300, working from a smaller total of signatures (412); and see Schwartz (1914–40) 2, 3, 2, pp. 72–83, 301 bishops plus seven presbyters signing for bishops. For Alberigo (1991) 75, subscriber lists are incomplete but two other sources say 500 or 600; in Sellers (1961) 104, over 500 or 520 bishops; and Pietri (1998) 75, 79 n. 2: 452 subscribers or alternatively, up to 630 in attendance, the last figure no doubt drawn from the letter of Vigilius of Rome, Günther (1895–98) 231.

11. "The bishop Ambrose said, 'You agree, Palladius'," Zelzer (1982) 357 and passim, every individual bishop and all collectively are called by their title; Gryson (1980a) 141, the deputy-target (as he may be called) *inpar stans iudicaretur*. But, alluding to Ambrose's irregular election, his target and opponent indirectly calls that election in question, Moorehead (1999) 112.

12. Address to a bishop's face as *sublimitas tua, sanctitas et peritia tua*, etc., Lancel (1972–91) 2.620, 622, 630, 632; reference in a bishop's letter to *he thaumasiotes sou*, Calvet-Sebasti and Gatier (1989) 166; Schwartz (1914–40) 1, 1, 3, p. 23, *ton panta theosebastaton episkopon*; bishops refer to a witness, *vir magnificus*, Mansi (1759–63) 8.185; Schwartz 2, 1, p. 279, of officials and the senate in Cple, *megaloprepestatos kai endoxotatos archontes kai hyperphyes synkletos*; *divinus vertex*, the emperor, Schwartz 2, 3, 2, p. 138; *sacratissimi*, etc., 2, 3, 1, p. 44.

13. Secular power deferred to, on secular matters not theological, cf. e.g. Meyendorff

(1989) 26, 32, 35f.; raised seating for dignity's sake, at Aquileia, Gryson (1981) 41; called *bathra*, Theodoret, *HE* 1.7.7; and Frend (1972) 40.

14. Gregory Naz., *De vita sua*, lines 1546ff. (*PG* 37.1135), recalling his surprise at the degree of violence that emerged and the absence of proper piety, *eusebeia*.

15. "Choruses," with *proedroi kai laou didaskaloi*, Greg. Naz., *De vita sua* 1535f. (*PG* 37.1134f.), Cple AD 381; instances of adversaries on each side, Chalcedon in Camelot (1962) 121; in Cple AD 536, Mansi (1759–63) 8.877.

16. Ranking of bishops is clear, e.g., at Ephesus I, where we can compare the quite intelligible order in first mention, Cyril to Acacius of Melitene, seven in all; then the order in which they offer comment, nos. 1, 2, 6, 3, 5, 4, 7; then in their final signing-on, in the order 1, 2, 4, 6, 3, 7, 5, cf. Schwartz (1914–40) 1, 1, 1, pp. 9, 14 and 55f.; ranking at Ephesus II, cf. Honigman (1942–43) 34, showing the presiding Dioscorus of Alexandria, then Rome's legate, then bishops of Jerusalem, Antioch, Ephesus, Caesarea in Cappadocia, etc.; in Chalcedon at Session #1, Rome's legates, bishops of Cple, Alexandria, Antioch, Jerusalem, etc., Schwartz (1914–40) 2, 3, 1, pp. 28, 39.

17. Schwartz (1914–40) 2, 1, 3, pp. 151–55; cf. one patriarch (of Alexandria) accusing another (of Cple) of being so "swollen with pride, he counts on ourselves signing on to his opinion along with everyone else, thanks to his intrigues and the power of his position", *dynasteiai tou thronou*, Mansi (1759–63) 4.1016B; and notice also the Ephesus bishop at Ephesus II signing for his suffragans with his assurances, *engyai*, that they wouldn't suffer for it, Schwartz (1914–40) 2, 1, 1, p. 88; for the practices in the Oriental bloc, ibid. 2, 1, 3, p. 30 [389] §122, at Tyre and read aloud at Chalcedon.

18. On the Orthodox, and the Nestorians hounded out of the empire in the AD 430s and again by the emperor Zeno, and the somewhat later and more gradual estrangement of the Monophysite and Jacobite churches, there is no obvious general treatment; but cf. Frend (1972) passim, Gero (1981) 21f., 47ff., and passim, Roberson (1988) 2ff., Zibawi (1995) 11–14, Pietri (1998) 23–29, and esp. Moffett (1998) on Nestorians, e.g. p. 200, and Brock (1996) passim; on the Jacobite, cf. Kidd (1927) 50, 90, Roberson (1988) 6, and Zibawi (1995) 11.

19. The best-known example of Cple's claims in Palladius, *Dialogus de vita S. Joh. Chrysos.* 48f. (pp. 84ff. Coleman-Norton); cf. Schwartz (1914–40) 2, 3, 3, p. 62; and regional solidarity among independent sees, e.g. Schwartz (1914–40) 2, 1, 1, p. 116, *hoi episkopoi hellados eipon*; but notice the Cple patriarch extracting reluctant signatures by the dozens from his suffragans, AD 544, in Hefele (1907–09) 3.18.

20. Evagrius, *HE* 1.10; a total at Ephesus II of 150 bishops, Honigman (1942–43) 34, of whom 23 were Egyptians (p. 41).

21. Janin (1923) 382–85; Schwartz (1914–40) 2, 1, 1, p. 65 (seating, where I cannot explain the "Illyric" contingent of bishops with Dioscorus, though scholars have no trouble with this group) and 56–64 (the list of 343 participants); further, Pietri (1998) 81f., in a chapter which seems to me the best guide for the council at the moment. Notice the reassignment of the texts of the early sessions (#2 = #3), p. 85 n. 22—correctly also in Schwartz (1914–40) 2, 3, 2.

22. Dindorf (1832) 1.589.

23. At the Cple council of AD 448, stress on the Extract, the "Tome", Schwartz (1914–40) 2, 1, 1, p. 121; why was it not read at Chalcedon?—pp. 83f.

24. Schwartz p. 84, cf. 2, 1, 3, pp. 49 (Bassianus) and 74 (Valerius), and Eusebius and Florentius, 2, 3, 2, p. 116, 4th Session of Chalcedon; and Ambrose at Aquileia, "Even now he's lying," etc., Zelzer (1982) 331.

25. Schwartz 2, 3, 1, p. 251, *scandalizaverunt animas simplices,* cf. p. 248, *quam maxime simpliciores . . . a pietate abstrahunt,* and above, Chap. 3 n. 35 and elsewhere.

26. Mansi (1759–63) 9.297; cf. 345, also quoted.

27. Mansi 4.1299, of 34 words, the first 29 in one sentence; p. 1323, more than 150 words concluding, "May the Divine [= emperor's] Ears be apprised of what is here offered;" other long synodal *"dixits"*, e.g. Mansi 9.189E, a 53-word sentence, or pp. 197f., or Schwartz (1914–40) 1, 1, 2, pp. 20 or 54; 1, 1, 5, p. 120, 121; 2, 3, 1, p. 127.

28. By exception, a spokesman named, Schwartz (1914–40) 2, 3, 2, p. 117, "Egyptian bishops through one of their number Hieracin said. . . ."

29. Schwartz (1914–40) 2, 1, 1, p. 84, on the *primikerios ton notariarion* (notice the Latin used for officialdom), where *primicerius* derives from the use of wax tablets for handy note-taking, before copying on to papyrus sheets.

30. Schwartz (1914–40) 2, 1, 1, pp. 67 (Chalcedon), 71–74 passim (at Ephesus I); 2, 1, 2, p. 79, *biblion* with the Nicene creed, cf. Mansi (1759–63) 6.956B; 2, 1, 1, p. 91, anthology of Cyrillian letters; cf. the anthology compiled in defense of his view by Eutyches in Cple AD 448, Lietzmann (1904) 92; again, the document, *charta,* which he had in his hand to read from at Cple AD 448, Schwartz (1914–40) 2, 1, 1, p. 141; Flavian's preparation of the condemnatory statement against Eutyches written out in full before the start of the trial (!), ibid. 2, 3, 1, pp. 167f.; and more on such compilations to govern proceedings, called *florilegia,* in use at Ephesus I and thereafter, in Alexakis (1996) 2, 6f., 10ff. For a crucial document introduced and much relied on at Aquileia, see "the Arius letter" in Zelzer (1982) 329 §5, Gryson (1980a) 277, and Tavano (1981) 162f.

31. Schwartz (1914–40) 2, 1, 1, p. 75; the complaints of use of force are quoted from the *acta* by Evagrius and testified to again in the 3rd Chalcedon session, Schwartz 2, 3, 2, pp. 28f. or 2, 3, 1, p. 44.

32. Honigman (1942–43) 41 finds only ten Egyptian bishops at Chalcedon who had also been at Ephesus II; the rest, scared to attend.

33. Schwartz (1914–40) 1, 1, 5, pp. 14, 128f. (*agroikoi*); more armed force at Ephesus I, Schwartz 1, 1, 2, p. 10; 1, 1, 3, pp. 12, 46f.; confirming details in Driver and Hodgson (1925) 108, 266; disruption of other councils, Tyre AD 335, Soz., *HE* 2.25.13 or Rome AD 501, Mommsen (1894) 429.

34. Hamilton and Brooks (1899) 46; more emphasis on compulsory signing, ibid. and p. 44; and p. 47, "Eustace of Berytus when he signed the Document [the "Confession of Faith" of Chalcedon] wrote in short-hand, 'This I have written under compulsion, not agreeing with it.' And he wept very much, as did others also who proclaimed the compulsion and exposed the hypocritical profession of faith which was made, because chief senators were present time after time and watched the proceedings of the synod." For other instances of signing only under compulsion, cf. (fourth century) Hilary, *Contra Constantium* 12 (Seleuceia); Sulpicius Sev., *Chron.* 2.43.2f. or Soc., *HE* 2.31.4 (Ariminum); Soz., *HE* 4.6.13 (Sirmium); Soc., *HE* 4.6.4; or (fifth century) Hefele (1907–09) 3.17f.

35. Careful explaining that signatures were not compelled, Schwartz (1914–40) 2, 1,

3, p. 94 [453], 97 [456]; the quoted extract, ibid. 2, 1, 1, pp. 92–94; for another, mass attempt to re-write the past so as to wiggle out of the present, cf. pp. 140f. (the Orientals contradicted by the Egyptians); and Nau (1919) 206–09 for a greatly abbreviated account of the AD 449 proceedings.

36. Schwartz 2, 1, 1, p. 112. The growth in Cyril's Christology is not always acknowledged, as if it were a unity; cf. e.g. Pietri (1998) passim; but cf. Baus et al. (1980) 99f., Meyendorff (1989) 192f., or Gray (1997) 198 and (1988) 287f. ("Cyril had in fact changed his mind").

37. Biblical citations, above, Chap. 3 n. 20; Schwartz (1914–40) 2, 1, 1, p. 120, "speak four-square," *anaischyntein*.

38. Schwartz 2, 1, 1, pp. 88f., with Dioscorus' words to describe the danger of misbelief, *phoberos* and *phriktos*.

39. Schwartz 2, 1, 1, p. 89.

40. Evagrius, *HE* 2.3 (*PG* 86.2193Cf.).

41. "Lied," Schwartz 2, 1, 1, p. 91, and after an interruption from the Orientals, the same Egyptian *phonai* are repeated.

42. Schwartz 2, 1, 1, p. 113.

43. Schwartz 2, 1, 1, p. 140.

44. Schwartz 2, 1, 1, p. 145, in the proceedings of AD 448.

45. Schwartz 2, 1, 1, pp. 3–8 and 29–34 (spoken) and 34–41, written; Chadwick (2001) 576; and eventual total of 520, in Honigman (1942–43) 43; but only 185 signatories to end the 17th Session, Schwartz (1914–40) 2, 1, 3, pp. 89–94 (448–63)—a figure that Sellers (1961) 112 and n. 2 mistakenly takes as the votes against Dioscorus.

46. Post-facto signing, e.g. Gryson (1980a) 131; Chadwick (2001) 282; Schwartz (1914–40) 1, 1, 2, p. 64, Ephesus I; Hefele (1907–09) 2.298f., 160 bishops present but 198 at the signing of Ephesus I and "more than 200" late-signers, Mansi (1759–63) 4.1212–25; Hess (1958) 9, Serdica; Soz., *HE* 4.19.5f., under threat at Ariminum AD 359; circulation of *acta* for post-facto signing, Schwartz 2, 1, 1, p. 123.

47. Schwartz (1914–40) 2, 1, 1, pp. 115f.

48. Schwartz 2, 1, 1, p. 117; the three names that Dioscorus invokes are the common ones, cf. e.g. the Flavianist Eusebius of Dorylaeum, at Cple AD 448, who adds Gregory Thaumaturgus and Gregory of Nyssa, ibid. p. 101.

49. Schwartz (1914–40) 2, 3, 1, pp. 41f.; 2, 3, 2, p. 132 (notice, I prefer the Latin to the Greek since, on comparison, the Latin seems a little more reliable, e.g., the Greek omits, 2, 1, 2, p. 117, an acclamation which is in 2, 3, 2, p. 123; and the Greek puts acclamations before a speech, 2, 1, 2, p. 139, which properly come after, 2, 3, 2, pp. 151f.); and Pietri (1998) 86f.

50. Schwartz (1914–40) 2, 3, 2, p. 120, with 121f. for the scene that follows.

51. Schwartz (1914–40) 2, 3, 1, pp. 44f.

52. Flemming (1914–17) 57 lines 31ff.; compare Schwartz (1914–40) 3, pp. 102f. where savage shouts are permitted and forwarded to the emperor. On the unbelievers' outraged comments about the violence of Christian disputes, see above, Chap. 3 n. 4.

53. Schwartz (1914–40) 2, 1, p. 410 (Greek) or 2, 3, 3, p. 60 (499).

54. Schwartz (1914–40) 2, 1, pp. 368f., cf. Chadwick (2001) 543f.; similarly, an individual's change accepted by a council at Rome, AD 496, Mansi (1759–63) 8.180ff.;

occasional mass changes, the most famous no doubt being the collapse of some 320 bishops at Ariminum AD 359, all together, after six months of being held in quasi-arrest, cf. Sulp. Sev., *Chron.* 2.41ff. (*PL* 20.152Bff.), esp. 153D, 154A; but other instances, e.g. by Sirmium participants post-eventum, Soc., *HE* 2.30.47 and Hier., *Altercatio Luciferiani* 19 (*CCSL* 79b.49); by the repentant bishops of Ephesus II; and by the council at Diospolis (Lydda) AD 415, grilling Pelagius but (with one outbreak of hissing, *susurrantibus quibusdam*) eventually finding no fault in his answers, Mansi (1759–63) 4.315–19 and *Varia scripta ad hist. Pelag* (*PL* 95.1708).

55. Lancel (1972–91) passim, where Marcellinus the friend of Augustine the initiator follows the emperor's mandate which is in the form of an indictment to begin with. Lancel the editor, 1.64ff., asserts Marcellinus showed no bias; but in fact he does, e.g. by his rulings at 2.708 §120; 3.948 §§45ff.; or 3.1041 §77.

56. Zelzer (1982) 334 §15, calls on a trustworthy speaker; changes subject, 332 §11 or 346 §34; solicits and dictates audience's response, evidently by turning to the audience as may be indicated by the *notarii* inserting, "*et adiecit*", 338f. §21f.340 §24; 341 §26; 345 §32; 348 §36; or 358 §53.

57. The preferred term is (Latin) *placet*, as a question and an answer, Turner (1899–1939) 1.453, 455, 465, 471, 493; some further illustrations in Munier (1974) 5ff., Carthage AD 345; Schwartz (1914–40) 2, 3, 2, pp. 16, 44, 113, 130; 2, 1, p. 458; Mommsen (1894) 444f., 446, Rome council of AD 502; Batiffol (1913) 11; and Sabw Kanyang (2000) 321f.

58. Soc., *HE* 2.39.15f.; Hefele (1907–09) 1, 2, pp. 946ff.

59. For Nicaea, Pietri and Pietri (1990) 270 and above, Chap. 2 n. 28; for Ariminum, see Sulpicius Severus, *Chron.* 2.41.1–3; for Cple, Soc., *HE* 5.8.4.

60. Aquileia, cf. Gryson (1981a) 138ff.; Arausio AD 529, Cappuyns (1934) 121; and Ephesus I, cf. Hefele (1907–09) 2, 1, p. 248.

61. Schwartz (1914–40) 2, 3, 2, pp. 15f. [274f.].

62. Schwartz (1914–40) 2, 3, 2, pp 130ff. [389ff.]; Sellers (1961) 119f.

63. The word *omnes/pantes* occurs all the time in acclamations, e.g. in Flemming (1914–17) 67; also the assertion that only heretics are silent, ibid. pp. 119ff., or Mansi (1759–63) 8.1057, 1064f. (in church, not council).

64. Schwartz (1914–40) 2, 1, 1, pp. 140 (from §487) to 143 §527.

65. Schwartz (1914–40) 2, 3, 2, pp. 125 (Carosus) and 127 (Dorotheus); 2, 1, 1, p. 87; the joint loyalty of the secular personages and assembled bishops at Chalcedon, 2, 3, 2, p. 4 §§3–4; and similar vociferous loyalty to the 318 from the monks gathered at Cple in AD 536, Mansi (1759–63) 1057f., "rejecting all fancy reasoning on one's discussions," *omnis in sermonibus subtilitas* (1064D).

66. A standard view, cf. e.g. Origen, *Contra Celsum* 1.66, in Chadwick (2001) 517; AD 325 at Antioch, Kelly (1950) 208; Constantine in Soc., *HE* 1.8.42; Eusebius of Caesarea, ibid. 1.8.49 and Philostorgius, *HE* 1.2; Eusebius of Nicomedia quoted in Candidus, *Ep. ad Marium Vict.* 2 (*PL* 8.1038); at Sirmium, AD 359, Hilary, *De synodis* 11 (*PL* 10.488Af.); Epiphanius, *Adv. haereses* 3.13 (*PG* 42.429); *Panarion* 69.15.4; Victorinus, *De generatione* 32 (*PL* 8.1036B); and Dindorf (1932) 1.641, Justinian's view.

67. Cyril's letter to Nestorius of AD 430, *Ep.* 17 (*PG* 77.108Cf.) = Schwartz (1914–40) 1, 1, 1, p. 34; the Twelve Anathemas, pp. 40ff. For compulsory cursing as a condition

of not being condemned as heretic, cf. e.g. Alzati (1993) 59, Antioch AD 344; Hilary frg 7 appendix i (*PL* 10.698Bf.), at Ariminum; Hier., *Altercatio Luciferiani* 18 (*CCSL* 79b.45); Augustine, *De gestis Pelagii* 25, in Mansi (1759–63) 4.320C, at Diospolis in AD 415; Schwartz 2, 3, 1, p. 127 (Eutyches in AD 448); Sotinel (2000) 278, AD 532; or Hefele (1907–09) 3.107ff., AD 553.

68. Mansi (1759–63) 6.953; Schwartz (1914–40) 2, 3, 2, p. 4 [263].

69. Schwartz (1914–40) 2, 3, 2, p. 5 [264].

70. For greater respect accorded to the greater churches' archives, cf. e.g. Munier (1974) 91 or Schwartz (1914–40) 4, 2, pp. 172f. For the accusation that words never spoken are entered by hostile *notarii*, see Lancel (1972–91) 2.678; checking of a council-copy by each person quoted, ibid. 2.576, 3.930; every person (meaning a half-dozen or more major sees) has his own *notarii* to record the sessions, Schwartz (1914–40) 2, 3, 1, p. 63; each side with its own, at Aquileia as at Carthage AD 411, Gryson (1980a) 54f. (objections about the Aquileian transcription, Zelzer[1982] 352f. §43, 354 §46, 357 §51, etc.); also Lancel 2.576 and Shaw (1995) 16 n. 18 on AD 411; at Ephesus II, Schwartz (1914–40) 2, 3, 1, p. 63; denial of accuracy of *acta* there, ibid. p. 131, at Cple AD 449, resulting in a protracted hearing, with the finding that Flavian or his deputies forged the *acta*, pp. 135f.; differing versions of *acta* evident today, e.g. Horn (1982) 125 n. 61, Syrian (Nestorian) vs. Latin; but a sense that there might be a better or approved version of the minutes, called a *kanon* in Schwartz 2, 1, 1, p. 180. At stretched-out councils the flow of sessions may be held up by a day or two so that the transcribers can do their work and present it for approval by vote.

71. Schwartz (1914–40) 2, 3, 1, pp. 137ff.; mis-report of Flavius, p. 153 §721; problems further, p. 157 §759, and steno's explanation, p. 158 §767. The standing of *notarii et presbyteri* shows well in the person of a certain Asterius, who appears at Cple AD 448, p. 78; then p. 198 as access-point to Flavian; also at p. 119 as announcer at a session; in AD 449 at p. 137; again pp. 140, 161. Very prominent; and another like him, Top-Wax Steno Diodorus in AD 553, in Alexakis (1996) 15.

72. Schwartz (1914–40) 2, 3, 1, p. 168, complaint by Asterius (above, n. 69).

73. Forged papal letters, Hefele (1907–09) 1.916, 924; 3.22; forgery of a Nicene canon by Juvenal of Jerusalem, meant to make his bishopric a patriarchate, but detected (Leo, *Ep.* 119.4, *PL* 54.1044A), so that he had to earn the promotion from the emperor two years later by betrayal of Dioscorus (above, at n. 47); and Schwartz (1939) 21, forgery detected by Justinian; "Athanasius'" letter, ibid. 18 and Gray (1988) 285; forged Clementine sermons to carry Eunomian teachings, Harnack (1893–1904) 1.214, 223; forged letter against Athanasius, *Ep. synodi Sardicensis ad universas ecclesias* 5 (*CSEL* 65.111); fake documents pro-Athanasius, Schwartz (1904) 390f.; fake letter of Cyril, Mansi (1759–63) 9.265f.; fourth century Messalian forgeries, Stewart (1991) 4, 24, and 70; fourth century Apollinarian forgeries, Cattaneo (1981) 52, Mühlenberg (1969) 100f., and Lietzmann (1904) 91–93f.; fifth century semi-Pelagian forgeries, Cappuyns (1934) 121f.; ibid. p. 135, fake "Augustine" tract; fifth century Monophysite fake, Gray (1997) 198; beginning of sixth century fake papal lives in aid of an anti-pope, Townsend (1933) 165, 168ff.; sixth century "Cyril" fakes, Hefele (1907–09) 3.88 and Outtier (1996) 379.

74. Text of the discovery (or first challenge known to me) in Munier (1974) 90f., the challenge respectfully voiced by Augustine's friend Alypius at Carthage AD 419; cf. also

Hefele (1907–09) 2.198, Guarnieri (1980) 349, Llewellyn (1977) 250, and Barnard (1983) 97f., 101f. On *acta*-archives, see a few details in the Carthage AD 419–discovery, and further in Schwartz (1914–40) 2, 3, p. 115. I have made no special search for these forgery-items, nor seen any general treatment of the subject.

75. In addition to a number of mentions in the present and earlier chapters, notice Lancel (1972–91) 2.515, re-writing of a fourth century council; Mouterde (1930) 35ff., or better, Horn (1982) 124f., Nestorian distortion; or Hefele (1907–09) 3.69f., sixth century re-writing of AD 553 council.

76. Council of AD 501–2, Aimone (2000) 73, 76ff. (with other forgeries, pp. 67f.)

77. Terminology of the two groups mutually in use, Schwartz (1914–40) 4, 2, pp. 184ff.

78. Nau (1919) 193 and Brock (1981) 92, 110 §41 (quoted); meeting in the "hepta-conch" triclinium under the Count of the Sacred Largesses, Strategius, and present also *clerici* and *monachi*, Schwartz (1914–40) 4, 2, pp. 169f.

79. Brock (1981) 94 §11.

80. Brock (1981) 94.

81. Gray (1988) 286; Sotinel (2000) 277ff., with Theodoret of Cyrrhus in the background, attacking Cyril's view of the Incarnation as occurring only in appearance, Flemming (1914–17) 93 lines 9ff.; the same charge against a second figure by Severus of Antioch, Treadgold (1997) 183 — Severus being a Monophysite leader. It was a further complication for the Occidentals that Rome's legates had found Ibas' letter orthodox, Schwartz 2, 1, 3, p. 39 [398] §161.

82. Brock (1981) 100, 102, §§18 (Chalcedonian *acta* read) –20 (quoted)– 27 ("demand that this be put in writing"); the Occidental version in Schwartz (1914–40) 4, 2, pp. 169–84, Innocentius' *De collatione cum Severianis*.

83. Treadgold (1997) 183, "arguments surprisingly similar"; screening, Schwartz (1914–40) 4, 2, p. 175 §36, 177 §43; diptychs, 180; the challenge, quoted, p. 68, Ibas and Theodoret *sicut rectae fidei suscepti sunt a synodo et sicut rectae fidei in divinis diptycis recitantur?"*

84. Schwartz (1914–40) 2, 3, 1, pp. 104f., repeated pp. 140f., bible texts are *firmiores*, whereas the Fathers *diversis modis locuti sunt*, even *in regula fidei* — a statement causing *perturbatio et mussitatio*.

85. Schwartz (1914–40) 2, 3, 1, pp. 117f.: Eutyches is quoted as asking, "in what text of the bible are the two natures found?," to which answer is made to him, "Yourself, then, show us where you find 'homoousios' . . .", to which he in turn replies, without rejecting it, "it's not found in scripture but it does lie in the teachings of the Fathers." The non-use of the word in the bible was a familiar stumbling block, cf. e.g. Hier., *Altercatio Luciferiani* 19 (CCSL 79b.48).

86. I omit mention of Justinian's Edict of AD 544 targeting three teachers as heretical, against whom also the Monophysites were rabid (his "Three Chapters"). One of them was Ibas in his Letter. The tract is convenient in Dindorf (1832) 1.664, quoted; 667, on the anonymous author of the "Ibas" letter, who aimed *pros apaten ton haplousteron* (cf. above, Chap. 3 nn. 35, 43); p. 670, the letter found in *biblia*; rejected at Cple II, Gray (1997) 202 and Chadwick (2001) 617.

87. Alexakis (1996) 16, the quoted words; further, on all the careful stage-managing and the flow of documents for all six sessions reflected in the *florilegia*, pp. 10–15.

88. On the strategy defined for Cple II, to set aside the letter and so protect Chalcedon, cf. Liberatus, *Breviarium causae Nestorianorum et Eutychianorum* 24 (*PL* 68.1049B); the Letter is abominated by Justinian in his summons to Cple II, Mansi (1759–63) 9.180; Ibas' letter "accepted by the Holy Council of Chalcedon" but a forgery, ibid. 297f., 345 (quoted), 346 (acclamations); and, at Session #7, the resumption of the letter's discussion is set aside, Mansi 9.345E–347A.

89. Mansi (1759–63) 9.229C.

Summary

1. Mansi (1759–63) 9.184C, *in mente habentes Dei timorem*. Justinian, as others would have noted to themselves, could find no hint of the term *homoousion* in St. Paul.

2. MacMullen (2003a) passim.

3. In addition to much obvious emotion in passages quoted above, passim, cf. mentions of weeping and dancing for joy, Hier., *Altercatio Luciferiani* 18, 19 (*CCSL* 79b.46, 49) or Hamilton and Brooks (1899) 47; outrage at injustice, Schwartz (1914–40) 2, 3, 1, p. 163; at cruelty, *inhumanitas*, p. 124; sarcasm, Mansi (1759–63) 9.297Af., *miranda est subtilitas sancti Chalcedonensis concilii*; clasping knees and feet, ibid. 2, 1, 1, p. 180 (Ephesus II); and comments like those of the presiding officials at Ephesus I, ibid. 2, 3, 1, pp. 45f. §46, after prolonged clamor: Please let things be orderly (and the meeting continued "when everyone was quiet").

4. At p. ix in his Introduction to the volume where his essay appears, R. Williams (1989).

5. Mansi (1759–63) 9.339A.

6. The "six" being, in the West, the Roman Catholic and the Arian, and in the East, the Syrian or Assyrian Church of the East ("Nestorian") and the Coptic Orthodox (Chap. 3 n. 27) with the Greek Orthodox or Melkite, and the Syrian Orthodox or Antiochene or Jacobite or Monophysite (on which see Chap. 7 n. 18). Against the terminology imposed on the eastern churches by western European church historians, and against much of their narration, Brock (1996) 23 rightly protests.

Bibliography

CCSL: *Corpus christianorum series latina*, Tournholt (Belgium) 1954–
CSEL: *Corpus scriptorum ecclesiasticorum latinorum*, Vienna 1866–
GCS: *Die Griechischen christlichen Schriftsteller der ersten drei Jahrhunderte*, Berlin 1897–
PG: *Patrologia graeca*, ed. J.-P. Migne, Paris 1837–
PL: *Patrologia latina*, ed. J.-P. Migne, Paris 1844–
PLRE: *Prosopography of the Later Roman Empire*, 1, ed. A. H. M. Jones et al.; 2, ed. J. Martindale, Cambridge 1971–80

Aimone (1998) — Aimone, P. V., "Gli autori della falsificazioni simmachiane," *Il papato di San Simmaco*, eds. G. Mele and N. Scappapelo, Cagliari 2000, 53–77.
Alberigo (1991) — Alberigo, G. et al., *Conciliorum oecumenicorum decreta*,[3] Bologna 1991.
Alexakis (1996) — Alexakis, A., *Codex Parisinus Graecus 1115 and Its Archetype*, Washington D. C. 1996.
Alzati (1993) — "Un cappadoce in Occidente durante le dispute trinitarie del IV secolo: Aussenzio di Milano," *Politica, cultura e religione nell'impero romano (secoli IV–VI) tra Oriente e Occidente. Atti del Secondo Convegno dell'Assoc. di Studi Tardoantichi*, eds. F. Conca et al., Napoli 1993, 59–76.
Atiya (1967) — Atiya, A. A., *History of Eastern Christianity*, London 1967.
Attridge (1978) — Attridge, H. W., "The philosophical critique of religion under the Early Roman Empire," *Aufstieg und Niedergang der römischen Welt*, eds. H. Temporini and W. Haase II, 16, Berlin 1978, 45–78.

Aubineau (1966)—Aubineau, M., "Les 318 serviteurs d'Abraham (Gen., XIV, 14) et le nombre des pères au concile de Nicée (325)," *Revue d'histoire ecclésiastique* 61 (1966) 5–43.

Bacht (1953)—Bacht, H., "Die Rolle des orientalischen Mönchtums in der kirchenpolitischen Auseinandersetzung um Chalkedon (432–519)," *Das Konzil von Chalkedon. Geschichte und Gegenwart*, eds. A. Grillmeier and H. Bacht, Würzburg 1953, 2.193–314.

Bagnall (1993)—Bagnall, R. S., *Egypt in Late Antiquity*, Princeton 1993

Baldwin (1981)—Baldwin, B., "The date of a circus dialogue," *Revue des études byzantines* 39 (1981) 301–06.

Bardy (1923)—Bardy, G., *Paul de Samosate. Etude historique*, Louvain 1923

Barnard (1978)—Barnard, L. W., "The antecedents of Arius," *Studies in Church History and Patristics*, Thessalonica 1978, 289–311.

Barnard (1983)—Barnard, L. W., *The Council of Serdica 343 A.D.*, Sofia 1983.

Barnes (1993)—Barnes, T. D., *Athanasius and Constantius. Theology and Politics in the Constantinian Empire*, Cambridge 1993.

Batiffol (1913)—Batiffol, P., "Le règlement des premières conciles africaines," *Bulletin d'ancienne littérature et d'archéologie chrétienne* 3 (1913) 3–19.

Battegazzore (1992)—Battegazzore, A., "L'attegiamento di Plutarco verso le scienze," *Plutarco e le scienze. Atti del IV Convegno plutarchea . . . 1991*, ed. I. Gallo, Genova 1992, 19–60.

Baus et al. (1980)—Baus, K., et al., *The Imperial Church from Constantine to the Early Middle Ages*, trans. A. Biggs, New York 1980.

Beard (1986)—Beard, M., "Cicero and divination: the formation of a Latin discourse," *Journal of Roman Studies* 76 (1986) 33–46.

Bell (1983)—Bell, D., trans., *Besa. The Life of Shenoute*, Kalamazoo (MI) 1983.

Bidez (1913)—Bidez, J., *Philostorgius Kirchengeschichte*, Leipzig 1913.

Bidez and Parmentier—Bidez, J., and L. Parmentier, eds., *The Ecclesiastical History of Evagrius*, Amsterdam 1964 [London 1898].

Blume (1989)—Blume, M., "A propos de P. Oxy. I, 41. Des acclamations en l'honneur d'une prytane confrontées aux témoignages épigraphiques," *Egitto e storia antica dall'ellenismo all'età araba*, eds. L. Criscuolo and G. Geraci, Bologna 1989, 271–90.

Boulhol (1994)—Boulhol, P., "Hagiographie antique et démonologie," *Analecta Bollandiana* 112 (1994) 255–303.

Bowman (1971)—Bowman, A. K., *The Town Councils of Roman Egypt*, Toronto 1971.

Brakke (1995)—Brakke, D., *Athanasius and the Politics of Asceticism*, Oxford 1995.

Brinkman (1989)—Brinkman, A., *Alexander Lycopolitanus*, Stuttgart 1989.

Brock (1981)—Brock, S. [P.], "The conversations with the Syrian Orthodox under Justinian (532)," *Orientalia christiana periodica* 47 (1981) 87–121.

Brock (1996)—Brock, S. P., "The 'Nestorian' church: a lamentable misnomer," *Bulletin of the John Rylands Library* 78 (1996) 23–35.

Brooks (1903)—Brooks, E. W., ed., *The Sixth Book of the Select Letters of Severus Patriarch of Antioch in the Syriac Version*, 2: *Translation* Pt. 1, Oxford 1903

Brooks (1924)—Brooks, E. W., "John of Ephesus. Lives of the Eastern Saints. Syriac text," *Patrologia Orientalis* 18 (1924) 511–698.

Brown (1970) — Brown, P., *Augustine of Hippo, a Biography*, Berkeley 1970.

Bury (1958) — Bury, J. B., *A History of the Later Roman Empire from the Death of Theodosius I to the Death of Justinian*, 2 vols., New York 1958.

Butler (1904) — Butler, C., ed., *The Lausiac History of Palladius* II: *The Greek Text*, Cambridge (UK) 1904.

Calvet-Sebasti and Gatier (1989) — Calvet-Sebasti, M.-A., and P.-L. Gatier, eds., *Firmus de Césarée, Lettres*, Paris 1989.

Camelot (1962) — Camelot, P.-T., *Ephèse et Chalcédoine*, Paris 1962.

Cameron (1976) — Cameron, A., *Circus Factions: Blues and Greens at Rome and Byzantium*, Oxford 1976.

Canellis (2003) — Canellis, A., ed., *Débat entre un luciférien et un orthodoxe (Altercatio Luciferiani at orthodoxi)*, Paris 2003.

Canivet and Leroy-Molinghen (1977–79) — Canivet, P., and A. Leroy-Molinghen, eds., *Theodoret de Cyr, Histoire des moines de Syrie, 'Histoire philothée'*, 2 vols., Paris 1977–79.

Cappuyns (1934) — Cappuyns, D. M., "L'origine des 'Capitula' d'Orange 529," *Recherches de théologie ancienne et médiévale* 6 (1934) 121–42.

Cattaneo (1981) — Cattaneo, E., *Trois homélies pseudo-chrysostomiennes sur la Pâque*, Paris 1981.

Chadwick (1958) — "Ossius of Cordova and the presidency of the council of Antioch," *Journal of Theological Studies*[2] 9 (1958) 292–304.

Chadwick (1972) — Chadwick, H., "The origin of the title 'oecumenical council'," *Journal of Theological Studies*[2] 23 (1972) 132–35.

Chadwick (1980) — Chadwick, H., "The role of the Christian bishop in ancient society," *Protocol of the 35th Colloquy . . . 1979, Center for Hermeneutical Studies . . . , University of California Berkeley*, Berkeley 1980, 1–14.

Chadwick (1993) — Chadwick, H., "Bishops and monks," *Studia patristica* 24 (1993) 45–61.

Chadwick (2001) — Chadwick, H., *The Church in Ancient Society from Galilee to Gregory the Great*, Oxford 2001.

Clark (1978) — Clark, M. T., trans., *Marius Victorinus. Theological Treatises on the Trinity*, Washington DC 1978.

Champeaux (1998) — Champeaux, J., *La religion romaine*, Paris 1998

Coleman Norton (1966) — Coleman Norton, P. R., *Roman State and Christian Church. A Collection of Legal Documents to A.D. 535*, 3 vols., London 1966

Coles (1966) — Coles, R. A., *Reports of Proceedings in Papyri*, Bruxelles 1966 (*Papyrologica Bruxellensia* 4).

Colin (1965) — Colin, J., *Les villes libres de l'Orient gréco-romain et l'envoi au supplice par acclamations populaires*, Bruxelles 1965.

Constantelos (1982) — Constantelos, D. J., "Toward the convocation of the second ecumenical synod," *Greek Orthodox Theological Review* 27 (1982) 395–505.

Creed (1984) — Creed, J. L., ed., *Lactantius, De mortibus persecutorum*, Oxford 1984.

Cuscito (1982) — Cuscito, G., "Il concilio di Aquileia (381) e le sue fonti," *Aquileia nel IV secolo*, Udine 1982, 189–253.

R. Davis (2000) — Davis, R., *The Book of the Pontiffs (Liber Pontificalis)*,[2] Liverpool 2000.

S. J. Davis (2004) — Davis, S. J., *The Early Coptic Papacy. The Egyptian Church and Its Leadership in Late Antiquity*, Cairo 2004.

Delehaye (1923) — Delehaye, H., *Les saints stylites*, Bruxelles 1923.

Desiderio (1992) — Desiderio, P., "Scienza nelle *Vite* di Plutarco," *Plutarco e le scienze. Atti del IV Convegno plutarcheo . . . 1991*, ed. I Gallo, Genova 1992, 73–90.

Devreesse (1945) — Devreesse, R., *Le patriarcat d'Antioche depuis la paix de l'église jusqu'à la conquète arabe*, Paris 1945.

Dindorf (1832) — Dindorf, L., ed., *Chronicon Paschale ad exemplar vaticanum*, 2 vols., Bonn 1832.

Dittenberger (1903–05) — Dittenberger, W., *Orientis graeci inscriptiones selectae*, 2 vols., Leipzig 1903–05.

Dovere (1998) — Dovere, E., "Contestazione religiosa e regionalismo: la *medicina legum* in Oriente a metà del sec. V," *Annuarium historiae conciliorum* 30 (1998) 1–30.

Driver and Hodgson (1925) — Driver, G. R., and L. Hodgson, *Nestorius The Bazaar of Heracleides newly translated from the Syriac*, Oxford 1925.

Duchesne (1886–92) — Duchesne, L., ed., *Liber Pontificalis*, 2 vols., Paris 1886–92.

Duval (1981) — Duval, Y. M., "Le sens des débats d'Aquilée pour les Nicéens. Nicée-Rimini-Aquilée," *Atti del Colloquio internazionale sul concilio di Aquileia del 381*, Udine 1981, 69–97.

Engelmann (2000) — Engelmann, H., "Neue Inschriften aus Ephesos XIII," *Jahreshefte des österreichischen archäologischen Institutes in Wien* 69 (2000) 77–93.

Evans (1996) — Evans, J. A. S., *The Age of Justinian. The Circumstances of Imperial Power*, London 1996.

Fedalto (1988) — Fedalto, G., ed., *Hierarchia ecclesiastica orientalis: Series episcoporum ecclesesiarum christianarum orientalium*, 2 vols., Padova 1988.

Fischer and Lumpe (1999) — Fischer, J. A., and A. Lumpe, *Die Synoden von den Anfängen bis zum Vorabend des Nicaenums*, Paderborn 1999. (*Konziliengeschichte*, ed. W. Brandmüller, Reihe A).

Flemming (1914–17) — Flemming, J., "Akten der ephesinischen Synode vom Jahre 449 syrisch," *Abhandlungen der königlichen Gesellschaft der Wissenschaften zu Göttingen, Philologische — historische Klasse*[2] 15 (1914–17) 1–188.

Forlin Patrucco (1983) — Forlin Patrucco, M., ed., *Basilio di Cesarea Le lettere*, Torino 1983.

Foss (1979) — Foss, C., *Ephesus after Antiquity: A Late Antique, Byzantine and Turkish City*, Cambridge (UK) 1979.

Frend (1972) — Frend, W. H. C., *The Rise of the Monophysite Movement: Chapters in the History of the Church in the Fifth and Sixth Centuries*, Cambridge 1972.

Gaddis (1999) — Gaddis, M., "There Is No Crime for Those Who Have Christ: Religious Violence in the Christian Roman Empire," Diss. Princeton 1999

Gain (1985) — Gain, B., *L'église de Cappadoce au IVe siècle d'après la correspondance de Basile de Césarée (330–79)*, Rome 1985.

Gaudemet (1974) — Gaudemet, J., "La participation de la communauté au choix des ses pasteurs dans l'Eglise latine," *Ius canonicum* 28 (1974) 308–26.

Gauthier and Picard (2002) — Gauthier, N., and J.-C. Picard, *Topographie chrétienne des cités de la Gaule des origines au milieu du VIIIe siècle*, XII: *Province ecclésiastique de Cologne*, Paris 2002.

Gero (1981) — Gero, S., *Barsauma of Nisibis and Persian Christianity in the Fifth Century*, Louvain 1981 (CSCOrient. Subsidia 63).

Granfield (1976) — Granfield, P., "Episcopal elections in Cyprian: clerical and lay participation," *Theological Studies* 37 (1976) 41–52.

Gray (1979) — Gray, P. T. R., *The Defense of Chalcedon in the East (451–553)*, Leiden 1979.

Gray (1988) — Gray, P. [T. R.], "Forgery as an instrument of progress: reconstructing the theological tradition in the sixth century," *Byzantinische Zeitschrift* 81 (1988) 284–89.

Gray (1997) — Gray, P. [T. R.], "Covering the nakedness of Noah: reconstruction and denial in the age of Justinian," *Byzantinische Forschungen* 24 (1997) 193–205.

Gribomont (1988) — Gribomont, J., "Le symbole de foi de Séleucie-Ctésiphon (410)," *A Tribute to Arthur Vööbus. Studies in Early Christian Literature*, ed. R. H. Fischer, Chicago 1988, 283–94.

Griggs (1990) — Griggs, C. W., *Early Egyptian Christianity from Its Origins to 451 CE*, Leiden 1990.

Gryson (1973) — Gryson, R., "Les élections ecclésiastiques au IIIᵉ siècle," *Revue d'histoire ecclésiatique* 68 (1973) 353–404.

Gryson (1979) — Gryson, R., "Les élections épiscopales en Orient au IVᵉ siècle," *Revue d'histoire ecclésiastique* 74 (1979) 301–45.

Gryson (1980) — Gryson, R., "Les élections épiscopales en Occident au IVᵉ siècle," *Revue d'histoire ecclésiastique* 75 (1980) 257–83.

Gryson (1980a) — Gryson, R., *Scolies ariennes sur la Concile d'Aquilée*, Paris 1980.

Gryson (1981) — "Les sources relatives au concile d'Aquilée de 381," *Atti del Colloquio internazionale sul concilio di Aquileia del 381*, Udine 1981, 31–41.

Gryson (1981a) — "La position des ariens au concile d'Aquilée de 381," *Atti del Colloquio internazionale sul concilio di Aquileia del 381*, Udine 1981, 133–42.

Guarnieri (1980) — Guarnieri, C., "Nota sull'elezione episcopale in Apulia all'inizio del V secolo," *Vetera Christianorum* 17 (1980) 347–56.

Guarnieri (1983) — Guarnieri, C., "Note sulla presenza dei laici ai concili fino al VI secolo," *Vetera Christianorum* 20 (1983) 77–91.

Günther (1895–98) — Günther, O., *Epistolae imperatorum pontificum aliorum . . . Avellana quae dicitur collectio*, Prague 1895–98 (CSEL 35).

Guy (1993) — Guy, J.-C., ed., *Les apophthèmes des pères. Collection systématique*, 2 vols., Paris 1993.

Haase (1920) — Haase, F., *Die koptischen Quellen zum Konzil von Nicäa*, Paderborn 1920.

Hall (1998) — Hall, S. G., "Some Constantinian documents in the Vita Constantini," *Constantine. History, Historiography and Legend*, eds. N. C.Lieu and D. Montserrat, London 1998, 86–103.

Hamilton and Brooks (1899) — Hamilton, F. J., and E. W. Brooks, eds. and trans., *The Syriac Chronicle Known as that of Zachariah of Mytilene*, London 1899.

Hansen (1902) — Hansen, G. C., *Anonyme Kirchengeschichte (Gelasius Cyzicenus, CPG 6034)*, Berlin 1902 (GCS² 9).

Harnack (1893–1904) — Harnack, A., *Geschichte der altchristlichen Literatur bis Eusebius*, 2 vols., Leipzig 1893–1904.

Hedde and Amann (1933) — Hedde, R., and E. Amann, "Pélagianisme," *Dictionnaire de théologie catholique* 12, 1 (Paris 1933) 675–715.

Hefele (1907–09) — Hefele, K. J., *Histoire des conciles d'après les documents originaux,* trans. H. Leclercq, vols. 1–4, Paris 1907–09.

Heim (1976) — Heim, F., "L'influence exercée par Constantin sur Lactance: sa théologie de la victoire," *Lactance et son temps. Recherches actuelles. Actes du IVᵉ Colloque . . . 1976,* eds. J. Fontaine and M. Perrin, Paris 1976, 55–70.

Hess (1958) — Hess, H., *The Canons of the Council of Sardica A.D. 343. A Landmark in the Early Development of Canon Law,* Oxford 1958.

Hill (1992) — Hill, E., trans., *Works of Saint Augustine. A Translation for the 21st Century. Sermons III, 4,* New York 1992.

Hirschfeld (1905) — Hirschfeld, O., "Die römische Staatszeitung und die Akklamationen im Senat," *Sitzungsberichte de Preussischen Academie der Wissenschaften* 45 (1905) 930–48.

Honigman (1942–43) — Honigman, E., "The original list of the members of the Council of Nicaea, the Robber Synod and the Council of Chalcedon," *Byzantion* 16 (1942–43) 20–80.

Horn (1982) — Horn, S. O., *Petrou Kathedra. Der Bischof von Rom und die Synoden von Ephesus (449) und Chalcedon,* Paderborn 1982.

Horst and Mansfeld (1974) — Horst, P. W. van der, and J. Mansfeld, *An Alexandrian Platonist Against Dualism. Alexander of Lycopolis' Treatise . . . ,* Leiden 1974.

Humfress (2000) — Humfress, C., "Roman law, forensic argument and the formation of Christian orthodoxy (III–VI centuries)," *Orthodoxie, christianisme, histoire,* eds. S. Elm et al., Rome 2000, 125–47.

Janin (1923) — Janin, R., "La banlieue asiatique de Constantinople. Etude historique et topographique," *Echos d'Orient* 22 (1923) 335–86.

Joannou (1962) — Joannou, P.-P., ed., *Discipline générale antique (IIᵉ–IXᵉ s.),* Roma 1962.

Jones (1964) — Jones, A. H. M., *The Later Roman Empire. A Social Economic and Administrative Survey,* 3 vols., Oxford 1964.

Jones (1966) — Jones, A. H. M., *The Decline of the Ancient World,* London 1966.

Jones (1971) — Jones, A. H. M., *The Cities of the Eastern Roman Provinces,*[2] Oxford 1971.

Kantorowicz (1946) — Kantorowicz, E. H., *Laudes Regiae. A Study in Liturgical Acclamations and Medieval Ruler Worship,* Berkeley 1946.

Kelly (1950) — Kelly, J. N. D., *Early Christian Creeds,* London 1950.

Kidd (1927) — Kidd, B. J., *The Churches of Eastern Christendom from A. D. 451 to the Present Time,* London 1927.

Kolb (1999) — Kolb, F., "Die Sitzordnung von Volksversammlung und Theaterpublikum in kaiserzeitlichen Ephesos," *100 Jahre österrechische Forschungen in Ephesos. Akten des Symposions . . . 1995,* eds. B. Brandt and K. R. Krierer, Wien 1999, 1.101–05.

Konstantinidis (1982) — Konstantinidis, C. S., "Les présupposés historico-dogmatiques de l'oecuménécité du II Concile oecuménique," *La signification et l'actualité du IIᵉ Concile oecuménique pour le monde chrétien d'aujord'hui,* Chambésy 1982, 63–91.

Krautheimer (1937–77) — Krautheimer, R. et al., *Corpus Basilicarum Christianarum*

Romae. The Early Christian Basilicas of Rome (IV–IX Cent.), 5 vols., Vatican City 1937–77.

Kreider (2005) — Kreider, A., "Beyond Bosch: the early church and the Christendom shift," *International Bulletin of Missionary Research* 28 (2005) 59–68.

Kretschmar (1961) — Kretschmar, G., "Die Konzile der alten Kirche," *Die ökumenischen Konzile der Christenheit*, ed. H. J. Margull, Stuttgart 1961, 13–74.

Lacey (1903) — Lacey, T. A., ed., *Apellatio Flaviani. The Letters of Appeal from the Council of Ephesus A.D. 449*, London 1903.

Lamberton (2001) — Lamberton, P., *Plutarch*, New Haven 2001.

Lancel (1972–91) — Lancel, S. ed., *Actes de la conférence de Carthage en 411*, 4 vols., Paris 1972–91.

Lanne (1971) — Lanne, J. E., "L'origine des synodes," *Theologische Zeitschrift* 27 (1971) 201–22.

Lavenant (1963) — Lavenant, R., ed., "La lettre à Patricius de Philoxène de Mabboug. Edition critique," *Patrologia Orientalis* 30 (1963) 721–894.

LeGoff (1988) — LeGoff, J., ed., *Histoire de la France religieuse*, 1: *Des dieux de la Gaule à la papauté d'Avignon*, Paris 1988.

Lewin (1995) — Lewin, A., *Assemblee popolari e lotta politica nelle città dell'impero romano*, Firenze 1995.

Liebeschuetz (1972) — Liebeschuetz, J. H. W. G., *Antioch: A City and Imperial Administration in the Later Roman Empire*, Oxford 1972.

Lietzmann (1904) — Lietzmann, H., *Apollinaris von Laodicea und seine Schule*, Tübingen 1904.

Lietzmann (1908) — Lietzmann, H., *Das Leben des heiligen Symeon Stylites*, Leipzig 1908.

Linderski (1982) — Linderski, J., "Cicero and Roman divination," *La Parola del Passato* 37 (1982) 12–38.

Llewellyn (1977) — Llewellyn, P. A. B., "The Roman clergy during the Laurentian schism (498–506). A preliminary analysis," *Ancient Society* 8 (1977) 245–75.

Lucchesi (1977) — Lucchesi, E., *L'usage de Philon dans l'oeuvre exégétique de Saint Ambroise. Une 'Quellenforschung' aux Commentaires d'Ambroise sur la Genèse*, Leiden 1977.

MacMullen (1966) — MacMullen, R., *Enemies of the Roman Order. Treason Unrest, and Alienation in the Empire*, Cambridge 1966.

MacMullen (1966a) — MacMullen, R., "A note on *sermo humilis*," *Journal of Theological Studies* 17 (1966) 108–12.

MacMullen (1984) — MacMullen, R., *Christianizing the Roman Empire (A. D. 100–400)*, New Haven 1984.

MacMullen (1988) — MacMullen, R., *Corruption and the Decline of Rome*, New Haven 1988.

MacMullen (1989) — MacMullen, R., "The preacher's audience (AD 350–400)," *Journal of Theological Studies* 40 (1989) 503–11.

MacMullen (1990) — MacMullen, R., *Changes in the Roman Empire. Essays in the Ordinary*, Princeton 1990.

MacMullen (1997) — MacMullen, R., *Christianity and Paganism in the Fourth to Eighth Century*, New Haven 1997.

MacMullen (2001) — MacMullen, R., "Punctuation and voice in expository prose," *The Litarary Imagination* 3 (2001) 1–17.

MacMullen (2003) — MacMullen, R., "Cultural and political changes in the fourth and fifth centuries," *Historia* 52 (2003) 465–95.

MacMullen (2003a) — MacMullen, R., *Feelings in History, Ancient and Modern*, Claremont 2003.

Maier (1987–89) — Maier, J.-L., *Le dossier de donatisme*, 2 vols., Berlin 1987–89.

Maisano (1995) — Maisano, R., ed., *[Themistius] Discorsi di Temistio*, Torino 1995.

Mandouze (1982) — Mandouze, A., ed., *Prosopographie chrétienne du Bas-Empire*, 1: *Prosopographie de l'Afrique chrétienne (305–533)*, Paris 1982.

Mansi (1759–63) — Mansi, G. D., ed., *Sacrorum conciliorum nova, et amplissima collectio*, vols. 1–9, Florence 1759–63.

Marasco (2003) — Marasco, G., "Church historians (II): Philostorgius and Gelasius of Cyzicus," *Greek and Roman Historiography in Late Antiquity. Fourth to Sixth Century A.D.*, ed. eadem, Leiden 2003, 257–88.

Marrou (1965) — Marrou, H.-I., *Histoire de l'éducation dans l'Antiquité*,[2] Paris 1965.

Martin (1985) — Martin, A., *Histoire 'Acéphale' et index syriaque des lettres festales d'Athanase d'Alexandrie*, Paris 1985 (*Sources chrétiennes* 317).

Martin (2004) — Martin, D. B., *Inventing Superstition: from the Hippocratics to the Christians*, Cambridge 2004.

Mateo Seco (1984) — Mateo Seco, L. F., "El cristiano ante la vida y ante la muerte. Estudio del Panegirico de Gregorio de Nisa sobre Gregorio Taumaturgo," *The Biographical Works of Gregory of Nyssa. Proceedings of the Fifth International Colloquium on Gregory of Nyssa . . . 1982*, ed. A. Spira, Cambridge 1984, 197–220.

Mathisen (1987) — Mathisen, R. W., "A reconstruction of the list of subscriptions to the Council of Orange (A.D. 441)," *Annuarium historiae conciliorum* 19 (1987) 1–12.

Matthews (2000) — Matthews, J. F., *Laying Down the Law. A Study of the Theodosian Code*, New Haven 2000.

May (1989) — May, G., "Das Lehrverfahen gegen Eutychen im November des Jahres 448. Zur Vorgeschichte des Konzils von Chalkedon," *Annuarium historiae conciliorum* 21 (1989) 1–61.

Mazzuchi (2002) — Mazzuchi, C. M., *Menae patricii cum Thoma referendario De scientia politica dialogus*,[2] Milano 2002.

McLynn (1992) — McLynn, N. B., "Christian controversy and violence in the fourth century," *Kodai* 3 (1992) 15–44.

Messeri and Pintaudi (1998) — Messeri, G., and R. Pintaudi, "Documenti e scritture," *Scrivere libri e documenti nel mondo antico*, eds. G. Cavallo et al., Firenze 1998, 39–53.

Meyendorff (1981) — Meyendorff, J., *The Orthodox Church. Its Past and Its Role in the World Today*,[3] trans. J. Chapin, Crestwood (NJ) 1981.

Meyendorff (1989) — Meyendorff, J., *Imperial Unity and Christian Divisions. The Church 450–680 A. D.*, Crestwood (New Jersey) 1989.

Meyer (2004) — Meyer, E. A., *Legitimacy and Law in the Roman World. Tabulae in Roman Belief and Practice*, Cambridge (UK) 2004.

Mitchell (1993) — Mitchell, S., *Anatolia. Land, Men, and Gods in Asia Minor*, 2 vols., Oxford 1993.

Moffett (1998)—Moffett, S. H., *A History of Christianity in Asia, 1: Beginnings to 1500*,[2] Maryknoll NY 1998.

Momigliano (1972)—Momigliano, A., "Popular religious beliefs and the late Roman historians," *Popular Belief and Practice. Papers Read at the Ninth Summer Meeting and the Tenth Winter Meeting of the Ecclesiastical History Society*, eds. G. J. Cuming and D. Baker, Cambridge 1972, 1–18.

Mommsen (1894)—Mommsen, T., ed., *Cassiodori senatoris Variae*, Berlin 1894 (*Monumenta Germaniae Historica. Auctores antiquissimi* 12).

Moorehead (1999)—Moorehead, J., *Ambrose. Church and Society in the Late Roman World*, London 1999.

Moreschini (2001)—Moreschini, C., "Quando un imperatore cristiano perseguita i cristiani," *Chiesa e impero: Da Augusto a Giustiniano*, eds. E. dal Covolo and R. Uglione, Roma 2001, 245–64.

Morley (1996)—Morley, N., *Metropolis and Hinterland: The City of Rome and the Italian Economy, 200 B.C.–A.D. 200*, Cambridge 1996.

Mouterde (1930)—Mouterde, P., "Fragments d'actes d'un synode tenu à Constantinople en 450," *Mélanges de l'Université Saint-Joseph* 15, 2 (1930) 35–50.

Mühlenberg (1969)—Mühlenberg, E., *Apollinaris von Laodicea*, Göttingen 1969

Munier (1974)—Munier, C., ed., *Concilia Africae A. 345–A. 525*, Turnhout 1974 (*CCSL* 149).

Nagel (1966)—Nagel, P., *Die Motivierung des Askese in der alten Kirche und der Ursprung des Mönchtums*, Berlin 1966.

Nau (1919)—Nau, F., ed., "Documents pour servir à l'histoire de l'église nestorienne," *Patrologia Orientalis* 13 (1919) 113–326.

Nau (1932)—Nau, F., ed.,"La première partie de l'Histoire de Barhadbesabba Arbaia," *Patrologia Orientalis* 23 (1932) 177–343.

Navascués (2004)—Navascués, P. de, *Pablo de Samosata y sus adversarios. Estudio historico-teológico del cristianismo antioqueno en el s. III*, Roma 2004.

Nollé (1998)—Nollé, "*Eutychos tois kyriois—feliciter dominis!* Akklamationsmünzen des griechischen Ostens unter Septimius Severus und städtische Mentalitäten," *Chiron* 28 (1998) 323–54.

Opitz (1935)—Opitz, H.-G., ed., *Urkunden zur Geschichte des Arianischen Streites 318–328*, Berlin 1935 (*Athanasius Werke* III, 1).

Ortiz de Urbina (1963)—Ortiz de Urbina, I., *Nicée et Constantinople*, Paris 1963

Outtier (1996)—Outtier, B., "Traditions et héritage de l'Orient chrétien: orthodoxie et nationalisme dans la tradition de l'Orient chrétien," *Traditions and Heritage of the Christian East. Proceedings of the International Conference*, Moscow 1996, 375–81.

Parmentier (1954)—Parmentier, L., ed., *Theodoret Kirchengeschichte*,[2] Berlin 1954.

Pharr (1952)—Pharr, C. et al., trans., *The Theodosian Code and Novels and the Sirmondian Constitutions*, Princeton 1952.

Pietri (1998)—Pietri, L., ed., *Les églises d'Orient et d'Occident*, Paris 1998 (vol. 3 in *Histoire du christianisme des origines à nos jours*).

Pietri (1992)—Pietri, L., et al., "Peuple chrétien ou plebs: le rôle des laics dans les élections ecclésiastiques en Occident," *Institutions, société et vie politique dans l'empire romain au IVᵉ siècle ap. J.-C.*, eds. M. Christol et al., Rome 1992, 373–95.

Pietri and Pietri (1990) — Pietri, C., and Pietri, L., eds., *Naissance d'une chrétienté (250–430)*, Paris 1990 (vol. 3 in *Histoire du christianisme des origines à nos jours*).

Pitcher (1994) — Pitcher, H. J., *Witnesses of the Russian Revolution*, London 1994.

Placanica (1997) — Placanica, A., ed., *Vittore da Tunnuna, Chronica. Chiesa e impero nell'età di Giustiniano*, Firenze 1997.

Pott (1992) — Pott, M., *Aufklärung und Aberglaube. Die deutsche Frühaufklärung im Spiegel ihrer Aberglaubenskritik*, Tübingen 1992.

Prestige (1956) — Prestige, G. L., *St. Basil the Great and Apollinaris of Laodicea*, London 1956.

Prosopographie chrétienne du Bas-Empire, 1: *Prosopographie de l'Afrique chrétienne (305–533)*, ed. A. Mandouze, Paris 1982

Prosopographie chrétienne du Bas-Empire, 2: *Prosopographie de l'Italie chrétienne (313–604)*, eds. C. and L. Pietri, Rome 2000.

Queyrel (1992) — Queyrel, F., "Les acclamations des inscriptions peintes du xyste," *Delphes: centenaire de la "Grande fouille" réalisée par l'Ecole française d'Athènes (1892–1903). Actes du Colloque . . . 1991*, ed., J.-F. Bommeleer, Leiden 1992, 333–48.

Roberson (1988) — Roberson, R. G., *The Eastern Christian Churches*, Roma 1988.

Roueché (1989) — Roueché, C., *Aphrodisias in Late Antiquity. The Late Roman and Byzantine Inscriptions*, London 1989.

Roueché (1997) — Roueché, C., "Benefactors in the Late Roman Period: the Eastern Empire," *Actes du Xᵉ Congrès international d'épigraphie grecque et latine . . . 1992*, Paris 1997, 353–68.

Roueché (1999) — Roueché, C., "Looking for Late Antique ceremonial: Ephesos and Aphrodisias," *100 Jahre österrechische Forschungen in Ephesos. Akten des Symposions . . . 1995*, eds. B. Brandt and K. R. Krierer, Wien 1999, 1.161–68.

Rousseau (1978) — Rousseau, P., *Ascetics, Authority, and the Church in the Age of Jerome and Cassian*, Oxford 1978.

Rousselle (1977) — Rousselle, A., "Aspects sociaux du recrutement ecclésiastique au IVᵉ siècle," *Mélanges d'archéologie et d'histoire de l'Ecole française de Rome* 89 (1977) 333–70.

Sabw Kanyang (2000) — Sabw Kanyang, J.-A., *Episcopus et plebs. L'évêque et la communauté ecclésiale dans les conciles africains (345–525)*, Bern 2000.

Savon (1997) — Savon, H., *Ambroise de Milan (340–397)*, Paris 1997.

Scherrer (1995) — Scherrer, P., ed., *Ephesos. Der neue Führer*, Wien 1995.

Schofield (1986) — Schofield, M., "Cicero for and against divination," *Journal of Roman Studies* 76 (1986) 47–65.

Schwartz (1904) — Schwartz, E., "Die Sammlung des Theodosius Diaconus," *Nachrichten von der königlichen Gesellschaft der Wissenschaften zu Göttingen, Phil.-hist. Klasse* 60 (1904) 357–91.

Schwartz (1914–40) — Schwartz, E., *Acta conciliorum oecumenicorum*, 4 vols., Berlin 1914–40.

Schwartz (1939) — Schwartz, E., ed., *Drei dogmatische Schriften Iustinians*, München 1939 (*Abhandlungen der Bayerischen Akademie der Wissenschaften, Phil.-hist. Abteilung² 18*).

Sellers (1961) — Sellers, R. V., *The Council of Chalcedon: A Historical and Doctrinal Survey*, London 1961.

Shaw (1995) — Shaw, B. D., "African Christianity: disputes, definitions, and 'Donatists'," in idem, *Rulers, Nomads, and Christians in Roman North Africa*, chap. XI, Aldershot 1995.

Sieben (1992) — Sieben, H. J., "Consensus, unanimitas und maior pars auf Konzilien, von der Alten Kirche bis zum Ersten Vatikanum," *Theologie und Philosophie* 67 (1992) 229.

Sillett (2000) — Sillett, H., "Orthodoxy and heresy in Theodoret of Cyrus' Compendium of Heresies," *Orthodoxie, christianisme, histoire*, eds. S. Elm et al., Rome 2000, 260–73.

Smith and Wace (1877–87) — Smith, W., and H. Wace, *A Dictionary of Christian Biography*, 4 vols., London 1877–87.

Soden (1909) — Soden, H. von, "Sententiae LXXXVIII episcoporum: das Protokoll der Synode von Karthago am 1. September 256," *Nachrichten von der königlichen Gesellschaft der Wissenschaften zu Göttingen, Phil.-hist. Klasse* 1909, 247–307.

Sotinel (1997) — Sotinel, C., "Le recrutement des évêques en Italie aux IVᵉ et Vᵉ siècles. Essai d'enquête prosopographique," *Vescovi e pastori in epoca teodosiana . . . XXV Incontro di studiosi dell'antichità cristiana, Roma 1996*, 1, Roma 1997, 193–204.

Sotinel (2000) — Sotinel, C., "Le concile, l'empereur, l'évêque," *Orthodoxie, christianisme, histoire*, eds. S. Elm et al., Rome 2000, 275–99.

Stein (1949–59) — Stein, E., *Histoire du Bas-Empire*, 2 vols., Paris 1949–59.

Stewart (1991) — Stewart, C., *'Working the Earth of the Heart'. The Messalian Controversy in History, Texts, and Language to A. D. 431*, Oxford 1991.

Stoop (1911) — Stoop, E. G. M. J. de, "Vie d'Alexandre l'Acémète. Text grec," *Patrologia orientalis* 6 (1911) 643–705.

Tacoma (2004) — Tacoma, L. A., *Fragile Hierarchies. The Urban Elites of Third Century Roman Egypt*, Leiden 2004.

Talbert (2000) — Talbert, R. J. A., *Barrington Atlas of the Greek and Roman World*, Princeton 2000.

Taylor (1981) — Taylor, J., "The first Council of Constantinople (381)," *Prudentia* 13 (1981) 47–54, 91–97.

Thiel (2004) — Thiel, A., *Epistolae Romanorum pontificum genuinae*,² Hildesheim 2004.

Thomassen (2004) — Thomassen, E., "Orthodoxy and heresy in second-century Rome," *Harvard Theological Review* 97 (2004) 241–56.

Thurn (2000) — Thurn, J., *Ioannis Malalae Chronographia*, Berlin 2000

Townsend (1933) — Townsend, W. T., "The so-called Symmachian forgeries," *Journal of Religion* 13 (1933) 165–74.

Treadgold (1997) — Treadgold, W., *A History of the Byzantine State and Society*, Stanford 1997.

Turner (1899–1939) — Turner, C. H., *Ecclesiae occidentalis monumenta iuris antiquissima*, 2 vols., Oxford 1899–1939.

Veyne (1999) — Veyne, P., "Prodiges, devination et peur des dieux chez Plutarque," *Revue de l'histoire des religions* 216 (1999) 387–442.

Vogûé (1994) — Vogûé, A. de, trans., *Quatre ermites égyptiens d'après les fragments coptes de l'Histoire Lausiaque*, Bégrolles-en-Mauges 1994.

Vries (1975) — Vries, W. de, "Das Konzil von Ephesus 449, eine 'Räubersynode'?" *Orientalia christiana periodica* 41 (1975) 357–98.

Walter (1970) — Walter, C., *L'iconographie des conciles dans la tradition byzantine*, Paris 1970.

Whitby and Whitby (1989) — Whitby, M. and M., trans., *Chronicon Paschale 284–628 AD*, Liverpool 1989.

Wilcken (1908) — Wilcken, U., "Aus der Strassburger Sammlung," *Archiv für Papyrusforschung* 4 (1908) 115–47.

Will (2000) — Will, G., *Papal Sin: Structures of Deceit*, New York 2000.

D. H. Williams (1995) — Williams, D. H., *Ambrose of Milan and the End of the Nicene-Arian Conflicts*, Oxford 1995.

R. Williams (1989) — Williams, R., "Does it make sense to speak of pre-Nicene orthodoxy?" *The Making of Orthodoxy. Essays in Honour of Henry Chadwick*, ed. idem, Cambridge 1989, 1–23.

R. Williams (2001) — Williams, R., *Arius: Heresy and Tradition*,[2] London 2001.

Wipszycka (1983) — Wipszycka, E., "La chiesa nell'Egitto del IV secolo: le strutture ecclesiastiche," *Miscellanea Historiae Ecclesiaticae* VI (*Congrès de Varsovie . . . 1978*, Section 1: *Les transformations dans la société chrétienne au IVᵉ siècle*), Bruxelles 1983, 182–201.

Wipszycka (1984) — Wipszycka, E., "Le degré d'analphabétisme en Egypte byzantine," *Revue des études augustiniennes* 30 (1984) 279–96.

Wipszycka (1992) — Wipszycka, E., "Le nationalisme a-t-il existé dans l'Egypte byzantine?" *Journal of Juristic Papyrology* 22 (1992) 3–128.

Zelzer (1982) — Zelzer, M., ed., *Sancti Ambrosii opera* 10: *Epistolae*, Wien 1982 (*CSEL* 82).

Zibawi (1995) — Zibawi, M., *Eastern Christian Worlds*, trans. M. Beaumont, Collegeville (MN) 1995.

Index